Gigging

A Practical Guide for Musicians

Patricia Shih

ALLWORTH PRESS
NEW YORK

08 07 06 05 04 03   5 4 3 2 1

Published by Allworth Press
An imprint of Allworth Communications
10 East 23rd Street, New York, NY 10010

Cover design by Mary Belibasakis
Author photo on back cover by Clyde Berger
Page composition/typography by Integra Software Services, Pvt. Ltd., Pondicherry, India
ISBN: 1–58115–275–2

Library of Congress Cataloging-in-Publication Data

Shih, Patricia. Gigging : a practical guide for musicians / by Patricia Shih. p. cm.
Includes bibliographical references (p.).
ISBN 1–58115–275–2 (pbk.)
1. Music trade—Vocational guidance. I. Title.
ML3790.S52 2003
780'.23'73—dc21
                                                                                    2003001462

Printed in Canada

Contents

Dedication

*To all those musicians who dare to
dream and make the leap.*

Acknowledgments

I would venture to say that no book in history has been written without much support to the author. This assistance could be through direct help with research, editing, or proofing; indirectly through inspiration or example; or simply through moral, financial, or practical support. *Someone's* got to cook and keep life going while the author is writing! I am indebted to the many people who contributed directly or indirectly to the writing of this book:

The good people at Allworth Press—my editors Jessica Rozler, Liz Van Hoose, and Nicole Potter, and publisher Tad Crawford, whose sonorous voice patiently guided me through the bewildering maze of publishing my debut book.

Michael Gross, Esq., from the New York Author's Guild.

My team of professionals/experts—Sy Buckner, Jim Coffey, Corey Davidson, Paul Foley, Joe Giardina, Paul Kendall, Howard Leib, Scott MacDonald, John McCutcheon, George Meier, Ron Meixsell, John Platt, Lawrence Re, Gary Roth, Charles Rufino, Jeffrey Seader, Willie Steel, Karen Sussman, and Fred Wolinsky, all of whom generously lent their authority, expertise, and time when agreeing to be sources for this guidebook. Also, Paul Glantzman of Progressive Tape Corporation for superb service always and for giving me valuable information for this book.

My dear friends—Janice Buckner, for being my mentor, role model, and creative advice–giver, and for changing the course of my musical career in this glorious business; Susan Gaber, Heather Forest, Elaine Greenspan, and Joe Martin, all enormously gifted, generous, and experienced in book publishing/writing/illustrating. Each advised, guided and encouraged me in this first endeavor. Also, Dave Gardner, for rescuing my manuscript from computer gremlins.

And lastly and most importantly, my family—my parents, Frank and Alice Shih, for giving me unconditional love, support, and the belief that I could do anything I set my mind to; my sister Dr. Christina Shih for moral support, great meals, help with the "Health" chapter, and sorely needed vacations; my daughter Jennifer Shih, for the very best reason to do all this; and my best friend, musical partner, and husband Stephen Fricker, for proofing, editing, researching, loving, entertaining, guiding, supporting, inspiring, and being the best protoplasm in the history of the universe.

Introduction

This book is meant to guide novice and intermediate musicians and singers through the maze of the music business. Although many books have been written on the subject, I believe one more is useful because, although I have made almost every mistake in the book, met every sleaze ball there is, and stepped on every landmine dotting the musical landscape, *I still think that being an artist is the finest vocation one can choose—it's just damn hard!* I have also been pretty fortunate, meeting kind souls who mentored and guided me and who, for the most part, were honest and well-meaning. But I would have also liked to have had a road map, in language I could grasp easily, with much of the information I needed in one place. Even at this stage in my long career, I sometimes feel as if I am re-inventing the wheel, when so many others before me have already been there, done that. If only I had access to their brains to pick! So, here is my brain and a few decades' worth of experience in the music business, for what they're worth.

This book's first assumption is that the reader is *ready* to make the leap from amateur to semi- or full professional; that his or her musical chops are up to par; and that the reader has the requisite talent, drive, and desire to make it in this very tough and unforgiving business. Even if the reader doesn't have the blind ambition and drive to be a "star," there's plenty of work for accompanists and other support roles for the shyer musician. But remember, we are talking about one of the *performing arts* here. If you don't like the stage and performing up in front of an audience, you might be better off being a studio musician, a music teacher, or some other kind of musician in a related field, and that's very cool, too. There are other books for you in that case.

So, on that same note, the assumption is that the reader is already at a certain level—not a rank beginner. For real beginners, the best advice is to practice, practice, practice until you are at a level where you are comfortable and technically ready to perform in front of an audience. Everyone starts small—playing in front of friends and family first, then on to small venues. Lots of people have the fantasy of being "discovered" while still green, but unless you are a musical prodigy, your talent isn't fully developed yet. I also assume that your ego has been toughened enough to withstand inevitable rejection—this business is full of it. A wiser person than I once said something like, "All the talent in the world won't get you success—there are many talented failures. It's *perseverance* that can make all the difference." If you truly believe you have what it takes, *don't give up!*

The objective of this book is to give practical, realistic, everyday hands-on advice to those who wish to make some sort of a living making music in the world. There is a resource section in the back that I hope readers will find helpful. There are some real-life stories in here—some not meant to discourage or break your heart, but to help you avoid pitfalls and real disasters. I hope you can turn to this book again and again, in different times and stages of your career, and that it will help you over rough spots, steer you around craters, and guide you in the right direction.

Although much of the information in here may be specific to one genre of music or another, I have tried to keep it somewhat general to apply to many fields—folk, rock, pop, classical, jazz, country, musical theatre, and more. There are problems and situations particular to some fields that would not apply to others, but for the most part anyone adventurous enough to enter into this crazy business can also be imaginative enough to make all this somehow fit into their own situation.

I learned long ago that if your dream is to make a living making music, you don't have to have a narrow definition or image of yourself in this profession. Even if your initial goal was to be the next Yo Yo Ma or Eric Clapton, you might also find yourself happy and fulfilled performing to four hundred elementary school kids to teach them about your joy in music. My own dear husband set out to be the next Steve Howe (guitar wizard for the progressive rock group Yes) but has happily navigated a very long career in musical theatre, country, rock, jazz, record arranging and producing, even playing bass balalaika and polka music before arriving at the present as my accompanist. I don't look at this as compromising or losing focus, but rather as a stellar example of creative thinking in a wide, wide field. For some, it's stardom or nothing. For others, just the pure joy of making music in front of seven or seven thousand is the goal. I want to show you that, with a little business acumen, you too can make a lovely living making music.

Using this Book

This book is organized into two parts. The first is about how to approach building a career from scratch. I'll tell you how to seek out venues and set up bookings, and how to put together a band and other personnel for your gigs. I'll also let you in on my approaches to setting up your home for optimum productivity. You'll learn how to care for your instruments, which details to ask about when booking a show, and how to grapple with difficulties like stage fright, slippery stage surfaces, and rain. And, once you've played a few gigs and have had a good response, I'll explain how to go about making a video or audio demo, getting on TV and radio airwaves, and booking a tour that hopefully will make you more than it costs.

The second part of the book is for your reference, both during the initial stages of setting up your gigs and throughout your entire career. Contracts, insurance, legal concerns, health tips, and other practical matters are addressed here, as are royalties, estate plans, and career alternatives to consider for the days if and when the joy of performing wears thin.

Finally, I offer an exhaustive appendix, where you'll find forms, contracts, and helpful resources—listing everything from performance rights societies to contact information for the people who helped me put together this book.

Happy trails—and remember, the reward is in the journey because the destination is illusive.

PART I

Building a Career —
Preparing for Gigging and Tours

Chapter 1

Moving from the Garage to the Spotlight

Okay, so you have your chops down, your "look" is right and consistent with your style, you are rarin' to get on that stage. You know your music has a lot to offer to the world. But how do you go about sharing it? Where do you start?

Well, it depends. Some rare and lucky ones can play in their rooms or on the street, get discovered, and be offered great gigs right away. Some think that blazing talent alone will have the world beating down their door, and they just have to wait until the world recognizes their genius. But if you rely on great gigs coming to *you*, then you will probably wait a very long time and become very frustrated. For the vast majority of musicians, the cold hard truth is that *you* have to go after *them*; *they* are not going to run after *you*, at least not until you reach a certain level. The name of the game is "exposure."

The more expensive, time-consuming, and complicated means of getting your name out there—entering contests, showcasing, building mailing lists, and sending out promotional flyers—will be addressed later on, after I've covered the basics of *preparing* for the world of gigging.

Meanwhile, take the time to review your creative assets, rearrange your home, get your instruments in order, and see how gigs can realistically fit into your present schedule. You're in for the ride of your life, but it won't be much fun (or financially rewarding) if you don't approach it with practical savvy and an optimistic yet realistic attitude.

But before you break down a wall in your home to set up a home office, or start choosing color swatches for your new rehearsal space, *take the time to talk up your act to everyone you know.* This is the most inexpensive, most useful, least risky first step to gigging out there.

Basic Networking

In many ways, you should approach getting a gig the same way you would look for any other job. You have to do some research, some homework, and some legwork. Read trade magazines and papers, visit likely venues, talk to other musicians in your field. The main point is to get out there and meet and *perform* for people. It's a cliché, but so true—it's often not *what* you know, but *who*. The right person can open doors that would stay locked up tight to ordinary schlubs who might spend years knocking on them to no avail. If you can find even one "right" person who loves your music and believes in what you are doing, that is worth more than gold. As in the rest of life, it is extremely valuable to cultivate your "people skills," because in very few other fields of work is communicating and relating to other human beings so important.

As mentioned above, one of the most effective (and cheap!) ways to promote yourself is to network with other like-minded musicians. Perhaps you have teachers, a mentor—people more experienced who can guide you. Don't be shy—pick their brains. Where and how did they get their start? How much time and money do they spend on promotion? What are some good resources for venues? Any mishaps to look out for? If you are bold and open to suggestions, you could ask someone you respect to come watch a show of yours, and then offer some constructive criticism to help you improve it.

Sure, some people are insecure enough to jealously guard their list of venues and contacts. But I have found if you approach fellow musicians with humility and genuine friendliness, most are willing to share. Everyone loves to "talk shop," and most musicians are generous souls willing to encourage the up-and-coming. Just remember who has helped you on the way up—it's a real truism that you will meet the same folks on your way down, too.

Once you've spoken with people immediately in your circle, see if they can recommend other musicians, promoters, producers, managers ... anyone in the music business. Or, anyone who knows anyone else in the music business. There are many people who aren't in the biz themselves, but hey, their cousin's wife's brother is a roadie for Paul Simon. Couldn't hurt.

Next, go to every venue that you think would even *remotely consider* your kind of music and get to know the owners, managers, waitresses, bookers, and other performers who have played there. They could suggest other similar venues. If they do, repeat the routine at these new places. In other words, get to know or shake hands with everyone who is remotely connected to the music business in your area. Then, when you go about building your venue lists—more on this in chapter 2—you'll have a lot of valuable information, such as names, numbers, suitability, and so forth. Plus, you'll have given the venue personnel a face to put with your name.

Building Your Skill Level — And Your Appeal

The more instruments you can play—and the more styles you can adapt to—the more venues and fellow musicians will be open to you. In other words, if you are very versatile, that is completely in your favor and you will probably get much more work than someone whose focus is more narrow. This, by the way, is a good point if you really want to work professionally as a musician: *broaden your styles* and you will be able to fit in almost anywhere, with anyone. Good studio musicians know this, and so they make themselves very much in demand because they can play anything, in any style, with anyone. Also, it is a real plus (and sometimes a requirement) if you can read music charts very well. Studios and orchestras are just some of the situations that demand good sight-reading. So, if you excel in this, put it in your résumé.

Speaking of résumés, some situations require them, while others just need an audition. Some places want to know whom you've played with, for how long, and where. They might want to know if you have had formal training—have you studied privately with anyone well respected, or at a conservatory? Some places may even need you to have a degree in music. But in the end, the true test of a musician is how well one plays. So even if you don't have any of the above and you are a self-taught but amazing musician, this may override another's fancy résumé. Read on to find out how to bring your talent and hard work into the spotlight …

Building Your Audience Fan Base

In a perfect world, this *should* be easy, following a natural course of events. You get the gigs, people hear and love your music, and they become fans. You take their names, addresses, and e-mail info, build a fan mailing list, and soon you're a popular, in-demand act whom everyone is clamoring for. Unfortunately, it's *not* that easy and it *doesn't* always follow a natural order. Artists lose momentum, have to drop out of performing for awhile, change styles of music, change groups—a thousand things can affect the upward trajectory of a career. In my line of music, which is performing for children and families, it's an unfortunate fact that my audience *keeps outgrowing me,* making it extremely hard to build up fans. Even though the kids and their parents love my work, sooner or later they abandon my music to listen to the latest pop music for the young teen set. I have learned to accept this. The good thing is, there is always a new crop of young'uns coming up the pike—a fresh new audience waiting to be turned on to quality music.

But my situation is fairly unusual and peculiar to the children's music genre. For the most part, your fans hopefully will stay loyal to you as long as you don't do anything *really* radical like switch from classical to rap, although Yo Yo Ma has experimented with other genres to no ill effect. Moving from pop to classical standards or musical theatre seems to work well, however—witness the fans of Paul McCartney, Elton John, Linda Ronstadt, Rod Stewart, and Billy Joel enjoying those artists' forays into other styles.

Anyway, the key to building a fan base is to be consistent, let your fans know when and where you playing, perform as often as you can, and offer them something new mixed in with the old. Most people like to hear the familiar pieces that attracted them in the first place, and they won't mind—indeed, they'll prefer—if you continue to play your older stuff. Some great examples of this are the Rolling Stones or Yes. Their fans would be sorely disappointed if they didn't get to hear and sing along with "Satisfaction" and "Owner of a Lonely Heart." Justin Timberlake of 'N Sync confirms this and says the group won't skimp on performing its older hits. "We know the fans want to see it, even if we're singing them for the thousandth time. *I know if I see the Stones, I want to see them do 'Satisfaction'*" (italics mine). But by the same token, you do want to offer your fans your newest material. You should never rest on your laurels, because you need to grow and stretch. Again, 'N Sync's Lance Bass says, "We're lucky we get to keep doing new things. You can only do so much before it starts getting repetitive."[1] Of course, there are plenty of acts that just do their old stuff on the oldies circuit, and they make a darn good living at it, too. But we are talking about you, an emerging artist who wants to build a new fan base. Fans who come to your shows again and again deserve to hear something new, as well as your old stuff. This goes for cover bands, classical artists, *and every musician*, really.

Your fans will not be able to support you if they don't know when and where you are playing. Read the Marketing and Promotion chapter—you don't want to market yourself just to industry wonks, but also to your fans, of course. Be sure to compile a mailing list and then be faithful about sending out notices of your gigs regularly. To cut costs, you can compile an e-mail list. And remind people to visit your Web site often (you do have one, don't you?), where your performance schedule should be updated regularly.

[1] Glenn Gamboa, "A New Twist on Celebrity," 5 April 2002, B39.

4

It goes without saying that the more you perform in public, the faster your fan mailing list will grow. If you only go out once a month, you won't be getting as many names as someone gigging every day. But even so, you can ask your fans to bring their friends to the next gig, to spread the word, or to give you the name and addresses of people they think would also like your music and want to be notified when you're playing. I also know artists who share their fan list with other musicians whose music is similar to theirs. The reasoning here is that if you like Mary Smith's music, you're going to love me, too, because we are in the same bag.

Don't forget to use your media mailing list (see chapter 7) to send out press releases regularly, especially if something unusual or newsworthy is happening with you. You won't always get press, but the law of averages suggests that you eventually will get into a publication's calendar of gig listings, a highlight, or maybe even an interview or article about your work. The more people hear of you and see your name, the more "buzz" there will be about you, and hopefully your career will start its upward climb. As Michael Dunne, promotions marketing manager for the club Mulcahy's on Long Island, says, "We're in business, too. What happens a lot is that the artists are very good but no one knows them yet. It's expensive to open for the night, and it's a big undertaking to do promotion and marketing for an unproven [band]…. We'll let bands develop first, and if we see there's a steady crowd seeing them every week, we'll try them."[2]

A wonderful opportunity to build your fan base is to open for a better-known but similar act. You can figure that if you are a talented jazz musician like Pat Metheny, then his fans will also love you if you have the good fortune to appear on the same bill. This can happen especially at festivals geared toward a particular style. It's amazing how quickly word can spread and how many musicians get their big break this way.

And lastly, always be nice to your fans. That sounds like it's a given, but you know when you are tired, it's late, you just want to pack up and go home, you have a splitting headache, and an audience member wants to come up and tell you all about the time he went to buy his guitar that looks just like yours and the salesperson tried to rip him off and where did you get yours and how much was it blah blah blah? The temptation is to blow him off because he's weird or whatever, but *everyone*, especially those who love your music, deserves to be treated with respect and to be given some of your time. These are your

[2]Jon Lane, "The Fans Will Come," *Newsday*, 31 March 2002, B7.

admirers, or maybe they're lonely. Whatever the case may be, you won't be building *anything* if you treat your listeners disrespectfully or with indifference. We all know of divas, both male and female, who won't autograph for fans, want to keep their distance, do the show, take the money, and run. The artists I admire most are those who take the time to talk with the people who wait for them after the show, and make each person feel special. Those are the artists who deserve my loyalty and money. I don't care how awesomely talented an artist is, how great her music—if she is not a decent person, I won't support the music. So, treat your fans well, and they will return in kind.

Chapter 2

Venues

Now that you've ready to get up and take the world of performance by storm, how are you going to go about finding a place to play? Where can you look to bring your music to the public? That is, of course, the object of all of this, unless you want to be solely a recording session player. The true value of playing music is that it must be heard by someone and shared. And the fullest appreciation of music occurs when it is heard live.

When you are just getting started, while you're seeking presenters who might book you for pay, keep your eyes peeled for places where you might be able to just show up and play for free. Many venues have "open mic nights" where beginners can try out their stuff. Places like nursing homes welcome enthusiastic and talented amateurs and aspiring professionals, where you will play for free but get invaluable experience. Some low-paying venues, like cafés or restaurants, which aren't necessarily "listening rooms," are also great places to start because much of the time—and don't be disheartened by this—the audience isn't really listening critically, or even *at all*. Therefore, you won't have a tough room scrutinizing every note, and you won't have to develop patter. In these cases you are adding ambience and mood to the place, not necessarily attention-grabbing virtuosity. For that reason, I call these gigs "wallpaper gigs." Although you might not build an audience here (or, then again, you might), you are still gaining valuable performing experience. Think of these gigs as "paid rehearsals."

The more experience you can get performing before a live audience, the better you can hone your act. As you perform more, you will start to interact with the audience more and develop rapport, patter, and the all-important stage presence. And remember, in many genres, that *really* is the measure by which performers will be judged. I have seen wonderful, enormously talented artists who could play circles around most others, but they don't have that on-stage charisma, that stage presence. That has to be learned and cultivated and refined through years of live gigging. If you are going to be a stage performer, you should have that presence. Audiences want to be wowed by great musicianship, but they also want to be entertained by an engaging personality.

Just by getting out there before a live audience, you will learn what "works" and what doesn't in a show. If you plan on being exclusively a recording artist (and there are many folks who make an extremely good living being studio musicians), a sideman, or other support musician, this "presence" is not as crucial.

Making a List of Venues

You will need all your creative thinking to come up with, and then research, what's most appropriate. When doing this, *do not overlook unconventional venues*. We all know about bars, restaurants, nightclubs, established concert halls; in fact, they are the first to spring to mind for just about every musician. Everyone wants to play the top juicy locations—the best-paying, the most prestigious. Thus, there is fierce competition for these jobs. But you may find it easier and even sometimes more gratifying if you break from the crowd and explore places that don't usually offer music and that may be less "prestigious." After all, no one says an audience needs to be more than a few people, or even of a certain age. All your audience needs is an appreciation for music, and you can find that literally *anywhere in the world where people gather*.

To jumpstart your search, below are possible venue ideas for different styles of music.

Acoustic, with genres including classical, jazz, ethnic, or folk music (including blues, bluegrass, singer-songwriter, and instrumental). Here the audience may or may not be "captive"—i.e., they may be transient. These venues are conducive to perhaps smaller, quieter acts or those that may not need amplification or electricity, and/or prefer a "listening" audience:

- **BOOKSTORES AND OTHER SPECIALTY STORES**
- **SHOPPING COURTYARDS**
- **WINERIES**
- **ANTIQUE SHOWS**
- **LIBRARIES**
- **HOSPITALS**
- **CRUISE SHIPS**
- **BED AND BREAKFAST INNS**
- **RESORTS**
- **SCHOOLS**
- **CONFERENCES**

- MUSEUMS AND ART CENTERS
- WEDDINGS
- NIGHTCLUBS
- COFFEEHOUSES
- BARS
- RESTAURANTS
- MUSIC CLUBS AND SOCIETIES
- SENIOR CENTERS
- NURSING HOMES
- PARKS
- STREET CORNERS, COURTYARDS, MASS TRANSIT STOPS (WHERE LEGALLY PERMITTED)
- PRIVATE PARTIES
- CONVENTIONS
- DEMONSTRATIONS AND RALLIES
- BENEFITS AND FUNDRAISERS
- CORPORATE FUNCTIONS
- PLACES OF WORSHIP
- FAIRS AND FESTIVALS
- MEETINGS

Electric or Louder-Volume Music, with genres including rock, rap, dance, big band, and orchestra. This may require electricity, and audiences may not be "listening" but rather dancing, chatting, shopping, strolling, or doing some other activity:

- BARS
- NIGHTCLUBS
- SHOPPING MALLS
- COUNTY FAIRS
- FESTIVALS
- DEMONSTRATIONS AND RALLIES
- BLOCK AND PRIVATE PARTIES
- CONVENTIONS
- WEDDINGS
- CRUISE SHIPS
- CONFERENCES
- PARKS
- PRIVATE PARTIES
- BENEFITS AND FUNDRAISERS
- CORPORATE EVENTS

Cabaret, musical theatre, and storytelling, with a stable or captive audience throughout the entire performance. This is for acts that require the audience's attention:

- COMMUNITY THEATRE
- SCHOOLS
- LIBRARIES
- FESTIVALS
- CONFERENCES
- PARKS
- CRUISE SHIPS
- RESORTS
- MUSEUMS AND ART CENTERS
- CABARETS
- SENIOR CENTERS
- PLACES OF WORSHIP

I cannot stress enough that you pick only *appropriate* venues—i.e., appropriate to your kind of music. There is hardly anything more frustrating or disheartening to a musician than to play your heart out to an unresponsive—or even worse, hostile—audience. These are truly "gigs from hell." It is painful enough for the audience to have to suffer through a mismatch, but it can be downright traumatic for the artist. Just imagine two teenage girls with acoustic guitars opening for a rock band in a coliseum before a rough and rowdy crowd ready to party. It's happened … to me, unfortunately!

One of my favorite stories is a sterling example of a performer being totally clueless and out of sync with the venue. At a showcase for PTA moms looking to book acts for their elementary schools, there appeared a solo guitarist/singer who obviously was new to this. It wasn't his style—he looked very hip, with Rasta dreadlocks and a cool electric guitar, and he sang reggae competently. Though his guitar was dreadfully out of tune, that wasn't his biggest mistake. He got up in front of a few dozen mothers scattered among a few hundred second-to-fourth graders and sang Bob Marley's "I Shot the Sheriff," then proceeded to advocate armed confrontation with authority. "Sometimes," he said, "You have to take up a gun and shoot someone." My bandmates, and the entire audience, in fact, could not believe what we were hearing. Needless to say, I never saw him again at a PTA showcase.

There are hundreds of other stories of gigs that went awry because of a mismatch of musical style to venue. Don't become a casualty because you're overeager or desperate to play *anywhere*. Most professional musicians have made this mistake early in their career.

Seeking Resources

The number of resources out there is astounding, limited only by your creative thinking. Once again, one of the best things to do is to network with other like musicians. It makes sense to seek out other artists whose work you admire and is similar to yours. Likewise, you probably already know the local haunts that would present your kind of music, so those are also good places to start.

But beyond the networking, where else can you turn to build your venue list? One logical place is the Internet. If you are a Celtic harpist, you might want to type "Irish music" into your search engine. If you know the names of other harpists (which I am sure you do), then search their Web sites. Often artists have links to other artists and venues that share their love of this kind of music. You could type in "Irish societies," "Irish pubs in Washington, D.C.," and so forth. The list is endless. You probably could spend the rest of your life online just researching on the Web!

There are a gazillion trade papers, magazines, and books you could either subscribe to, buy, or borrow from the library or from friends. Newsletters from organizations who might like your music also can give you leads. I keep a file folder of possible venues that I add to whenever I come across anything in print that might be helpful; or, if someone tells me about a place, I jot it down and throw it in my file. When I have time, I take the file out and either call to inquire or add them to my venue mailing list if they look like a likely prospect.

There are also quite a few trade organizations you can look up. Most of them advertise in the trade publications, and people in your music world will also know of them. You might want to consider joining a musicians' union, which exists to help musicians. For more information, see chapter 16.

Maintaining a List of Venues

Once you've drawn together all of your research findings, make a list of all possible venues. Be sure to get not only mailing addresses but also phone numbers. On mailings, I don't tend to use actual names of bookers because they turn over frequently. Instead, I address it to "Program Director" or "Cultural Arts Coordinator" or some other title. Of course, when you are calling someone directly, it is very helpful if you know, or can get, her name for that personal touch. This mailing list will be invaluable to you once you are ready to really market yourself. I have found my mailing list, which I have cultivated over many years, to be one of my most valuable resources. I have gotten gigs simply by direct mail, without so much as an audition.

Once you start a mailing list, be sure to maintain it. Weed out those that don't appear to be useful, and keep addresses and phone numbers up to date. Otherwise, you will just be throwing postage and brochure money down the drain. The addresses can be updated by printing "Address service requested" on the face of your mailings. The post office will return the ones that can't be forwarded, with the new address if it is known. If some are not known and can't be forwarded, you want to know that, too, so you can delete them from your list or research where they've gone.

Hot and Cold Calls

Now that you have your list, start visiting, start mailing, start calling. If you are a good talker, you might be able to convince the powers that be that they need your kind of entertainment. If you're more on the shy side or schmoozing isn't your thing, then at least ask if you could send a demo tape and press kit as an audition. Or, if you are playing somewhere else in the area, you could invite them down to hear you live. Many bookers prefer either a live demo tape or a chance to see an artist work a room. Once again, you might be a fantastic musician, but can you hold an audience *and be entertaining*? Because unless you are Eric Clapton or Midori or some other dazzling prodigy, why should someone leave a comfortable living room, go out, and spend good money to listen to you as opposed to a recording? Even though your mom could listen to you play your violin for hours, strangers need something a little more compelling in order to part with their bucks. An exception to this would be as background music in a restaurant, bar, or cocktail reception.

What good is a cold call? The booker has never heard of you or might never have considered your kind of music for the venue. These calls are always hard to do, and it will take all your chutzpah and powers of persuasion to even get her to give you five minutes on the phone. If you are a good salesperson, you might get as far as getting the booker to consent to listen to your demo tape. Chances are, she gets literally dozens of demos every week. Why listen to yours? Well, maybe because there is that slight chance that something you say might intrigue her enough to make her want to take the next step, which is actually listening to your music. What makes *you* unique? I always feel that, as hard as cold calls are to make, you really have nothing to lose except a little time and a few pennies for the call. The upside is that you might just get a gig, and your ego is learning to withstand the inevitable battering of rejection this business dishes out. Also, a tip I learned from another seasoned pro is, if you can make the person on the other end of the line laugh, you might just make the catch.

Now, "hot" calls are much easier to make. Let's say you have managed to create a buzz in the industry, say as an emerging artist, or someone has recommended you. I believe in striking while the iron is hot. It's a mistake to wait too long to make that call. People have short memories and are busy, and "buzzes" fade quickly. Audiences have short attention spans and can also be absurdly fickle, as can bookers. But if your style is "hot," use it to your advantage. Tell the booker that you sing in Spanish, or that you wowed the audience at a festival that was similar to hers. Drop the name of the person who recommended you, and tell the booker all the superlatives that fans and presenters used after your concert. By the way, I also

12

make a practice of collecting quotes (only superlative ones, of course) about my work from notable people in the biz—which are very useful as recommendations.

Auditions

The next step after getting your foot in the door is the audition. This could be live or by demo. If you are sending a recording, make sure it is the best quality you can make and of the best material you have. There is a separate section in chapter 7 that addresses demos. So let's concentrate on the live audition. By telling you about three of my failures, I will illustrate some examples of what *not* to do.

Let's say the booker has consented to hear you live. She may want you to come to her venue and do a set or two, to see how you work with an audience. Or she may just want you to play for her in her office. It's a most peculiar fact that it's harder to play for just one or two people than it is for a thousand. The most nerve-wracking live audition I ever had was for Richard Nixon's inauguration gala (yes, I've been in the business *that long!*). The booker came to my manager's office, where my partner and I had to sing two songs as if we were singing for the whole nation. At the time we were very young and inexperienced, and couldn't manage to pretend we were singing for millions instead of just one guy. That, plus the fact that our songs were of the liberal bent—not exactly the kind of music Nixon's supporters would go for. Needless to say (and looking back, I am ever so grateful for this), we didn't get the audition and therefore didn't get to sing for Dick. This was one of only three auditions I ever failed in my long career.

I learned from this mistake. Many years later, I again had to audition in an office, this time in front of several people (and a baby!) for a new children's television show called "Tell Me a Story," which was under development. This time, much more experienced and confident, I sang as if there were three thousand people listening to me instead of three. *Then*, when the producer told me that he definitely wanted me as a guest, but he was also looking for a host, I seized the moment, pitched myself on the spot, and I got the gig as the regular daily host for the whole season (on TV, that's fall until summer). Following that season, we *almost* became a national show on a special channel devoted to storytelling and music. Unfortunately, the big boss pulled the financial plug on the channel, and the entire new project died. But the moral of the story is, you should audition for one as if there were hundreds or even thousands in front of you.

And this means *being yourself* in front of three people, in the same way you'd be yourself in front of thousands. My second failed audition not only falls into the "inappropriate venue" column discussed earlier, but also the one titled, "it's phony and futile to try and fit *their* mold." I auditioned for *Star Search* at the recommendation of my former singing partner, who had passed her audition for the show and had gone on to actually appear on national TV in competition. Her audition video was smashing. It was really *her* and everything that made her special: her style, her song, her look. But then she made what I believe was a fatal mistake. She decided she needed to remake herself over in the image of the other female singers so prevalent on *Star Search*, and when she finally appeared, she was a clone of everyone else: She had *their* look and sang a popular song that wasn't her own composition, in *their* style. Unfortunately, as talented as my friend was (and still is), she got beat out by the other woman contestant. Anyway, her initial success at the show inspired me to try as well, but I didn't learn from her mistake. I auditioned for a few people in a studio, and I, too, tried to make myself into what they were looking for. I even hired a choreographer to help me move, because none of the "girl singers" on the show used a guitar, and I felt awkward without one. Again, needless to say, I failed that audition because I was trying to be someone I wasn't. *Star Search* was not my kind of "venue," and I wasn't their kind of singer. The moral of this one is, if you try to be someone you are not, you end up being nothing.

My last failed audition was caused by lack of preparation. When you audition, of course you want to do your very best material that you know inside and out, material that shows off your best qualities as an artist and musician. I had the opportunity to audition for a TV show as a musical personality. This was for a new show for Nickelodeon. Not being familiar with mainstream culture (I live in a cave, under a rock) I didn't know just how big Nickelodeon was, and didn't take the audition very seriously. When I went to the first audition I sang one of my own songs, which of course I knew backwards and forwards. I passed that first one and was called back for a second about a week later. Again I did a familiar piece and passed. The third time I was called back, they sent me a tape of the theme song to learn in advance, and I was very half-hearted about the whole thing. I didn't bother to memorize the lyrics, nor did I really pay much attention to the melody, which was in an impossible key for me (as well as for most of the other women auditioners). Well, I fluffed that third audition because I didn't prepare. At least, that was a factor. It could also have been that I wasn't what they were looking for, after all.

An easier and more natural live audition involves performing before "your" audience. Let's say you scoped out the venue and determined that it fits your kind of music. (Again, I stress that this is extremely important; an audition in front of an unresponsive or hostile audience is hard work at best and disaster at worst.) Now you are going to do an "open mic" or a few sets, or maybe even a whole night or concert in front of this unfamiliar but hopefully friendly audience. If you are going to be doing only a few pieces, it goes without saying that you should choose your strongest material. I like to show my versatility by picking three pieces that are very different from each other in style, tempo, theme, and dynamic. You might like to show off your musical virtuosity, your sensitivity, your sense of humor, your stellar songwriting, or your spectacular voice. Whatever it is, this is your chance to shine and dazzle. You want to *blow away* the audience and the booker. This is where all the nights of free or "little" gigs pay off, where you show off what you've learned about working an audience. This is where what is called in the music biz "paying your dues" finally pays you back. You will want to make your audience laugh, or cry, or sit up and take notice, or preferably, all three. Most of all, you want to touch them in some way. Bookers see a tremendous number of performers, and are pretty jaded when it comes to auditions. But they also know quality when they see or hear it. And you must have all your gears clicking at an audition, because you may not get another chance at this same venue. You've got to show them *why* they should hire you and risk their audience on you.

Before auditions, just like at any other performance, I like to warm up my voice, stretch my body, and breathe deeply. Long ago, when I was first starting out, I would get a bad case of the jitters before auditioning. Nowadays, it's no big deal unless it's a very important one for a big gig. Anyway, if you do this preparation, it works wonders for calming your nerves, as well as for getting your body ready. See the section on stage fright in chapter 5.

Pre- and Post-gig Forms and Logs

Once a presenter calls to book you, you'll need to be ready to gather all of the pertinent information about the venue. You must be prepared to provide all of the information and material they need, in addition to detailing to them your specific needs from the venue itself. One thing that I started to do early in my solo career was to keep logs of each and every concert. There are many reasons to do this, and I have found the practice to be invaluable in many ways. I can find a past gig quickly if I keep up an index.

Once a month, I go into my Microsoft Access sponsor mailing list and, using this index, add the information about when and where I played that month.

Here is my method for keeping track of future and past performances. Let's start at the beginning:

INTAKE/INQUIRY FORM

When a presenter calls, or if I make the call, I have an intake/inquiry form (see appendix A). This form will help you to remember all the pertinent details you will need to know about the gig in order to write a contract. My form is just a suggestion—you should customize whatever details you need. Sometimes a presenter is just calling to get information, and it never gets any further than the inquiry. I keep these records for about six months, during which time I make follow-up and gentle reminder calls. Sometimes, the presenter does intend to book you, but life gets busy and if your name is not right in her face, you'll get overlooked. At times like these, presenters often appreciate the follow-up call. Just make sure you don't do it too often, or you will be perceived as a pest. I usually wait a week or two, then call to see if they are still interested. If they still seem to be, I ask when would be a good time to call again. If not, I *may* pitch their form in the trash. I keep all inquiry forms in a folder, which I take out from time to time when I am free to make these calls.

On the inquiry form at the top, there is a place to record the dates of your calls. This is important, because you want to see how the inquiry is "aging." If you find you are making too many follow-up calls, maybe you are chasing a lost cause. You also want to space your calls out, again so that you are not pestering them. There is that fine line between being a pest and being persistent! After the date of the call, I write a code that tells me the result of that call— something like "LM" for "left message" (on an answering machine or with a live person, both of which can be unreliable about relaying your message), "cb" for "call back" (and make sure you mark a callback date), "wcb" for "*they* will call back" (again, try and pin them down to a date for their call back), and "wcii" for "will call if interested." If it's this last category, I'll throw the form out after about six months but keep the venue in my mailing list. Again, turnover for bookers can be high, and if you're not the first guy's cup of tea, his successor may like you. You will find the best method for yourself.

Under the dates of the calls, I put contact information, including the name and title of the contact person, mailing address to send the contract, day, evening, and cell phone, and fax numbers. This is very important information, because if the gig does come your way, you will no doubt be speaking and corresponding with this person directly. I always ask how to spell the contact's first and last name, because some people get really irked if their name is misspelled! If there is a question about the pronunciation of the contact person's name, I write it phonetically in parentheses so that I won't embarrass myself next time I talk to him. I also ask for the mailing address because sometimes it is not the same as the performance address.

Next, I get or confirm the performance address if different from the mailing address. You'll want to get an actual street address and the site's phone number for when you are driving there. The phone number should be of someone who will be available just before the gig—it's for you to use in case you are late or lost.

Under this I put "type of program," because I have many different kinds—family, adult, and children, plus different titles for each of my programs. Maybe you have a Gershwin, a Cole Porter, and a Rodgers and Hammerstein show. If the performance is to be for children, I also ask the age range so that I can target my songs better to the audience. (There's nothing worse than singing songs that go "above their heads." I take that back—what's worse is singing too-babyish songs for older kids. They will kill you.) Then there's the length of the concert. How many sets? How long?

Date, time of concert, and arrival time are, of course, crucial. I always also put down the day of the week of the concert, as a double check. It's easy to put down a wrong date, but if you consult your calendar, you can generally catch a mistake if you also know the day of the week it's supposed to be on. Determining the arrival time is for the benefit of both you and the sponsor. You want to let the venue know when to expect you, to make sure it is open and ready for you. You might also want a space for sound-check time.

Ah, the fee: Setting it will be covered in its own section in chapter 14. But here is where you will put the total fee due you, including any other charge that is relevant, such as hotel expenses, meals, per diem fees, and so forth. If you want separate checks for your various accompanists or support personnel, you will note that here, too, with the amount each person is to be paid spelled out clearly. Many places will also want Social Security or tax numbers. You can put those in your contract or in a cover letter.

An alternate date and site are for when there is danger of cancellation or change due to weather or anything else unforeseen, such as illness. I try not to cancel altogether—I try to get them to commit to a rescheduling if possible. Also, if the performance is to be outdoors, you might try and ask for a rain site, again so that you don't have to cancel or reschedule.

Other bits of information you should obtain—just to make sure that you and the presenter are on the same page—include the following:

- ♫ *Backup. For me, this means how many and what kind of accompanists the booker wants and can afford. Does she want the drummer? The second guitarist? A go-go dancer? (Only kidding.)*

- ♪ *Audience size. I ask this because I want to know what to expect. Often the venue can only guess, but you may want to know the room's capacity. Are you performing for forty, four hundred, or four thousand?*

- ♫ *Room description. Are you playing in a church? An auditorium? A gym? A bar? You want to know this for the size of the room, the acoustics, and so forth. Will there be a stage? What size? Lights, and what kind? Will the audience be seated on chairs or on grass?*

- ♪ *Sound system. Who will provide it? What kind of equipment do they have? Will you need to supplement it with your own stuff? Will there be someone acting as sound technician?*

The answers to the above questions will lead to other questions. For instance, if the location is in a park, will the presenter supply you with electricity if you need it? This sounds silly, but if you're playing outdoors and you need it and they don't have it, you have problems. We have had outdoor gigs where the show was in the middle of some green space, far from any kind of electricity, so they brought in a generator that was too loud. We had quite a time trying to sing and play over that. That wasn't the only problem; this generator somehow put out too many amps or watts or whatever, and blew up my PA amp, which quit working mid-show. This was a disaster all around, costing me my voice from trying to sing to hundreds of kids outdoors without a sound system, plus the $125 it took to fix my PA. From that incident, we learned to request *no* generators. If there is no electricity for our sound system and amps, we don't play unless we can get away with a totally acoustic set, such as in a small room.

Speaking of small rooms, even in such a space, I like to use a PA system. This gives some presenters pause, but I explain it's not for volume so much as for *presence*. I find it very hard to sing with sensitive dynamics acoustically unless it's in someone's living room. So even a small sound system is preferable to none in a small space. I have three different systems for different purposes and space sizes.

Below this go other details: Can I sell product? This is important to know up front, although some artists go ahead without asking first anyway. They figure it's easier to get forgiveness than permission! But some venues will not permit the selling of anything, and will get pretty perturbed if you do anything that smacks of commercialism from the stage. If they do allow it, see if they require a commission of sales. Some do, some don't. A typical commission is 10 percent.

Then, there is the "please provide" space. Here is where you tell them everything that you will need from them: Water? Volunteers to help sell CDs? Driving directions? Hotel and meals? A massage and sushi backstage? Oh, I wish …

Lastly, there is a space for what the presenter needs from me: photos, posters, press release information, biography, demo tape, video, and so forth. Keep a record of what you send her.

You will, of course, customize your own intake sheet. But whatever information you need, be sure to put in on this sheet. It will help you when you go to contract, and if there is any dispute about who was to provide what. (See chapter 15, the section on performance contracts.)

PERFORMANCE FORM

After I've secured the gig, I have one more form that I take to the gig. Here is what I have on that form:

- *Date, time, and arrival time of gig*
- *Presenter and location*
- *Length of concert—number of sets and how long*
- *Kind of audience*
- *My equipment checklist*
- *My sets*

At the bottom I have an evaluation, for my purposes only. No one else sees this form; it's for my benefit and eyes only. I write my sets beforehand so that I have an idea what I want to do, but I also stay flexible so I can change, add, or delete songs in the middle of a concert as I read the audience. After the show, I make any revisions to the set list so it's an accurate account of what I did that day or night. This information is very valuable to me later on, especially if the venue hires me again soon after this first gig and they want me to perform different—or the same—material.

The checklist is important so that I don't forget something either going to the gig or after the show while loading my van. I make the checklist the day before the gig, so I have plenty of time to revise it, and I'm not rushing and frantically trying to remember what I need the day of the gig.

The evaluation is valuable to me so that I can remember the gig a little better. It tells me how big the audience was, what its makeup was (kids, adults, seniors, mixed, teenage Albanian shoemakers …), how much product I sold, and whether the gig was worthwhile. Then I have a space for my comments. I always try to write these right after the gig, so the memories are fresh in my mind. I want to know if they loved the concert. Did I get an encore? Did it seem I was right for the venue? Did I have fun? Should I come back in the future or should I never set foot there again? Over the years you will have gigs in thousands of venues, and it will become impossible to remember them all. You want to recall all this information—forewarned is forearmed, as they say.

I clip any pertinent paperwork to this performance form as it comes in—contracts, correspondence, directions, invoices, and so forth. Then I put all the packets for each upcoming gig in a big folder in chronological order, to be pulled out week by week. At the start of each week, I review the upcoming gigs so I know what's in store for me. I also try and call each venue a few days ahead of the concert date, just to touch base and to remind them of my needs and when to expect me. I have found that they often forget that I requested water, that they didn't send directions as I'd asked, and so forth. I recheck when the sound check is going to be. I ask that the stage be cleared and broom-swept. You would not believe the clutter some venues stash onstage, expecting the artist to clear it! I've had to move an orchestra's worth of music stands and folding chairs more times than I'd like to remember. Again, I take this whole packet of paperwork to the gig. You would be surprised at how much you will need all this info while you are there at the venue.

After the gig and after I've made all my evaluations, I staple the packet together, punch holes, and put the whole thing into a three-ring binder that's got dividers by month—and I keep the packets in chronological order. I used to have one binder per year's worth of gigs, but once I got real busy and the paperwork started multiplying, I began using three two-inch binders per year, which I label by months and year. In this way I have a systematic record of every gig I've played through the years. I know what songs I played, how the audience reacted, who my contact person was … everything. I refer back to these logs constantly, especially when I have repeat shows at the same venue. I also use these logs as a reference when people ask where I've played in their area.

I have a hard-copy master index of venues I've played arranged by state and town, year by year, so that I can find them quickly. This I can take to showcases, while a computer list in Microsoft Access allows me to type in the name of the venue and find the performance history instantly. Of course, both the index and the computer program need updating regularly, so there is a lot of clerical work involved. But if you do a little bit at regular intervals, it's manageable, and *so* worth it!

Finally, post-gig, some artists like to send a follow-up/thank-you letter to the presenter. One time, to an extraordinary presenter who bent over backwards to make us feel appreciated as "stars" and welcomed as honored guests, I sent flowers and a nice card as a thank-you. This is gracious and a gesture of goodwill, and hopefully they will remember you when they want to book again. Of course, this is only in the event of a successful show! You will find that presenters often talk to each other, and a good evaluation of your show will help you create a buzz. Likewise, a poor show could hurt you with other venues, but that's another story.

Folksinger John McCutcheon has a good suggestion: If a presenter loves your show so much that she asks you to return, you can say, "Sure! And I'll play for the same fee, even if I bring in a larger crowd, as long as you invite x number of *other* presenters to the next show to see it." This works with festivals, schools, and clubs.

Creating Your Own Place to Play—Concert Production

Oftentimes artists decide to self-produce a concert. Maybe they have just released a new album, maybe they want to help a cause or charity through music, or maybe they just want to put on a great concert featuring themselves and, possibly, some other similar artists. Whatever the reason, producing your own concert can be a wonderful thing—or not!

It's a good idea to pick the brains of others who have experience—their advice could save you a lot of headaches and dollars. You, in turn, will have total (well, almost total) control of the experience, and you will reap the profits (if there are any!). Then again, you might find yourself spending too much time as a concert producer and too little time as a musician. Producing carries with it a hefty set of responsibilities, and you'd do well to know what you're getting into before you start.

𝄢 *Venues*

WHERE?

Of course, you will need a space. This might be your single biggest expense. But get creative—maybe you know someone with a big house or yard that might be willing either to lend it or to rent it for a small fee. Houses of worship also often rent their spaces out, for not too much. Elks, Lions, and Moose lodges, firehouses, libraries, meeting halls, barns, parks ... the list goes on. Call around; you might be surprised at what is available. If you are producing a benefit or fundraiser, even better, as people are more likely to lend their space for a reduced fee or even for free if they support the cause. Features to consider when choosing a space are:

- ♫ *Location and parking. Can your audience find the place easily? Once they get there, is there adequate parking?*

- ♪ *Capacity. Will the space hold the anticipated crowd? By the way, if you are unsure of the number of people you'll attract, it's always better to use a smaller space. There is something very discouraging about seeing two hundred people in a thousand-seat hall. Better to have to put out extra chairs or have standing room only for those two hundred people crammed into a smaller venue. It looks and feels better for both the artist and the audience.*

- ♫ *Acoustics. What kind of music will be played here? Acoustic or electric, big band or solo cello? Bring someone with you to check this out. By singing or playing several bars of loud and soft music, you can get an idea of the reverb of the room and of any "slapback" or dead spots. Remember, music in a roomful of people sounds quite different than music in an empty room. Will you need amplification?*

- ♪ *Heat and air conditioning. Pretty important when it's freezing or stifling. You don't want your audience to be so uncomfortable that they pass out or have to leave. I have been trapped in the audience in an extremely uncomfortable hall for a three-and-a-half-hour music revue (way too long!) in ninety-degree heat. Horrible! If the audience is wilting, think of what the musicians will feel like working under lights in those conditions. Conversely, players' fingers and listeners' ears don't work well chilled to the bone, either.*

- ♫ *Rest rooms. Make sure there are adequate facilities for the number of people you anticipate. Any woman will tell you that there are NEVER enough restrooms for females! Check out the cleanliness and who will stock them with supplies.*

♪ **Kitchen facilities.** *If you plan on serving or selling food or drink, especially alcohol, make sure you check with the venue first for approval to have refreshments. Many places forbid or restrict it.*

♫ **Lighting and electrical.** *Is there separate lighting for the stage area and the house? Will you need supplemental lighting? What is the current capacity—will you blow circuits if you add lights or have lots of huge amplifiers or other electricity-sucking equipment?*

♪ **Stage.** *Is there one? What kind, how high, and what is the access? See chapter 10 for advice on the technical aspects you should look into before you perform on a stage.*

WHEN?

After finding a space, you will need to secure a date. Make sure you have a good calendar that is marked with any holidays that could possibly interfere with your concert. Also, it's a good idea to check with other organizations whose audience you wish to draw from: Will they be having any events on the same night that might split the audience? You will want to pick a date that is *at least* three months away from right now. Ideally, you want at least six months to produce a concert successfully. Of course, Friday and Saturday nights are usually first-choice nights for events, as most people don't have to get up early the next day. But those nights are also usually the most expensive to rent spaces, so you might want to consider a weeknight or Sunday afternoon, knowing that it may be harder to draw an audience then.

If you are providing the sound system, you will need not only an adequate one but also someone who knows how to set up and run it. More is covered on this topic in chapter 10. If you need to rent a system, figure that into your overall budget. You will still need to familiarize yourself with a new system, so give yourself time *well before* the show to learn it.

HOW MUCH?

Setting the admission fee is tricky. You don't want it so high you discourage people from coming, especially if the act is unknown or doesn't have a draw; yet you don't want it so low you lose money on the event. Try to gauge what other similar concerts charge. If it is a fundraiser, people are more likely to shell out a higher admission fee because they want to support the cause, not necessarily come to hear the artist. If it is possible, you might consider a sliding or lower fee for children, seniors, students, or hardship cases. I like to make it possible for anyone to come to hear great music, regardless of the listener's financial situation. I have often found that it's the less well-heeled that make the best audiences.

REACHING YOUR AUDIENCE

Publicity is *the most important key* to producing a successful concert. You might have the most talent in the world, the best sound system, a beautiful space, and the perfect date. But if no one knows about it, it will flop. Press releases need to get to monthlies two months before the targeted publication date; weeklies, six weeks; and dailies, four weeks. Direct-mail flyers and e-mail should ideally go out one month before the concert date. See chapter 7 for some fresh ideas.

There are other resources where you can turn to if you want more details on concert production. It is my hope that you will want to try your hand at producing—it's rewarding, frustrating, and a huge amount of work, but it will certainly add to your knowledge of the music business. And, if your first show is a success, why not do it again? I know several artists who have created small listening rooms—mini concert halls, if you will—with a regular schedule of concerts. It makes some sense to do this, for once you've produced one concert, you have the know-how and resources to make a series.

Benefits and Fundraisers

Sooner or later, you may be asked (or you may volunteer) to do benefits and fundraisers. This, in fact, is a very good way to get started in the music business, since everyone loves musicians at events but no one wants to pay us. It's a way to get exposure to new audiences, and everyone talks about "exposure" in this business. It's true—you need to be seen and heard to build an audience. And at the beginning, if someone isn't willing to pay you what you think you're worth, heck, play for free this time. Next time, after she is dazzled by your music, someone in the audience or the benefit producer may offer you a paying gig. Just don't get carried away and *always* give away your work for free! For more on these kinds of gigs, see chapter 5, "Giving Back and Getting Back."

Chapter 3
Other Musicians

Part of the fun and magic of performing music is doing it with others. There is something lovely and simple about a solo voice or instrument, but with two or more you get harmony, volume, richness, interplay ... so much of what makes music interesting. It's no wonder that musicians often seek out others to play with; it's like a dance, a conversation, a cooperative effort that gives listeners chills when it's right. Two people performing together *more* than doubles the effect of a single musician.

How to Find and Hook Up with Others

As you'll read in the section on accompanists in chapter 9, you will find other musicians for your group by looking, listening, and asking around. However, unlike a front person–accompanist relationship, in a group presumably everyone is a peer, with equal or nearly equal say in decisions, pay, billing, and so forth. Once you are playing out in public, you will meet others who appreciate and play your kind of music. If you play the blues, a logical place to start would be the blues clubs in your town. Networking is extremely valuable here because you want the people making up your group to be not only musically compatible but also personally compatible. It's much harder to get both if you are auditioning complete strangers. But that certainly is another way to go and well-used.

Many musicians, especially if they are new to an area, look in the classifieds of their local paper (preferably a trade/music paper) for groups to join. Also in some areas, especially large urban ones, there are organizations and businesses especially for the purpose of hooking up musicians with each other. Some charge a small fee for a limited time for searchers to read through big binders of groups looking for musicians and musicians looking for groups. Others may ask you to join as a member to give you access to their musician files. Music stores also often have bulletin boards expressly for this, and they are free. Groups looking to fill a spot advertise for like-minded musicians, and, conversely, musicians looking for situations also place ads. Be sure to read (or compose) these ads *carefully*. Don't even bother showing up to audition if the ad asks for heavy metal guitarists aged eighteen through twenty-two if you are thirty and have a strong background in Sixties rock. No one will be happy, and it will be a waste of everyone's time.

Just as with your search for a good venue, the Internet is a good place to find and hook up with other like-minded musicians. There are countless Web sites and virtual organizations (meaning they exist only on the Web rather than in any other kind of formal setting) in every genre of music there is. But like anything else on the Net, you want to be careful about making contact. I don't have to tell you there are a lot of nuts, crooks, and frauds out there.

Most musicians want to work with others in their own area for ease of rehearsing. So you may be concerned with not only musical and personal compatibility, but also geographic proximity. More on this in chapter 9.

Another idea you can explore to find other musicians is to start or join a formal or informal organization, such as a folk club, blues jamming group, mandolin orchestra, songwriters' forum, and so forth. This is a great, no-pressure way to meet other musicians who like similar styles of music. You will have a wonderful time playing together, get to "audition" many musicians, and have the chance to form lasting friendships this way. It needn't be anything elaborate—meet at someone's house over a potluck, rent a church space monthly … whatever your imagination and budget will allow. You can advertise this in all the usual places, as well as in some unusual ones like grocery store bulletin boards and school hallways.

Band Mates

I define "band mates" as people who perform together in a more or less equal-status situation. There may be a leader or organizer, and there may be an equitable but not necessarily equal division of labor, where each person does what he or she likes or does best. Maybe one person is great on the phone, one writes exciting and colorful copy for brochures and press releases, and one is the muscles who likes carrying, setting up, and tinkering with equipment and instruments. If a group is to last, whether an orchestra, rock group, choral group, or whatever, you want to make sure everyone feels a part of it and has an investment in it. Otherwise, there will probably be high turnover and hard feelings. No one likes to feel that he is carrying more than his fair share of the load, and no one likes to feel unappreciated. Everyone, presumably, is there for somewhat the same reasons—to have a good time making wonderful music that others will enjoy. If being part of a group becomes burdensome or oner-ous, if there are personality clashes and much fighting, or if there is any sort of major ongoing, unresolvable unpleasantness, what is the point of staying in the group?

At the very beginning, some sort of groundwork should be laid out for making decisions, handling money, sharing responsibilities. Up to a point, this can be a simple, informal, verbal agreement. But after that crucial point (see the "Contracts" section in chapter 15) you'll need a formal, written contract spelling everything out. As group members change over time, these guidelines will help smooth transitions so there will be fewer misunderstandings. Also, these "rules" may change with the personnel. The main thing to keep in mind is that you are there to make your kind of music together (and hopefully enough money to do it full time!), have fun, and respect each other. If you lose sight of any of this, you might as well go get a straight job.

I know of some groups whose members live, work, and play together. There are, of course, advantages and disadvantages to this. I say, if it works for you, more power to you. It certainly works for my husband and me! For others, it's just too much togetherness, and people feel they need their space away from each other. The advantages of having a close-knit group are pretty obvious—scheduling and finding space for rehearsals are very easy to do in this situation. Also, by living together you may find that you get very much "in sync" with each other, and this may carry over into your performances, with everyone almost reading each other's minds onstage. It makes thought-ful, respectful, and fair decision-making all the more crucial, too, because when living together, you are forced to work things out—no one can just leave and go home! The disadvantages are also obvious: It's harder to get away from each other, and if there's professional friction, it may carry over into the per-sonal and vice versa. It's a special group that can be both band mates and housemates.

Bill Mates

I use this term to mean artists who share a performance or an event but remain separate acts. Hopefully, everyone's music is somewhat compatible, i.e., in roughly the same genre, unless the diversity is the whole point of the show. A very typical example of bill mates would be a main act and one or more opening acts. The reason I address this topic here is because of the issue of professional courtesy. Many "main acts" don't like the idea of having an opening act because of the very real concern of their audiences' attention span. Most people, except in certain circumstances like a festival, cannot sit for longer than sixty to ninety minutes at a stretch before becoming aurally or physically "fatigued." If the opening act's set is too long, too incompatible, or not engaging, the audience may become somewhat fatigued or restless even before the main act goes on. Unless the opener is very good, some audiences won't tolerate the evening's time being taken away from the artist they really came to hear. So, most openers perform anywhere from a mere two songs to maybe forty-five minutes. Another reason why a main act might not want an opener is because of incompatibility of styles, or even professional insecurity—maybe the opening artist is so dynamite, the main act becomes overshadowed!

WHY ARE BILL MATES EVEN CONSIDERED?

When there *is* an opening act, it can be good for everyone. The audience gets warmed up and excited. Introduced to new faces and sounds, they get more "bang for their buck." The opening act gets further exposure, can possibly win more new fans, and gets the chance to perform for a larger audience than is usually available to it. If the main act is very well-known, the cachet of opening for this act adds to the opener's résumé and reputation. If the match is well-made, the main act benefits by having a warmed-up audience who is put in a good, relaxed mood by the opener and who is now eagerly awaiting the "star." Plus, maybe the main act will make new contacts through the opener, and friendships may form.

There is also something to be said for the responsibility well-established acts have of giving a leg up to newcomers, as they themselves were probably helped along during their career. I have had the help of many generous famous "mentors" like Tom Chapin, who not only graciously shared a stage with me but who, after hearing and enjoying my music, helped me along in other ways, from introducing me to record companies to performing on one of my albums. It has been a thrill to finally meet and share a stage with my heroes. Whenever I have the chance, I try and do the same for those newer and less known. Of course, it might be the concert producer or venue who has a say in whether there's an opening act, rather than the "star's" people.

ORDER OF APPEARANCE

Beyond main act and opener—when there are three or more acts on a bill—an order of appearance needs to be set. If the venue or producer doesn't make this decision, if everything else is equal and the acts are deciding among themselves who goes where, my favorite place to be is somewhere in the middle. Opening an evening or an event is hard because you are the audience's first taste of what is to come. Expectations may be high and hard to fulfill and late-comers may miss your set. You have a "cold" audience *you* have to warm up. For these and other reasons this is often considered the least desirable spot. On the other hand, unless you are the main act who everyone's waiting for, the last spot is kind of crummy, too, because of the fatigue factor again, and because it may be very late into the night as well.

The middle is optimum, in my opinion, because the audience is still somewhat fresh, you can blow them away and leave them excited to hear more, and you haven't pushed anyone's tolerance or patience level. In any case, you never want to overstay your welcome. Leave your audience wanting more. If you sense your audience drifting, it is best to cut your set short. End with your best number and the audience will appreciate it.

SHOW SOME RESPECT

I also want to stress here the importance of cooperation and camaraderie among bill mates. It does no one any good when hostility, impatience, and professional jealousy rear their ugly heads. Superstar egos or prima donna attitudes should likewise be held in check. If the situation is stressful, like maybe at a showcase or festival when set changes need to be made quickly, a calm and cooperative demeanor will be appreciated by sound and stage techs as well as by the other acts. It can taint an event if someone throws a hissy fit because someone else didn't leave the stage quickly enough or didn't like her placement on the bill.

I have found that by offering to share equipment, adjusting a set length, or giving some other kind of accommodation in a difficult situation, I can diffuse a lot of the tension that occurs naturally at performances. In order for everyone to do their best, an atmosphere of relaxed and efficient professionalism is the most effective.

FRIENDS, COLLEAGUES, STARS, AND "RIVALS"

It goes without saying that music is a gregarious form of art. It's more fun to play with others, and most magical when played by live musicians for a live audience. You probably already know that musicians are some of the most generous, friendly, and fun people on the planet. At the same time, they can be the most egotistical, insecure, neurotic people one can encounter. But unlike visual art—which is often created by a solitary, isolated artist, then separated from its maker and subsequently viewed by an "audience" far removed from the artist—music depends on a certain social interaction between its makers and the audience. So it follows that musician friends and colleagues should form and maintain amiable relations, with music as a bond.

Most of my close friends are musicians—some fully professional, some part-time, some strictly amateur. But when we get together, music is somehow involved, more often than not. We perform on each other's recordings and at each other's concerts. We share mailing lists, tips, and tales of woe. We call each other up for "pep talks" or advice when something's not working. There is no room for jealousies; we revel in each other's triumphs, and we support each other during the down times. This network helps sustain us in this very trying business. I think this an *extremely* important thing to have if you are trying to make it in music. You will, no doubt, hear many, many stories of backstabbing, cutthroat behavior in this business. It's bad enough that our society might devalue what we do without a fellow artist trying to sabotage or undermine our efforts. So try and surround yourself with positive, giving, trustworthy people. Likewise, try and be that kind of friend yourself. Having a "we're all in this together" attitude is part of being in the gracious community of musicians.

WHEN GENIUSES ARE UNGRACIOUS

Thankfully, there have been very few real stinkers among fellow musicians that I have met, performed with, or otherwise gotten to know over the decades. I just avoid those unhappy souls, their music, and their whole game. It's disappointing when you meet people whose music you really admire but who turn out to be real losers. How can someone who makes such great, beautiful sounds be so ugly inside? This is especially disenchanting if that person is a "star," because we tend to think that people should be like their public persona. We want to think that that wonderful songwriter is deep and thoughtful and sensitive, not a sexist jerk or a creep. We hope that that amazing musician put as much time into his own character as into practicing chops, and thus, is a god worthy of worship. We forget that that guitar god is also just a flawed human being like the rest of us.

This is one reason I have difficulty with the whole "cult of personality/celebrity" thing. As much as I admire and respect my music heroes, I have to remember they were once struggling and started much like

I did, that they snore and yell and break things, too. What I am saying is, don't be so overawed by your idols that you put them on a pedestal. And I personally won't support even the greatest musician if he's a boorish jerk.

WHEN OTHERS OUTGIG YOU

On the subject of "rivals," I like to look at it this way: There will always be musicians who are better than me, who will climb higher on the ladder of success, who will get the gigs I don't. But on the other hand, I have had a certain level of success that some others only dream of. I make a good living doing what I love, and at the same time feel I am doing good in the world. You can get eaten up with envy and jealousy over what you *don't* have, or you could choose to be grateful for what you *do* have. Whenever I meet someone who is a potential "rival," I try and make friends with him instead. I prefer to have a cooperative mindset over a competitive one.

Also, try to get secure about *your* talents and position in *your* career. Jealousy and envy go hand-in-hand with, and indeed *arise from*, insecurity. If you think of the music business as having enough jobs and goodies for everyone who is talented—that is, if you have a *prosperity* mentality instead of a *poverty* mentality—then whatever anyone else gets doesn't seem like it's being *taken away from you.* Even in a real contest or competition, winning and losing doesn't really mean anything in the objective world, since the quality of art and music is sometimes rather subjective. You may lose one contest or a gig to someone else, but you will also have your share of being in a winning situation from time to time, too. What I mean is, you don't *really* have any rivals. You and your music are unique, and you will find people who appreciate what you have to offer. What anybody else gets or has doesn't matter in your life.

Chapter 4

Instruments and Equipment

Before you pack your car, round up your band mates, and strike out to make your mark in the world, take a moment to inventory what instruments you've got to work with and what necessities you may still lack to do your best work. Furthermore, it is wise to consider the value of your items before dragging them with you on a plane or to a rainy pavilion. Insurance (which I'll address in chapter 18) won't save you the heartache of losing your precious Martin guitar to some thief at a showcase.

Remember, our instruments are extensions of ourselves, our tools that enable us to express our creativity, our dear friends and valuable investments. I know many musicians who would have to think twice when deciding to save their drowning spouse or their overboard instrument! But, seriously, many of us are so attached to our beloved instruments that we actually grieve if we get parted, through loss, sale, theft or destruction. Of course, there are those for whom one guitar is interchangeable with any other, and others who have so much money to throw around that even if one valuable Stradivarius is lost, it's no big deal to get another (I exaggerate a tad here). But if you are like me, the care and feeding of your friends is of paramount concern. Remember, it is partly your instrument that makes you sound good enough for people to pay money to hear you, so taking care of it is taking care of yourself and your career.

Depending on what kinds of instruments you play, more or less maintenance is required. But *all* instruments and equipment need to be kept in shape in order to sound and play their best (including our own bodies—see chapter 17).

Woods

Instruments made with any wood parts are particularly vulnerable because of the nature of the material. Wood is affected by temperature, humidity, oils and grease, and impact. Acoustic, hollow-body stringed instruments like guitars and violins are particularly sensitive because of the thinness of their bodies' wood. Those made of solid wood as opposed to laminated wood are of better quality and more expensive, but less sturdy than the latter. According to luthier Scott MacDonald of S. B. MacDonald Custom Instruments, laminated instruments need less maintenance because they are less susceptible to environmental factors. Solid wood instruments need more care.

Strings put tension on the wood, so the kinds of strings you use affect the stress level it must withstand, as well as the sound it makes. Strings for various instruments usually come in a variety of material (ie., nylon, steel, bronze, silk) and gauges (extra light, light, medium, heavy, and so on). You will need to experiment with several to find what is optimum for your instrument, your playing, and your sound. It is also helpful to check with the manufacturer of your instrument, if possible, to see what kind and gauge is recommended. Put too heavy a gauge string of the wrong material on a fragile or old guitar and see what happens—it's not a pretty sight. More on strings later.

Varnishes also affect the sound and look of an instrument. You don't have much choice about this, unless you get yours custom made or restored. Usually, professional musicians want as little varnish as possible so that the wood can vibrate well. Over-varnished instruments may look new and shiny, but the wood won't respond and "sing" as well.

Scott stresses the importance of a good setup when you first get your instrument. With regards to fretted stringed ones, often the action (how high the strings are off the fingerboard) needs to be custom-set to the gauge string you use, as well as to your touch. A good setup will allow you to play with the greatest ease and get the best performance out of your tool.

HEAT AND FREEZING WEATHER

If you leave your wood instrument in the freezing cold (heaven forbid), you can not only craze the varnish (where it cracks and looks like a spider web), but actually crack the wood. When I was young and stupid, I did just that. In my ignorance I left a lovely classical guitar in the trunk of my car overnight in winter. To my heartbreak the next morning, I found it split from sound hole to bottom. Later I got it repaired (glued), but the crack will always be there, marring its appearance and altering its sound. Likewise, a dear friend of mine put his valuable Martin acoustic guitar in the trunk during a four-hour drive in the dead of winter. He was lucky and got away with only crazing the varnish, which also can be fixed, but it's a big job—the whole instrument must be stripped and revarnished, and doing so may devalue both the instrument and its sound. As Scott MacDonald points out,

> *It's a* **big mistake** *to refinish if you are concerned with the tone and value of the instrument, as opposed to its appearance. Revarnishing a vintage or valuable instrument destroys the value because the original finish, no matter the condition, is still more valuable than a restoration. Changing the finish can also change the sound for the worse. For this reason, people buying a vintage instrument should research to make sure the finish is original.*

Heat seems to affect woods less, other than perhaps softening and loosening glue and making the whole darn instrument fall apart. At the very least, a stringed instrument sitting in full sun at the height of summer outdoors will go nuts and refuse to stay in tune. But I wouldn't subject my beloved instruments to *any* extremes in temperature. Remember, wood was once a living thing and, like us, it doesn't tolerate extremes.

HUMIDIFYING AND DEHUMIDIFYING

The environmental factor that affects wood the most is humidity—too little and it shrinks and cracks, too much and it swells and distorts. It's the real devil to watch for. My husband and I keep our instruments stored in their cases unless we are actually using them. In the winter months, when our house is warm and dry, we put humidifiers in our instruments themselves as they are stored. There are many kinds of commercial humidifiers you can buy for all kinds of instruments. But you can easily make your own humidifiers with a damp sponge in a small plastic bag poked with holes. Make sure the sponge has been wrung out well—you don't want drops of moisture getting on your instrument. This bag must be placed inside the sound hole if there is one, down into the body of the instrument. If there is no sound hole, such as with autoharps, then place the bag into the case. You will have to periodically check all humidifiers to add water. You can also humidify one whole room and keep all your precious tools there. This approach works for those who have many instruments or who want to keep them out of the cases so they are ready to play.

Acoustic hollow-body instruments are more susceptible to all of these factors than electric solid-body ones, although electric fretted instruments have their own reactions. When dry, the fingerboard shrinks and the fret ends stick out and feel sharp. If there is binding along the neck, the frets could actually crack it. Before this happens, the frets need to be filed down.

In the summer months my husband and I usually do not use dehumidifiers, because dryness is actually worse than humidity. Some new instrument cases come with silica gel packs to keep them dry in transit, but *do not keep these packs in your case*, as excessive dryness can crack your instrument. If it's particularly muggy in the house, use an air conditioner, for your comfort as well as for your instruments. You will find that with high humidity, the instrument is more difficult to play and will feel sticky. Relative humidity of 40 to 70 percent is ideal for both humans and wood—or, in the words of Scott MacDonald, "Instruments that are made of wood are happiest in the same climate and weather that we are."

In our town we have a two-month-long summer arts festival where, six nights a week, there is music, dance, and theatre for free in the park. The arts council that presents this fabulous festival prides itself on having the show go on, regardless of weather. Even in light rain or on very hot and humid nights, the audience and the artists soldier through. The stage is covered to protect the artists from rain, but that, of course, does not protect against humidity. On one particular night several years ago, there was a classical string quartet from Russia playing, and it was very hot (in the nineties) and the humidity was very high. Can you guess what happened? Cindy Clair, who served as the executive director of the Huntington Arts Council during that period, recounts the incident:

> *The group performed on this very hot, humid night and were most concerned about staying in tune. They made it through most of the concert, but in the final movement of the final piece, the neck of the violin played by the first violinist just broke right off. There was an audible gasp in the audience. These musicians were traveling with no extra cash and no spare instruments. An angel of a man came backstage afterwards—he happened to be a music teacher and stringed instrument repairman. He repaired the instrument free of charge and did it in time for them to catch a noon ferry to Connecticut the next day. He told us later the violin had been glued together with inferior glue, and that the humidity adversely affected it.*

Just another sad tale about humidity's ravages …

GREASE AND SWEAT

My husband is the instrument tech in our business, and he handles and cares for them all like a loving parent would a baby. After each concert (in fact, sometimes after each set if there is a long time between them) he will wipe down the necks, strings, and bodies of all guitars to remove sweat and oil. Bodily fluids can both mar and deaden your instrument's looks and sound. Some guitarists use a sweat guard under the place where their strumming and picking arm rests. Those who don't guard against sweat on their instruments find that, over time, there will be the wearing down of the varnish and possibly the wood if it gets that far. Oils from our fingers deaden the strings and so should be wiped off as soon after playing as possible to extend the string life.

MORE ABOUT STRINGS AND THINGS

Speaking of strings, opinions vary about what kind to use and how often one should change them. It varies from instrument to instrument within the same family, and from family to family in general. Violin strings are very different from guitar strings, which are very different from charango strings. But, of course, the rule of thumb is, the kind you use is really up to you and your own taste, as long as it's appropriate for the instrument. As for the replacement frequency, I know many pros who change their acoustic guitar strings daily, or at least before each gig. Others change them when they remember to, when the sound is so dead it reminds them to, or when the darn strings break! Once again, the kind and gauge of string will also have an impact on how often you change them.

And speaking of impact, don't. Not on your precious instrument! Willie Nelson's beloved acoustic guitar notwithstanding, you really only need the sound hole that was provided by the manufacturer. (Willie has had his Martin so long and it's traveled such hard roads that there is a second unintentional hole by the original sound hole.) If you treat your instrument like it is a baby, it will last you many generations. Keep it in its case when not in use. (Not recommended for human babies.) Not only will its humidity and temperature level stay more constant, but it will be protected. Violin maker Charles Rufino adds, "Whenever an instrument is in its case, the case should be closed and latched, not left lying open. Many accidents result when cases that are shut but not latched are picked up and the instrument spills out!" Try and get the best case you can afford for your instrument, because that's part of its insurance. This is especially true if you tour a lot, and especially on planes. I do believe the airlines hire thugs just to spot and destroy instruments going into baggage compartments. There are Fort Knox-like cases that you probably could drop from a great height (don't try this at home, however) or drop a piano on, and no damage would occur to the instrument inside. These are enormously expensive, but worth it if your instrument is valuable or precious to you. Charles advises, "Whenever possible, keep instruments, especially cellos, out of aircraft cargo holds. If you have no choice, ask for special handling in the loading and unloading of the instrument. Incidentally, packing an instrument in a cardboard box changes its status from 'luggage' to 'freight' and, while economical, dramatically increases the risk that it will be bumped off your flight onto a later one! It is also not treated as kindly as luggage."

Here's more advice from Rufino's violin shop: After playing, the hair on violin bows should be loosened and the instrument wiped down with a soft dry cloth; the tip on the bow should be protected from impact as it breaks easily and is quite expensive to repair, despite its small size; for the best tone, use as little rosin as possible and try and never touch the hair—the oils in your hands cause the bow hair to become slippery and lose friction; lubricate pegs with peg compound and string grooves with pencil lead each time you change strings, which should be whenever they are frayed or unraveling, or at least twice a year; once a year, have your bow rehaired.

As with violins, the other parts of other wood instruments also need attention from time to time. Tuning pegs may need to be lubricated or replaced, frets filed, bridges and nuts adjusted or replaced. Your instrument will let you know when something needs work. There will be buzzing, creaking, squeaks, or something just won't feel right. Get to know your instrument like an extension of your body, and you will be able to listen and feel when something's about to go bad. And just like a bodily ailment, the sooner you can catch what's wrong and fix it, the better it will be for your instrument and ultimately, of course, for your career. It's not a bad idea to have one or more "backup" instruments for when yours is in the shop or not feeling well.

STAGE STANDS AND WALL HANGERS

Stands are specially designed to hold a particular kind of instrument, and you should get one that fits the instrument well, doesn't tip over easily, and stays open for home, studio, and stage use. Another consideration for both wall hangers and stands is to make sure that the rubber parts that may touch the instrument are "finish-safe" or nonreactive. This means that they are not petroleum-based rubber, which could melt into an organic finish and ruin it.

I believe that stands onstage are crucial. We cringe when we see musicians lay their valuables on the floor onstage, or worse yet, lean them against amps or chairs. Can I tell you how many have come crashing down and were destroyed, or were stepped on or crushed accidentally? Enough to make one weep. Of course, even with a sturdy and well-designed stand, accidents happen. We were performing at one festival in the plains of Canada during an impending violent thunderstorm and later heard about one artist's guitar that got blown off its stand. It came crashing down and its head snapped clean off. I myself had a near disaster happen to my precious vintage Martin guitar when performing on a platform that was neither well-balanced nor sturdy. It was sitting on its stand at one end of the platform when another artist innocently jumped onstage at the other end. The darn stage seesawed and catapulted my baby clean into the air! It crash-landed a few feet away, but was miraculously unscathed. I was lucky that time. From that point on, you can be sure that I've checked every stage for sturdiness and stability!

Even with the most careful artist, instruments may get damaged. Again, accidents happen and the best we can do is try and be alert to any possible danger. Once, I was rehearsing with my daughter, who was to play violin with us in concert. Somehow, she knocked over her music stand, which then toppled onto my most valuable, brand new, shiny, perfect guitar, which I was holding. I just didn't get out of the way fast enough. Luckily, it just put a large scratch in the varnish (maybe the wood, I can't bear to examine it closely), but it could have been worse. Trying to put a positive spin on it, we reasoned, "Well, now I can distinguish mine from all the other exquisite, expensive, beautiful pearl-body guitars out there." My heart (and my guitar's value) sank a little tiny bit that night. Anyway, this is to illustrate that instrument insurance is a good idea if you can afford it. (More on that in the chapter on Insurance.) You will also want to get friendly with your local instrument repair person. Think of this person as your "doctor," who will keep your precious tool in top playing condition and repair any damages that may occur.

Brass and Woodwind Instruments

This is not my area of expertise, so I defer to the wisdom of others. Woodwind musician Paul Kendall notes that winds are pretty hardy, much less sensitive to the vagaries of the environment than stringed wood instruments. However, they, too, can be affected by humidity. Don't leave them unprotected in basements or other damp areas, as they can rust. Temperature can somewhat change the tone of woodwinds—too cold and the pitch is lowered, too hot and it's raised. It's easy enough to warm a cold woodwind simply by blowing into it for awhile. Other than that, the only other maintenance it needs is a little oil on valves and the changing of reeds regularly.

Percussion Instruments

I am turning this section over to George Meier, an authority on percussion. He is a professional drummer and percussionist who performs not only on an acoustic kit but also on electronic drums, hand drums, and other percussion. George says that although most drums and hand percussion instruments are low-maintenance, quite sturdy, and made to take a beating (no pun intended), under wet/humid conditions the heads of drums will deaden. Extended moisture can damage heads permanently, but an occasional soaking won't hurt them too much. In this case, you should take the heads off after the gig and clean all the rims and wood. Metal parts can rust with extended exposure to moisture. Most kit drum heads are made of plastic and are more impervious to moisture than skin heads, which you will find more on Latin, Asian, or African hand drums. Heat from a blow dryer or even a candle held judiciously close will tighten skin heads that are soft and loose by pulling the moisture out.

How often one changes the heads on drums is as individual as the drummer. Variables include how often they are played and in what conditions. Plastic heads last longer than skin because they are less variable, being synthetic and manufactured to exact measurements. If the metal rims get bent, it's easier to replace than fix them.

Drums and percussion instruments react much less to temperature extremes than hollow-body wood instruments, although wooden drums can crack with extreme fluctuations in temperature. Because most drum shells are laminated wood, they are quite hardy, but again, don't leave your drums in extreme heat over long periods of time, because the lamination can degrade. A damp cloth will clean shells easily.

All chrome parts (rims, lugs, housings, and all hardware) should be cleaned with a good commercial chrome polish, such as the cotton pad cleaners that are readily available from any drum shop. They are easy and convenient to use. Also, the lug housings should periodically be taken apart and lubricated with petroleum jelly.

Cymbals need even less maintenance—only some polishing with a nonabrasive metal cleaner, mostly for appearance's sake. Some drummers even prefer to leave them dirty because they feel the dirt "mellows" the sound. "Eventually, with enough dirt," George says, "some of the overtones get taken out. Some guys like it, some guys don't. Some guys like the brightest sound possible."

George claims that even less maintenance is necessary on electronic drums (not drum machines), as there are no heads to replace or cymbals to clean. The pads are sturdier than heads and would only need to be replaced if they get ripped. There *are* "pickups" (piezos) on these instruments which have to be replaced from time to time once triggering problems start to occur. Also, the wires probably will go bad before anything else. Treat the brain module with care, as you would any other kind of computer. Clean all pads and parts with a soft cloth, and follow the owner's manual for any other routine maintenance.

The packing of percussion instruments requires some care, as certain kinds like hanging chimes have strings that can get tangled. It's also easier to access smaller instruments in a common trunk if they are packed in separate bags, and pairs of instruments like maracas or claves won't get separated if packed together that way. The kinds of cases you choose for all your instruments depends on the kind of traveling you do, as they come as soft bags, fiberboard, and hardshell cases which give increasingly better protection. For a weekend drummer, the fiberboard cases hold up quite well, but again, get the very best you can afford to protect your real investment.

Electronic Instruments and Equipment

It's best to have someone you trust in your address book unless you know how to work on these things yourself. You can really do some damage, to yourself and to your equipment, if you don't know what you are doing. If you are experienced with tube amps and so forth, certain simple maintenance and repairs could be done by you.

For professional expertise, I turned to Corey Davidson of Davidson Electronics Corporation, who says that some of the most important aspects of safeguarding electronic instruments and equipment, and of getting the best performance from both, are to have high-quality cables and good road cases.

There is *absolutely* a difference between instrument cables and speaker cables, even though both may have the same terminals, such as $\frac{1}{4}''$ jacks, and look the same. Many of you may go, "Duh, Patricia!," but I didn't know this, and have mixed the two kinds or used them interchangeably. Don't do this! Instrument cables are shielded, meaning they have a thin inner wire at the core that is surrounded by a heavy braided one. These cables cannot handle the heavy current of a power amp. Conversely, speaker cables are not shielded; their wires are thicker, separated, and not surrounded by an electrical ground, and can therefore carry a heavier current. From the outside, you cannot always tell the difference between these two kinds of cables. If, however, you use the wrong cable (e.g., an instrument cable for speakers or speaker cables for your instrument), it's not disastrous, but you will definitely hurt your sound (by a reduction in the higher frequencies) and over time could harm your amplifier outputs. Also, it is ideal to use equal-length cables when using them for speakers, and the thicker the cable, the better. The disintegration of the plastic insulation is also an issue. Check your cables often for this and replace any that start to show signs of degradation. On the stage floor, I keep all wires as taut as possible to prevent tripping—in fact, we duct-tape down every wire that might be a hazard.

Basic maintenance is a lot of common-sense stuff, such as keeping gear clean. If you see any kind of contamination on the outside of a piece of gear, depending on the material, you can use a glass cleaner and paper towels. A thorough vacuuming is also helpful. Watch out for wetness, especially with electronics. Get good (preferably waterproof) cases for your sound system and amps. When you're performing outdoors, your equipment and instruments can get pretty dusty or dirty, so be sure to inspect and clean them before putting them away. Dirt wreaks havoc with electronics!

If subjected to very cold temperatures, wires become stiff and less flexible, but there is no risk of failure. With regard to moisture, however, any contact with it, including humidity, can affect your equipment adversely. Corey says,

> *What can happen in the presence of moisture is a phenomenon called "induction." It can cause anything from noise to failure. Moisture can be a conduit for unwanted electrical phenomena. It also causes the degradation of material, like rusting and corrosion. So, after playing outdoors when moisture is high, you should carefully check your equipment and then store it in a very dry environment. From time to time you might want to open equipment cases and let them dry out in the air.*

According to Corey, dryness is never a problem with electronics in a live performance situation. Where it *is* a concern is with digital equipment in a studio, where static electricity in a very dry atmosphere can wreak havoc. Most reinforcement gear does not use static-sensitive components in its design. However, computer- or microprocessor-based equipment often does use static-sensitive devices. Depending on the piece of equipment, static electricity can possibly harm components, *even without the power being on*. Static electricity is insidious because it conducts through even plastic, cloth, or metal.

If there is sand or salt air, you might need to open up the gear itself and chemically remove any film that has formed on the circuit board. Musicians should not attempt this themselves, but instead have the equipment serviced at an authorized center. Delicate gear such as drum machines and computer-based musical equipment should not have constant exposure to salt air, as it will not hold up for a long period of time under those conditions.

With tight-fitting road cases, the gear is better protected, since the cases act as a barrier. Addressing road cases, Corey says, "Rough transit is often the cause of the problems that we see here. Road cases will protect against this. The better the road case, the more that unit will be able to sustain in rough handling."

Extreme temperatures matter less than the *transition* from hot to cold or vice versa. Electronics can sustain subzero or very hot temperatures without damage. But if gear has been heated up to a relatively high temperature (outdoors in the summer or after being in a hot vehicle) and then immediately goes into an air-conditioned environment, condensation can form inside the gear. Conversely, in the winter, going from the very cold outdoors to a warm room and immediately turning on equipment, which heats it quickly, can cause separations and fractures. The best thing to do is to avoid extreme transitions. Don't keep electronics—or any instruments, for that matter—in vehicles in any extreme temperatures, especially for a long period (like overnight). If your gear has been subjected to extremes, try and wait a good while to let it acclimate to the room temperature before turning it on or using it.

Electronic keyboards contain a lubricant for the keys. Dust, dirt, and contamination can inhibit their movement, so keyboardists should keep their instruments clean. Once there is a problem, however, take it to a reputable service center for lubrication. Speaking of how musicians can find a good center, Corey advises, "Unless they can be personally referred by someone who has had first-hand experiences, they should always call the manufacturer of that product for a referral. Do not go by hearsay, do not take the recommendations of music stores." There is no recourse if things don't work out with the latter recommendations, but there is if the manufacturer refers. Furthermore, Corey maintains that it is better to ship your equipment to a referred center than to take it somewhere locally that is untried. Although there are no regulations or licenses for service centers, you should try and check that the center has proper insurance, certifications, credentials, and authorizations to work on your products. Don't trust your expensive, precious equipment to a service center without doing some research first.

Lastly, Corey says with a straight face, "Don't eat or drink over your gear. We see a lot of stuff in here that is the result of spills and contamination."

Accessories

Add these to your checklist or keep them in instrument cases. How easy it is to lose or forget those small things like tuners, picks, reeds, sticks… Believe it or not, our drummer once forgot to pack his sticks. In his defense, he usually packs his equipment into his truck himself, and this time he had someone else do it and it was that person who forgot. But he failed to check, and so showed up without that crucial detail. We were playing in a school. Now, normally this would be no problem—schools usually have bands or orchestras, or at least a music teacher. Usually they have lots of musical stuff around, although it might not be of the highest quality. But for some reason, this school didn't have any sort of music program or equipment, and we were stuck. We had to improvise, and he ended up playing with paintbrush handles! Anyway, the lesson here is, keep everything you need together, and have spares for every little thing. We have more than enough cords, batteries, tuners, picks, capos… you name it. We carry extras for everything—even spare rolls of duct tape!

Instruments and Travel

One thing that I do is keep my most treasured instruments at home, to be brought out only for very special gigs and where I know there will be good security. Playing festivals, for instance, is great fun, but oftentimes their instrument security leaves something to be desired. For some of these types of gigs, I have a second, less-expensive or less-cherished instrument. I feel fine carrying this one on tours and turning it over to baggage handlers on planes.

Speaking of planes, if you must travel with your expensive instrument and money's not an issue (ha ha), you might consider buying it its own seat so that you can have it in the cabin with you. Some other musicians I know carry their prized guitar in a flimsy gig bag instead of a hardshell case, hoping that it won't get put into baggage but instead gets carried on and stowed in a closet or overhead. This is not, however, guaranteed, especially these days, with tightened security and less storage space. Others, on the other hand, buy the very best heavy-duty cases that can withstand amazing punishment. These cases cost a fortune, but they are well worth it if you need to go that route.

Another suggestion: If you want to save your equipment from travel damage, rent equipment in the towns where you are touring. The trouble with this, though, is that you probably will get pretty crummy stuff if you can't afford to rent the best. Also, the costs cut into your profit, and if you travel from town to town, what happens if you can't rent everywhere you go? You could rent in your hometown for the duration of the tour. When I have chosen to rent on tour, we had been touring a region but were based in one place, so we could return the equipment where we rented it. I charged enough and worked enough to cover the rental costs and make my profit.

You could also ask the venue to supply the instruments you'll need, although they do expect you to bring your own unless it's a piano or maybe drums, and some won't even supply you with a PA system. Many musicians hate to play on unfamiliar instruments for many reasons, not the least of which is the questionable quality of what you'd be getting. If the venue supplies the instrument, the musician then has to play on whatever is offered, until he reaches a certain level and can demand a high-quality instrument. Heck, once you reach a certain level, you can travel with your own piano with its own tuner and technician and climate-controlled tractor-trailer!

Sound Systems

Your sound should be the most important part of your show career. You might sound terrific unamplified, playing acoustically in a beautifully resonant room designed and built specifically to showcase music perfectly faithfully. But chances are, those situations are few and far between. You may need some sort of sound reinforcement system, no matter what kind of music you play. For me, the most consistent and reliable means is to have your own system. As I mentioned before, I like some sort of amplification, even in small rooms, not so much for volume as for presence. Some listeners also have mentioned that they can understand lyrics better when the act uses a sound system.

Read up on all the different brands of pickups, speakers, and amplifiers, as well as the models within those brands. Test out as many as you can. Ask other similar acts what they like. Only through experience and experimentation will you find what works best for you. Most music stores may sell you what's "best for the store," as they are commission-driven. Corey Davidson weighs in with his opinion about the best way to build a system: "Go through a consultant that makes a living in sound systems. This person can be found through a professional sound company. It should cost under $100 for a basic 'what-to-buy' consultation, but it's well worth it. You can also go online and check out companies not in your area, as well as manufacturers' Web sites." There are also some manufacturers that provide 800 numbers to answer sound system questions for free.

If you need it and can afford it, get a PA amp with more channels than you think you need, as your needs may soon outgrow something small that has just a few channels. Look for an amp in which each channel has its own EQ settings (for adjusting the highs, mid-ranges, and low frequencies), so that each voice or instrument can be tweaked by itself. It's also very useful if each channel has its own monitor level adjustment. The more expensive amp heads have *several* separate monitor outputs and EQs, which is mighty helpful for those groups who want their separate monitor mixes. There are all kinds of bells and whistles you can spend enormous amounts of money on. Try and anticipate what you will need in the near future, and don't be seduced by features you won't use in a hundred years. Corey advises that sound system needs are determined basically by three factors: (1) the size of the rooms you'll be playing in, (2) the size of the band, and (3) portability.

Get the very best microphones you can afford, because that is the first "filter" your music goes through in a system, and lesser-quality mics can detract from the true sound. Likewise, choose wisely your pickups for acoustic instruments, which act like mini-mics. If you can find a knowledgeable sales-person whom you trust, pick her brain about the different qualities different brands and models offer. Some mics are especially designed for the voice; some work better for certain instruments. Be sure to try many out and see which reproduces your sound most faithfully. As for mic stands, I like boom stands over upright or gooseneck. You don't want to accidentally run into your stand or hit it with your instrument, and booms allow you to stay far away from the actual stand yet still get close to the mic. Whatever stand you get, make sure it is sturdy and won't tip easily.

Speakers should be more than adequate for the kind of music you play, where you expect you'll be playing, and what instruments will be going through them. For example, if your music uses a lot of heavy bass, either from a kick drum or bass guitar, and if the instruments go through the PA, you will need at least fifteen-inch speakers in order to accommodate these lower frequencies. Anything smaller will get "blown" or shredded in no time. Corey warns, "As soon as you start miking drums or bass and they go through the

PA, look out—everything changes." If you expect to play solely in small meeting rooms in libraries, you can find self-contained units with the amp and speaker in one relatively light and portable cabinet. Madison Square Garden, of course, requires a bit more.

Maintenance of sound systems is pretty easy—find a qualified technician and your big problems are solved! I wouldn't try and service my system myself unless I knew a great deal about electronics and acoustics. My maintenance is confined to keeping well-made, weatherproof covers on amps and speakers when they are in transit or not in use, and keeping everything clean. My mics are protected in hardshell cases, with all wires carefully rolled and secured without twisting or bending.

WIRELESS OR NOT?

Many musicians, nowadays, if they are amplified, like to go wireless because of the freedom it affords. No more cords to trip over or get tangled, the stage looks cleaner, and you can roam as far as the signal will let you. As with anything, there are advantages and disadvantages. But in my opinion, the plusses outweigh the minuses.

When my husband and I first made the decision to go wireless, we couldn't afford the very best system, so we got what we *could* afford. It's not flawless—we have silently cursed out the manufacturer plenty of times when it has broken down. Luckily for us, though, the manufacturer and repair shop are only minutes from our house, so though we are greatly inconvenienced whenever it does break down, we don't have to ship anything off and wait for weeks. But, again, we love the freedom of being wireless. We can walk through the audience if we want to. It makes sound check a breeze, as one of us can walk around in the audience area and still play. There are all kinds of wireless systems for different instruments. We have different frequencies, of course, for each instrument and mic.

I chose a handheld mic as opposed to a headset or lavaliere (clip-on mic). Although this choice meant being restricted to one place when playing my guitar (the handheld is then clipped to a mic stand), I don't like the way any of the headsets make you look—kind of like you are a pilot or a telephone operator. Of course, now that everyone is using them, audiences have gotten used to the look and it's kind of chic, but I still don't like that ball in front of my face. Also, I am not aware of any affordable lavaliere that is high enough quality for singers. Of course, Broadway shows use tiny mics hidden in wigs and costumes for their singers, but those systems are very expensive.

Whatever wireless system you use, be sure to keep plenty of spare batteries on hand, as they suck up a lot of juice, and you will need to insert fresh batteries often. It's horrible having a dying battery during a performance!

The downside of going wireless is that, once again, you are at the mercy of technology. There have been times when our wirelesses have picked up radio stations (nothing like singing along with a Madonna song coming out of your amp!) or another singer in the next room on the same frequency. There have been times when the receivers have just stopped working or caused horrible sounds because of a bad connection or some other reason. For this reason, we always keep spare cords and mics onstage so that we can quickly recoup and go back to being wired. But for the most part, we find that wireless is the way to go. If you are a down-and-dirty rock or rap group, you won't be able to prowl the stage or jump around without wireless equipment.

You can get whole books and manuals about different kinds of amplification. They are too varied and complex to explain in a single chapter—or even a single book. The point is, you should look out for and guard your sound vigilantly, because that is your main asset. A bad or inadequate system can sabotage or frustrate your intentions.

Security

If we are going to take such good care of our instruments and equipment when they're around us, it stands to reason that we are equally (or more) vigilant when they are out of our sight. The first line of defense, obviously, is to try not to let your stuff out of your sight, but that is often impractical. We have meal breaks and leave our stuff onstage, our instruments are trundled off on conveyor belts at airlines, our set isn't until later, or we want to watch other acts at a festival, on other stages. There are a million scenarios in which our stuff will have to be trusted out of sight. How can we help prevent theft, loss, or damage?

LOSS

There are many sad stories of musicians who, out of haste, forgetfulness, or neglect, have left instruments and other equipment behind when going to or from a gig. A very simple solution to this is to use checklists. If you pretty much use the same stuff from gig to gig, it's quick and easy to make one checklist that can be copied and used again and again. You would use it to pack up to go to the gig so that you don't forget something crucial, and again when the gig is over and you are packing your van or car. Also, designate one person to do a "sweep" of the stage and backstage area before you leave.

If your stuff changes from gig to gig, make a comprehensive list of *every possible thing* and check off only what you take to each gig. Before we took this one simple step, we were constantly "reinventing the wheel" before each gig, trying to think of everything we needed, and we sometimes left stuff at the gig. Once my husband even left his precious blue Stratocaster in Pennsylvania on a tour! Luckily, we were headed back that way very soon after and didn't have to make a special trip to retrieve it, and luckily it was at our hosts' house and thus secure.

Another tip that may be helpful for those who do take the same equipment to every gig is to pack the van, car, or truck the same way every time. That is another way to check to see if everything is there. If, like a puzzle, the equipment doesn't go together the same way, or if it doesn't look the same, something may be missing.

And, finally, always, always be aware, even when in a hurry, of your surroundings. Don't nonchalantly set your instrument down on a sidewalk, even if it's just to fill a parking meter on your way to meet a friend—the unfamiliar surroundings will make you liable to forget what you've been carrying—or not carrying.

There is a story about Pete Seeger, who was on his way to a gig. He needed a nap and so pulled his vehicle over on the side of the road. He took his famous banjo—the one he's had forever and made himself—out of the backseat, put it on the roof of his car (intending to put it back into the car), crawled into the backseat, and slept for a while. Refreshed, he jumped into the driver's seat and took off, completely unaware that he had left his banjo on the roof. Needless to say, it fell off and was lost. He was heartbroken and went to the media to publicize his loss, apparently forgetting he'd misplaced it and thinking it had been stolen from his car. (It was dangerous to put his prized instrument on the roof in the first place, even if he had intended to put it back in the car.) But Pete was lucky several times over. For one, the banjo wasn't damaged when it fell off the car. Two, it didn't land on the road where someone could have run over it. Three, the person who found it was honest and responsible. And finally, it was returned to him intact.

Another musician left his guitar on his stoop—just forgot to pack it in his car when he was going to a gig. Luckily for him, too, it was there when he got back, but it sure was an inconvenience (to put it mildly) when he got to the gig with no instrument, and a scare too. Not all such stories have happy endings. Be aware of where your stuff is at all times—both in your sight and out.

THEFT

Mark your stuff—instruments *and* cases—indelibly in an inconspicuous (or even conspicuous!) place. Use something easily identifiable, like stickers or bright colored tape, to distinguish your case from others. You can use a permanent marker inside your acoustic guitar, and an engraving pen on electronic equipment or inconspicuous areas of an instrument's metal parts—on drum rims, for example. You should use materials or tools that won't decrease the value of the instrument nor affect its sound.

Even if you have the misfortune of losing an instrument or having it stolen, at least you will be able to identify it if it ever shows up again. Furthermore, clearly and obviously customizing or marking your belongings with your information will in and of itself act as a deterrent to a thief. Things are much harder to sell or be pawned when they're so identifiable. (Of course, with *famous* musicians, rather than being a deterrent, a label may be an incentive because it's proof it belongs to the celebrity. The thief won't be able to easily sell it or publicly acknowledge having it, but there are a lot of unscrupulous collectors out there.)

Many places that use lots of musicians have instrument lock-ups, which are usually available at conferences, showcases, clubs, and festivals. I always check to see if the area is completely and truly secure, and that the temperature and humidity levels (especially at outdoor summer venues) are acceptable. If not, I leave my instrument in my hotel room or other more secure place and go back and forth to get it. If it all checks out, however, I leave my stuff in the lock-up, always with reservation. Make sure, again, that your stuff is clearly marked, because so much looks the same, and it's easy to make mistakes. Also, make sure you don't lose your claim ticket or you might have a dickens of a time convincing the stewards of what's yours!

When on tour and not at the concert venue, I trust my instruments to the hotel room. I *never* leave *anything* in the car or van, even if it means loading, unloading, and schlepping up flights of stairs or many floors on an elevator several times. Hotel and motel parking lots and garages are notoriously unsecured. Hotel rooms are a little more secure—at least your stuff is out of sight and only a few people have keys. If there are other storage options, weigh them. Personally, I'd rather be a little cramped with my stuff in my room and in sight, than not.

Also, when loading and unloading at the gig, *never* leave your vehicle unlocked and, even for a moment, unattended. It only takes a few seconds for someone to swipe something—why make it easy for her? Ideally, you will have more than one person at load-in and load-out, with your people watching the equipment at the venue and at your vehicle at all times. Likewise, never store stuff in plain sight in an unattended vehicle, even for a short while. Thieves break into trunks hoping to find anything—what a bonus if they get your valuable instrument. I have walked into restaurants with my instrument rather than leave it in my van. Once there, you can ask to check it into the coatroom, or, better yet, put it near or under your table. If you can't or don't want to do this, try and park where you can see your vehicle from your table.

Make and keep a list of the make, model, serial number, and replacement value of all your instruments and equipment. You can also make a record of distinguishing marks like scratches, dings, and dents. Take photos or videos to further help identify your instruments and equipment. If you can afford it, get instrument insurance. If your instrument is lost or stolen, report it immediately in the town where you lost it. If you can, publicize the lost or theft in trade publications, the Internet, and elsewhere—musicians are sympathetic to others' losses and will keep an eye out. You may just be able to get it back. Of course, the best protection is prevention. Let only those you completely trust handle your instruments and equipment.

Chapter 5
Professionalism

If you just want to have fun and work part time and just enjoy, more power to you. If you want to do this full-time, for a living, long-term, then everything about you, not just your abilities as a musician, must be on par with other professionals. Many, many wonderfully talented musicians never turn or stay pro because they couldn't cut it in the other areas of their lives. But why shouldn't talent alone be enough to earn success?

One reason is because now the stakes are so high. Many years ago, musicians didn't command the high fees they get now. Musicians were considered lowly, or else they were "pets" of high society and royalty. Even today, respect eludes some areas of music even if wealth and fame are achieved. Let's face it: Deservedly or not, musicians have the reputation of being flaky, druggy, drunk, and irresponsible.

Well, mostly we *are* on the fringes of mainstream working society, as are most artists—that's one of the reasons many are drawn to the arts, because they are "outside" and "different." But being unconventional doesn't necessarily mean you are irresponsible, unreliable, shady, or dopey. If you are, and want to make it in music or anything else, you'd better have darn good people around you, propping you up and rescuing your butt when you fall down. Because now, with so much wealth to be made in music, presenters, agents, and others don't want to invest their good money, time, and energy on someone who is going to screw up, no matter how talented. I have heard so many stories about presenters who won't hire a big star again because of her attitude or unprofessional behavior. It can positively sink your career, or even derail it before it gets started.

Again, the ones who last in this business treat others as they would like to be treated, and they take their careers seriously. A perfect example of someone like this is the highly regarded bass player Tony Levin, who has worked with such diverse musicians as Yes, Judy Collins, Paul Simon, Cher, and Al DiMeola, among many others. Accompanying critics' praise for his playing are legions of stories about what a wonderful person he is to work with—totally reliable. Do you think he would be so in demand if he weren't completely professional?

You want your look, act, behavior, and so forth to show that you are serious about your music and that you mean business. It's not a pastime or hobby for you; you are ready for the big leagues.

Presentation

By "presentation," I mean how you present yourself in all areas of your daily existence: onstage, on the phone, in your promo, out on the street. We are musicians, not actors; there probably isn't too much of a schism between who we are in public while working and our private selves. How do we want to be perceived, in public and in private? Even artists in a heavy metal thrash band, if they want to be around for a long time, have to maintain some semblance of professionalism, or else have great people covering for them. We aspire to being pros, so everything should say that we are—from our printed promo to our stage clothes.

Your promo should be well-designed and should portray the image you are trying to project. If you hand-letter your brochure on copy paper with a poor and out-of-focus photo carelessly duplicated on it, it screams *amateur*, and you won't be perceived as serious. The same message gets sent if you show up for an important gig—maybe a wedding or a formal concert—in sloppy clothes, unprepared or under-rehearsed, or hung over from a bad night out. If, when a presenter calls to book you, you can't find your calendar, a pen, or your map of the United States, that speaks poorly of your ability to deliver the goods when it's called for. *You need to get your act together, both musically and personally, to succeed.*

MAINTAINING AN APPROPRIATE DEMEANOR

Surly rock star. Arrogant diva. Menacing rapper. These are icons we all recognize. Of course, some are just facades, image, show business. But some artists have really bought into their own image. The public generally expects musicians to have a different demeanor than, say, librarians. As a whole, musicians tend to be looser, more uninhibited kinds of people—we have to be, in order to get up in front of strangers and perform. Does it mean we can act like creeps and jerks, as many uninhibited people do? Some musicians think so. We have to remember that for the most part we work *in public*. We are not like some corporate cogs working in some cubicle, out of sight, hearing, and mind. We are in people's faces. We are performing. In many ways, we are exhibitionists. We *want* to be heard and seen. We do have an image we want to project, that which is consistent with our music and presumably our inner selves. Our demeanors should truly portray who we are and what we want to convey with our music. If we act accordingly, we should also understand and accept the reactions of those who watch and hear us. If someone is a rapper or a heavy metal guy who walks, talks, dresses and preaches hatred and violence, we shouldn't be at all surprised if violence erupts at his concerts. Thus, demeanor is tied to music and its makers.

Timely Arrival

Part of being professional is *being punctual*—for rehearsals, gigs, and meetings. For some reason, many musicians are lousy at this. Maybe it's because many are thinking of loftier things than the clock and the calendar. But it is the height of inconsideration, to the point of rudeness and arrogance, to keep your band mates, audience, colleagues, presenters … *anyone* waiting. When two or more people set a time for something, it is an informal pact, not just a suggestion. Singer John McCutcheon, one of the most respected musicians in folk music, agrees:

> *I made it a special point that I was going to have a reputation of always being on time, and that I always did what I said I was going to do. I remember somebody saying, "You know, we decided to hire* you *rather than musician X for our music series because you always deliver. You do what you say you're going to do, you show up on time, you're pleasant to work with."*

Don't discount the value of your off-stage reputation—remember, presenters talk to each other all the time.

It has become commonplace, unfortunately, to start concerts up to an hour later than the ticket says. I don't know why audiences put up with this. To me, constant tardiness shows disrespect, like no one has anything better to do than wait for the artist. It has become a sign of the diva, the arrogant artiste. Or of sloppiness. It gives musicians a bad rap, not undeserved. This doesn't have to be, and people are very pleasantly surprised when, if an artist says he'll be there at 9:00, he shows up at 9:00 instead of 9:30. Likewise, if you promise that something will be delivered by such-and-such a date, it's a matter of integrity and point of pride to see that that deadline is met. Punctuality is a show of reliability.

Some time before leaving for the gig I will whip out my map (and I keep piles of them, detailed ones for any areas I gig regularly in) and trace the route so that there will be no surprises. Sometimes the directions given to you are wrong, and if you don't find this out until you're on route, you will lose time getting lost and possibly get there late. While I'm driving, my navigator is reading the directions and map so I don't have to. You can get lost or get into an accident if you are trying to negotiate reading directions and a map, *plus* watching your driving at the same time. Of course, if you are traveling solo, you don't have much choice. A quick trial run on the map before you leave will help in this case as well.

Battling Stage Fright

My feeling is that stage fright is the fear of something going terribly wrong, and/or humiliating oneself in public. Stage fright is so common that I would venture to say that most, if not all, performing artists have experienced it at one point or another. Even the most seasoned performer sometimes gets the jitters before going on stage. Maybe it's a new venue, or an unusually big or "important" audience. Maybe the performer hasn't totally learned the material or is uncomfortable with it for some reason. Many artists have had anxiety dreams about performing—maybe appearing onstage naked, forgetting lines, or losing their way to a gig. It is so typical that it's truly nothing to worry about, *unless* it becomes so pervasive that it stops you from getting onstage time after time. It's a normal reaction to a stressful situation—you are supposed to get up in front of a group of people and basically show off. Hey, that's why it's called *show* business!

After a certain length of time performing in front of an audience (and it will vary wildly from person to person), stage fright will eventually lessen and may disappear forever. Or it may return from time to time. The trick is to not let it overcome you so powerfully that you can't perform. I know some people get such a strong reaction to performing that they can't do it any more. They even experience such extreme and violent reactions as vomiting or passing out. For those people, a career onstage is not in the cards.

However, for those of us who occasionally experience milder forms of it, here is a trick I learned from Heather Forest, a wonderful storyteller-musician friend of mine: *Fear has the same symptoms as excitement.* You know the feeling—heart pounding, breaking out in a sweat, clammy hands, a certain light-headedness. These symptoms can stop you cold and actually prevent you from performing well. Or, you could tell yourself that you are *excited about getting out there* and showing your stuff. It's kind of like fooling yourself. If you tell yourself you are scared, it will only spiral downward, and the fear will increase and be harder to shake off. It could affect your performance. But on the other hand, if you tell yourself you are *excited*, you may find it will spiral upward and you can *use* that excitement, that adrenaline, to put on a stellar show.

Try and remember that all stage fright is is the fear of something going terribly wrong, of humiliating oneself. The real key to fighting stage fright is to be meticulous in your preparation. If you know your material inside and out, if you are confident in your look, your abilities, and your act, then you will realize there is nothing to be frightened of. It will also let you operate on "autopilot" long enough for you to relax and get comfortable onstage. The less you have to struggle to remember onstage, the better. Stage fright is the opposite of confidence. Of course, if you have to face a hostile or really important audience, there is something real to be nervous about. But if you are confident in yourself and your music, *that's* what you can control. Everything else is out of your control anyway, and you might as well just enjoy yourself and go with the flow. Stretch, shake yourself out, and then, just before stepping onstage, take several deep breaths to *relax yourself*, or jog in place to *pump yourself up*— whatever you need to do your best. And remember, you are doing this because music is wonderful and playing is *fun*.

Devising Your Program

Your music program is one of the most important parts of your presentation. How you structure it (assuming that you have some control over this) and the pieces you choose are crucial to your show. A well-planned program is a beautiful thing, and planning it is an art in itself. Personally, I want to take my audience on a kind of journey, starting off with some excitement to bring them in, adding dynamics through a change of tempo, volume, and mood with subsequent pieces, then building to a climax with my most impressive piece. During the concert, I like to make my audience laugh, cry, groove, and think. I want to have the last song of my last set be a powerhouse, and to leave my audience wanting more. If you have control over how long you play, like a good houseguest, you never want to overstay your welcome. You will know if your audience is getting restless. This means that you either need to change the dynamics or end the show. They are growing tired of listening to the same kind of music, or they just don't like you and what you're doing! It's a *real* bad sign if you see numbers of people yawning, looking at their watches, or getting up and leaving! You know something is *really* wrong if you clear the room …

TIMING YOUR SETS

Most times, the length and number of sets or the program is determined by the venue. A general rule of thumb for club sets is, "forty on, twenty off." This means you play a forty-minute set, take a twenty-minute break, play another forty minutes, and so forth. A typical night might consist of three to five sets like this. If you have a transient audience (bars, restaurants), you can get away with repeating your first set as your last, or reintroducing certain popular or familiar songs throughout the night.

Also, if the presenters want to determine the length of the program (and they usually do), try and make them understand from the beginning that *more* is not necessarily *better*. In fact, when I am quoting my fee, I tell them that it is the same whether I'm performing two songs or a whole night. After all, they are not paying by the song, but rather they are hiring me for the day or night. I then try to explain that I am creating a show and they have to trust my experience as a performer to structure the very best program—again, I want to leave them wanting more, not overstay my welcome. Most people's ability to sit and listen without interruption lasts about 45 to 60 minutes, 90 at the very most, and it is actually counterproductive to try to do more in one set.

INTERACTING WITH THE AUDIENCE

Many artists like to take requests if they are performing cover tunes, or if it's *their* audience who is familiar with the artist's own music. This makes for a very nice camaraderie between the audience and the artist, because it shows that *you* are really listening to *them* by honoring their request, as well as *them* listening to *you*. It builds a rapport and makes everyone feel as if they are among friends. The only problem with this is that you had better know your full repertoire inside and out and be prepared to perform any piece in it.

Other artists hate taking requests and will only stick to a predetermined set. The upside of this is that there are no surprises and the set unfolds as the artist planned, with all the dynamics in place. The downside is, if something isn't working, or you suddenly get inspired or otherwise need to change the set, you are locked in and the show may spiral downward. The best situation is one in which you can have some control over the program and are ready to change the sets to accommodate your audience and the situation.

The wonderful thing about live performance is that there is interaction between artist and audience through immediate feedback. The act will know if the audience is "getting it" and enjoying the show, or if something needs to be done to rescue a ship that is sinking. In the worst-case scenario, the artist senses a "downward spiral," with the audience losing interest and the performance affected by frustration, even desperation. Beginners may get totally flustered and make mistakes or worse. The audience picks up on this and the whole ship starts to go down. There is a point where it's unsalvageable, and you might as well cut your losses and get off stage.

A good show, on the other hand, should "spiral up" for everyone—artists feed off a responsive audience and usually get energized and work harder, and the performance grows more inspired. In return, the audience becomes more excited by the performance and gives the artists greater applause, laughter, whatever. This upward spiral ideally ends in encores and standing ovations, with both the artists and audience truly transformed by the performance.

Respecting Your Audience and Keeping Your Cool

If you have a manager, agent, or other rep, you will have less contact with the venue management than if you are self-booking. Either way, maintaining your professional attitude is important. If you do have representation, make sure your reps' values and attitudes accurately represent yours as well. I have experienced situations where the rep believed she was speaking for the artist, but in reality gave the *exact opposite response* from what the artist would have given. You and the venue have common goals: Both want to bring the audience a quality show, and both want to make money and hopefully fill the space with happy people as often as possible. If you alienate the audience, the venue management, or their workers, if you come across as a space cadet—not showing up on time, not being prepared, and not knowing what the hell is going on, and if you have tantrums or make unreasonable demands, then you will have a very short career. I know, I know, there are entertainers who have made millions by insulting their audiences and abusing everyone around them, but once again, I maintain that those people are few and far between, and chances are, no one likes working with them. Sooner or later, the audiences will tire and the act will grow old. Presenters talk to each other all the time, and if the artist has a reputation of being difficult, no matter how talented, he or she will find it hard to get booked.

Respecting your audience is way up there at the top of the "musts" of being a professional. Here's an example of what *not* to do:

I was part of a group of children's performers who were invited to perform at the family stage at Woodstock '99. Naturally we were very excited about going and playing, but we also liked walking around the grounds as audience members, taking in the other acts. We caught the set of a well-known TV comedian who, to be fair, was known for his coarseness. Well, he must have gone over the top this day because his act was not only unfunny but so crude, insulting, and laced with so much profanity that even this wild young crowd didn't stand for it. They started booing him and swearing back at him. This exchange went on for quite some time, until finally he was loudly booed off the stage. He left extending a particular digit on each hand to the audience. Even though this behavior is what he is known for, I am sure that on that particular day, he alienated many more people than he made fans. This act may be "cool" and trendy for a while, but it gets old and tired *really* fast.

Now, that is an extreme example, but you get the idea. I always like to think of every performance as kind of a "date" with someone. You want "your date" (i.e., your audience) to like you and think you are really cool. You want your audience to want to see you again. You want to excite them, entice them, maybe have fun with them, connect with them. You are, in some fashion, flirting with your audience, building some kind of a relationship, even if just for an hour. You are sharing something precious—your talent, your music—with total strangers, creating an intimacy that can't be created any other way. You don't know if someone is seeing you for the very first time, or the hundredth. Regardless, you want to give your very best, each and every time, no matter how you personally feel that day. When you get onstage, all the problems in your life should be put on the back burner, as you are there to work, to entertain. If you are mad, depressed, sick—your audience doesn't want to see it. They came to forget *their* problems, and want you to help them do that. And it's strange, but often a very peculiar thing happens: If you can manage to appear happy (or at least not unhappy) onstage, once the show is over, you probably will actually feel much better than you did before you went on. Music has the power to do that, so it's beneficial to both the audience *and* you.

So anyway, present your best, in appearance and performance. Oh, and do everyone a favor—be sure your instrument is perfectly tuned, to itself and to the rest of your group! It seems ridiculous to mention, but out-of-tune instruments during a performance are more common than they ever should be, and the off-pitch notes scream *"amateur!"*

HECKLERS AND OTHER FLAK

Now, what about hecklers? There are as many ways to deal with them as there are artists. Sometimes the heckler is drunk. Sometimes he is just some jerk who enjoys challenging musicians. Some artists like to heckle right back. Some ignore it, hoping it will stop on its own. Some deal with it using humor from the stage, which I personally feel is the very best approach. This way not only do you (hopefully) disarm and stop the heckler so that you both maintain some dignity, but you also gain the rest of the audience's respect. If it gets really bad and doesn't stop, the best thing to do is to ask the management personnel to step in and handle it if they haven't already, especially if the heckler is drunk or really belligerent or unruly.

In any event, what you don't want to happen is to let the heckler get the upper hand and ruin the show. Part of being a professional is learning how not to get rattled when unexpected things happen. The audience is looking to you to see how you handle such situations. I once saw guitarist Steve Howe perform solo in an intimate setting. The small concert hall was filled with his adoring fans. One woman seated next to me was obviously drunk and kept yelling out slurred comments like "Steve! I love you!" at very inappropriate moments, like during a quiet, sensitive instrumental. Steve, always the classy performer, chose to ignore her. Too bad the rest of the audience, myself included, didn't pounce on her and evict her. It ruined the night for many of us, but Steve never lost his focus.

At one of my concerts I had a cell phone ring, and the ensuing loud conversation interrupted right in the middle of a song. It took everything I had to stay focused on the song and not on her conversation, and to not react so that the audience's attention would be drawn away from me to her even more. When the song was over, instead of following my instinct to leap off the stage and grab her phone and throw it through a window, I calmly asked in the sweetest voice I could muster that all cell phones be turned off or taken outside if they must be answered. A more clever artist might have handled the situation with a joke. The audience appreciated how it was handled, the offending party wasn't unduly embarrassed, and the show went on. By the way, I have learned from this and now request that whoever introduces me also makes the request to turn off cell phones and beepers or set them to "vibrate" *in advance.*

One other caveat: there may be times when an audience member is just plain rude, like talking out loud throughout your show, as if he were in his own living room watching the TV, for heaven's sake! This has happened to me more times than I would have wished. If I were to follow my impulse, I would be equally rude to that person; instead, I try to ignore that behavior, or sometimes just give an unbelieving look. But you don't want to *embarrass* folks like this, because they might not even be aware that they are talking so loudly. Furthermore, there have been times when the offending person turned out to be someone who books another venue! I usually am very happy when I don't turn ugly on them, in any case.

MISTAKES ON STAGE—AVOIDABLE NO-NOS AND INEVITABLE SLIPS

On the subject of mistakes: Everyone makes them onstage, even Yo Yo Ma, Billy Joel, and Aretha. Bad notes are played or sung, lyrics forgotten, places in the music lost. What is so hard for us musicians is that we make them *in public*, in front of dozens or thousands of people! Long ago, my first manager gave me an invaluable piece of advice. He said, "If you make a mistake, in live performance it's gone in an instant. Unless it's being recorded in some way, forget about it. But most importantly, *don't 'telegraph' it!*" This means that a professional doesn't make a face or otherwise convey to the audience that she's made a small blooper. It seems obvious that an artist certainly shouldn't stop in the middle of a piece, break down, and walk off the stage if there's a mistake. It is a natural reaction to want to shrink and crawl away, but a professional rides right over it and keeps on going.

Of course, if the mistake is *so* bad or obvious, the best way to deal with it may be to use humor. I've seen singers (and I've done it myself, more times than I care to admit) who have completely blanked out on lyrics who then make up new ones on the spot or "blah blah blah" their way out, often to hilarious effect. Some instrumentalists play off the blooper by exaggerating it or comically pointing it out. I've seen Bruce Springsteen actually start a song over because it started badly. If you are part of a group, hopefully your band mates will cover for you. But in any case, believe it or not, making mistakes oftentimes endears you to your audience, because it shows your human side. If you can keep your cool and laugh it off, you will win your audience to your side even more. The more mistakes you make onstage, the easier it will get to deal with them when they happen, and hopefully they will lessen. Even though you can't anticipate all possible events, you might practice or plan your response if something goes awry. Such as …

Falling asleep onstage or "zoning out." I have done this a few times, mostly when I am so exhausted I can barely stand up. Sometimes I zone out if I am bored or distracted at the gig and my mind is wandering—a really bad sign, because if *I'm* distracted while singing, what could the audience be feeling? Actually, what I mean by both falling asleep and zoning out is when your mind either wanders or shuts down during a performance. I have dealt with this by being so well-rehearsed that my mouth and hands can continue with the song while my brain falls asleep with my eyes still open. There have been times when I have literally "awakened" later in the song and found I haven't missed even a single beat, much less a whole verse or two. Sometimes I'll be singing about some lofty subject, yet thinking of what to make for dinner. This is, of course, a dangerous thing to happen, as well as a sign that you are too much on auto-pilot and not "in the moment" or present, which you need to be at all times when performing. Every audience deserves your full attention, and every performance should be "special" rather than routine. Of course, if you are truly so fatigued that you fall asleep onstage, you might want to rethink your priorities and schedule.

Giving Back and Getting Back

Like many beginning musicians, at the start of my career, I played for free at a lot of benefits and fundraisers for the exposure. Now, I pick and choose the benefits and fundraisers carefully, mostly because of my limited time. I do believe that everyone needs to "give back." It's also a wonderful way to support organizations or causes you believe in, and music adds so much to an event that musicians are almost always welcomed as volunteers. Of course, once you reach a certain level, your name and "star quality" will lend appreciable weight and draw to the event. But until then, it's a creative way to be a social activist. Maybe I can't lobby Congress or canvass door-to-door raising money, but maybe I can raise funds and public consciousness by doing what I do best—making music. When you have attended such events, remember how relieved and appreciative everyone was when there finally was entertainment? How many speeches can anyone sit through, anyway? You can tailor your music to fit the event. Maybe you can play songs that have meaning to the particular cause and that will inspire the audience. If you are a songwriter or composer, perhaps you could even write a new piece just for that event. You'll be surprised how inspired you can be if you really believe in the cause, and how, in turn, you will inspire others with your music. This is no small contribution that you are making—it is indeed as valuable as a financial one.

There is, however, a peculiar phenomenon at some benefits, one that I've experienced too many times: The less someone pays for your performance, the worse you might be treated. At benefits and fundraisers, you would think that if you are volunteering your time and talent, the producers would fall all over themselves to be nice to you, but the opposite is often the case. Maybe you can't get the bottled water or equipment you need and have asked for. Maybe you are spoken to or treated in a condescending or rude manner. After years of experiencing this, I've come to this conclusion: *The more someone pays for something, the more valuable it's perceived to be, and conversely, the less someone pays, the more it's devalued*, no matter what its real value.

The only thing I stipulate now, at this stage of my career, is that I expect to be treated with respect. Once you have built a reputation, this respect comes more automatically. You won't find anyone dissing Eric Clapton at a benefit. But even before you reach stardom, you can and should expect to be treated well. I explain that my usual fee is relatively high, and that I am happy to lower it or waive it completely because I believe in what the event is doing, but that doesn't mean that what I am doing or giving is to be *devalued*.

There are certain things I need in order to do my job well and to perform optimally. I need bottled water and a safe place to put my stuff. A parking space and help with my equipment is appreciated. If it's appropriate, I ask whether it's permissible to sell my albums at the event. I point out that since I am volunteering my time and talent, it would be mutually supportive of them if they would allow me to sell product to audience members who liked my music. Almost always, I offer to give a percentage of all sales to the organization, as a further show of my support. I will gladly continue to work with organizations and events that subscribe to all of this, and I won't return to those who don't. Like all good relationships, this one should be built on mutual respect and support. Again, remember that as an artist, you deserve and need this too.

Chapter 6
Your Office and Creative Space

As artists, we don't like to have to think about the mundane things like the business and clerical sides of our lives, but until we are successful enough to hire others to do things like typing, faxing, and filing, we are going to have to do them ourselves. And we will need a place and equipment to organize the business end of our artistic lives.

Good time management here is key. Many artists simply dread the thought of doing the business and clerical end of things, and tend to either put things off or refuse to learn to do them. I find that time management is like money management, which is also like business management; *if you can prioritize and take care of the big things right away*, you won't fall behind and you won't feel so overwhelmed. One big secret of succeeding in the music business, as with all businesses, is not just to be talented but to be *organized*. A well-designed office and good time planning facilitate this.

Unfortunately, a disproportionate amount of our time will be spent in this business space—probably more time here than in the recording studio or onstage—so we might as well make it as pleasant, efficient, and functional as possible. At the beginning, I'm assuming that you'll be working from home. When the royalties and performance fees start rolling in, you may want to consider renting a separate space; then again, you may not.

Personally, I like having a home office and studios. I like being able to roll out of bed, have my office in the room next door, amble down to the kitchen for a snack, and toddle upstairs into the recording studio or downstairs into the rehearsal room. You can enjoy the separation, similar to having an offsite place, as long as it is understood by your family members and roommates that when you are working, *you are working just as if you were to leave the house*, and interruptions should be kept to a minimum. In my own family, my then-eight-year-old daughter once made me a sign on her own that I have kept on the door to my office: "Is it important? If not, SEE YA!" She knew at a young age that, although I was still available to her always, when Mom's in her office she is only to be interrupted for *important* reasons. Of course, when she was younger, that often meant to play a really important game of Monopoly or to see a dance she had just made up …

If you don't have a separate room, can you at least find a sacred space that is all your own? Maybe a corner of the dining room, bedroom, or kitchen where you can set up a desk and a computer near a phone? I do think it's important that other people living with you respect this space, however informal or small it may be. You need to know that the contract you are working on and the files you have built remain undisturbed when you are not there. It's very frustrating to have your papers moved around, lost, or thrown out.

Likewise with your creative space. I know artists can create almost anywhere—we all have worked in our cars, on the subway, holed up in a motel room, or even in the john—but again, the ideal situation is a space where you can leave your instruments, music stands, writing tools, tape recorders, and so forth and know they will still be there, just as you left them, when you come back. Personally, I find it extremely difficult to try to create when I can't find my stuff, there are phones ringing, and people are coming in and out. I need a long span of quiet alone time in order to write, arrange, or practice. Your friends and loved ones will just have to understand that this isolation is necessary for the creative process to take place. And that isolation means space, time, and quiet, inside and outside of your own body.

But first, let's go back to the office. This is where the "business" part of "the music business" takes place, and just as you need to spend time and money building your creative life, so will you need to spend on this part.

Office Equipment

The most basic things you will need are a desk, a comfortable chair, a phone, and a computer. I suppose there are some artists who can get by with just the first three items, but I honestly don't know how anyone functions without a computer nowadays. At the beginning of my career and for many years, before computers became ubiquitous and affordable, I ran my business with just a typewriter (boy, does this date me!). But every time I had to write a contract, update my performance schedule, or write a "personalized" form letter, I had to start from scratch. What a pain. Among the manual skills a musician should have is typing. I know many people think they don't need it—after all, they are *artists!*—but that's a big mistake. It's one of those basic life skills, like driving, that really handicaps you if you don't have it. Anyway, nowadays it seems just about everyone has a computer and is online. More about computers later in this section.

I try not to skimp on my equipment in the office, like I try not to skimp on my musical equipment. These are the tools of your trade, as surely as your instrument is, and you want the best you can afford because it will make your life easier and help you do your job better. If you are just starting out, any kind of desk surface will do; it just has to hold your computer and phone, and maybe some office supplies. The chair you choose should be comfortable, if not ergonomic, because you will spend long hours sitting in it, and you don't want it to contribute to fatigue. It's bad enough that you have to sit in your office working instead of making music; you shouldn't have to be uncomfortable or actually hurt by your furniture! Beware the dangers of carpal tunnel syndrome, exacerbated by poorly-designed or badly-arranged desks, chairs, and computer keyboards. This condition can be disastrous to a musician.

PHONES, PHONE LINES, AND MESSAGE SYSTEMS

A simple phone is enough to start with. You just need to be able to make and receive those gig calls. But one nice kind of phone that you might like to get right off the bat is a cordless one or one with a headset. This will enable you to move around your office. A speakerphone feature will also serve this purpose, allowing you to talk while at the computer or when your hands are otherwise occupied. At times you may want to play your instrument into the phone, too.

You might want a separate line and number just for your business. I also find the call-waiting feature to be rather important, because I am on the phone so much. I don't want to discourage callers who might get hours of a busy signal. Later on, as you climb the ladder of success, you can add more phone lines, DSL, caller ID, all kinds of fancy stuff; but at the beginning, keep it simple, and keep it cheap. Whatever you choose, *make sure your phone number is stable.* You will be advertising this information on all your promo, and you want to make it easy for people to find you. They can't do this if you keep changing your number! Using a cell phone as your business number accomplishes this, in addition to having other benefits.

I believe having a cell phone is absolutely essential. Being the Luddite that I am, it took me years to get talked into having one. But since I got mine, I can't imagine getting into a car without it. Since most musicians will be traveling quite a bit, even if you only play locally, you need a cell phone in case you are lost, late, or in trouble. I can't tell you how many times I've relied on it while away from home and office. (Just don't use it and drive at the same time! Be aware of state laws regarding handheld cell phones while driving.) If you get a nationwide calling plan, you can call home when you are touring, retrieve your messages, and return calls—in other words, you can continue to conduct business while on the road. It is helpful if all the members of a band have their own, to keep in contact when separated.

You will need a good answering machine attached to your office phone, one that is reliable if the power goes out and that can hold many messages of extended length. In fact, investing in a voicemail box with the phone company may be a worthwhile endeavor. Some services will take messages when you're on the phone, eliminating the need for call waiting. Others will also pick up when you're online if you don't have a dedicated line or DSL for this. It's fun to be creative with your outgoing message—but remember to be professional and don't make it too lengthy. No one likes to sit through a very long, overly clever answering machine message more than once. And by the way, it's a good business practice to answer your calls promptly, say within a day or two at most, even when touring. The people you will be dealing with will appreciate you all the more for not being the stereotypical flaky musician. Also, I never say on my outgoing message that I am away on tour. This could invite burglary.

COMPUTER HARDWARE AND SOFTWARE

The computer you get should be as fast and up-to-date as you can afford. Once again, it's frustrating and time-consuming trying to work on outmoded equipment. You want as much memory and the best and latest software that you can afford. You might want to write, store, edit, and record music on your computer. The programs available now to musicians are staggering. Nowadays, you don't have to know how to transcribe music to be able to write and print beautiful sheet music, or (and this is a disturbing fact) even know how to play competently in order to record dazzling solos! Although discussion of making music using a computer is beyond the scope of this book, there are plenty of other books and courses you can take if you are interested. We will mainly be concerned with the clerical uses of the computer here.

The most basic program you will need is a word processing one. You will use this for writing, editing, and storing lyrics, contracts, performance calendars—just about anything. Most, if not all, basic computers come loaded with such a program. They are easy to learn and use. It helps, if you are a computer dummy like me, to have friends to lean on who are more conversant in computer stuff. Of course, there are books and courses you can take, too. Again, think of this as a basic life skill, like cooking, driving, or playing scales.

Also extremely useful is a reliable database program; that's where you will keep your all-important mailing lists of fans, media, and venues. It should keep your mailing list in such a way that you can arrange, edit, and access it easily. Maybe you want just clubs in Maryland, or just libraries in Louisiana. Microsoft Access is a good program for such a list. It allows you to sort by last name, zip code, or "code." For instance, you'll want to keep your sponsor mailing list separate from your fan list. You can attach codes (something like "S" for sponsors and "F" for fans; other subcodes might be "SL" for libraries, "SF" for festivals, etc.). in Access to accomplish this. In this way, you can pull up that person who moved and whose address needs updating, everyone on your fan list in Minneapolis, or all library sponsors.

And, in order to keep a reliable record of your income and outflow, make sure you purchase a good spreadsheet program like Microsoft Excel or Quicken. These make it easy for you to keep meticulous records of expenses and income for tax purposes (which will be discussed in chapter 14).

Attached to your computer you will want a modem, as you will want to be online. Some people like to have a separate phone line or cable for their modem so their business phone isn't tied up when they are online. Since being online will make you vulnerable to miscreant virus writers, you will want a good anti-virus software to protect your hard drive, e-mail address lists, and program files.

Plus, you must have a good-quality printer. I bought the best I could afford, a laser printer, because the output is better than other kinds and it's fast. You might also want a color printer for producing displays—especially if you get into doing your own artwork, layouts, brochures, and so forth. By the way, you can save yourself tons of money if you learn to design and lay out your own promo. The services of good artists are expensive, in addition to the printing costs. That's also why, on a good photocopy machine I've purchased (see below), I print most of my own "insert" promo, from articles and reviews about my work to performance and fee schedules and more. That way, I can use more of my promo budget for a commercial printer for my brochures, CD covers, and other print material that must look really great, be made of glossy material, or be mass-produced in full color. I save not only money this way, but also precious time. (For more on doing your own promo, refer to chapter 7.)

OFFICE ODDS AND ENDS

Other extremely beneficial office machines include faxes, scanners, and copiers. These are now relatively cheap and getting cheaper. Again, in all cases, it pays to get the best you can afford because better resolution, faster speed, and other useful features will come with the higher-grade models. Nowadays, there are great machines that combine a plain-paper fax, speaker-phone, copier, scanner, answering machine, and coffee maker (I'm lying about that last one). A good photocopier is certainly a luxury for struggling musicians, but once you can afford one, it will make your life so much easier. Think about how many times you need to run out to the copy center to duplicate sheet music, contracts, promo, and so forth. For my office copier, I tried to get the fastest, heaviest-duty one that makes good-quality reproductions of photos on different sizes of paper. Mine also enlarges and reduces, an indispensable feature for many reasons. It's a good idea to get a service contract on your machine for routine maintenance and cleaning, as well as for when it breaks down. It's horrible to be in the middle of a big mailing, have your machine break, and have to wait for a repair person *and* pay through the nose.

Other office furniture you may need are filing cabinets, bookshelves, horizontal file shelves for quick promo collating … on and on. Once your business starts growing, you may need to hire an office manager or assistant, and he will need a place to work, too. You are limited only by your imagination, budget, and space. There is more on clerical help in chapter 9.

Accessories you'll need are good maps (regional or national ones if you are touring), wall calendars and appointment books, good lighting, and a postage scale or meter. I pin up my regional and national maps right on the wall so I can be looking at them when a presenter calls me. This helps me not only locate the town but also figure out travel time and fees—and I can plan a tour that is geographically logical.

A Rented Office

If you are lucky enough to have a separate space for your office, that's a big bonus, because you can go there, shut the door, and have peace and quiet (we hope) to do your office work. Some folks are successful enough to have an office in another building away from their homes, thus *really* being able to separate their work life from their home life. Like everything else, there are advantages and disadvantages to this.

The distractions of home—personal calls, family interruptions, *a cozy bed*—aren't there and you can really concentrate on work. When you are at this office, you are *really at the office*, just like a stockbroker or CEO. This may be anathema to most artists, but you can also make it as personal and artistic as you wish—after all, like your music, this space makes a statement about you. Here is a wonderful place to be creative as well as practical. Here is where you may take meetings, where you can show off those framed awards and be the business professional. You also might like to have your rehearsal space and recording studio in or near your office. And at the end of the day, you can shut the door and *go home*.

The disadvantages are the added expense of your office's rent, heat, electricity, phone, and so on, the commute, and the inconvenience of having your "stuff" in different places. Remember, the more monthly expenses you incur, the higher your income requirements.

Creative Space

I love having my own space and time to create, and consider it crucial to my life and career to guard and maintain it. As was mentioned above, it's supremely hard to create with distractions. Try to carve out *some place* that is yours alone to write, arrange, practice, and rehearse. Maybe it's as simple as your bedroom, or as elaborate as a full-blown rehearsal and recording studio.

Regardless, make it as conducive to creativity as possible. Make sure your instruments are happy, safe, and secure there (a controlled temperature and humidity are important to them, as is a strong lock). The space should be quiet and peaceful and beautiful—or stimulating—whatever you need to get the best out of your music. Maybe you need a window with natural light and a beautiful view; or maybe you don't want that distraction. Maybe you need a black box with neon or candlelight. In any case, make it inviting to you and your muse. The very least you will need is some kind of good lighting, maybe one or more music stands, a tape recorder, maybe some sort of keyboard, and some place to write. You will want to install some shelves for your favorite inspirational and reference books. And you'll probably want a place to store refreshments so you won't have to leave when you are inspired and on a roll. Soundproofing is a wonderful luxury—perhaps a necessity, if you can afford it—for both you and your neighbors. A cheap trick is to use old carpeting, foam, or even egg cartons tacked onto walls and ceiling (but watch out for their flammability). As you put it together, remember that this space, more so than any other, is your sacred space.

Likewise, *carve out time* for yourself to create. I find, what with all the other details of a busy life, that my creative time is often last on the list. This is unfortunate, since I need extended hours alone to write music or create a new show, and often it's hard to find that stretch of hours. And as sociable as music is, creativity usually requires solitude. Sometimes, significant others, children, and friends tend to forget that, as artists, we *need* that solitude and space to focus. There are so many other demands on our time and attention. But let us never lose sight of *why* we became musicians and artists in the first place—to express ourselves in this most beautiful medium. Demand that creative time and space—*you must have it*—or go work at something else.

Obtaining Helpful Knowledge and Skills

As mentioned before, basic clerical skills are useful, as are basic computer skills. Until you are ready to hire someone to take over these chores for you, you will be doing them yourself. And the longer it takes you to do these oner-ous things, the less time you will have for your real heart's desire, and that is making music. Much of what you will learn will only come from experience—no book can give you everything. You will need to learn how to find resources for problems that come up—where to turn for answers you can't find by yourself. Get friendly with librarians, computer mavens, electricians, sound techs, and designers—believe it or not, all will help you achieve your goals in music. Because one of your ultimate goals is to make an independent living playing or singing, you will have to depend on your own knowledge and skills as much as possible. And you'll also need to know when to delegate and rely on others.

So, besides working on your musical chops, it helps to develop your busi-ness, clerical, and human relations chops. You don't want to be at anyone's mercy. At your local university, there probably are adult education, continuing education, and college credit courses in music business, computers, account-ing, and so forth that you can take, as well as privately-run seminars, courses, and conferences everywhere. Of course, you can't be the master of all know-ledge, and that's where you foster relationships with others who are willing to help you. Pick the brains of anyone and everyone you meet, whether or not they are in music, because you can learn a lot about other fields and then apply them to your own. Again, remember, knowledge is power, and you are the master of your career. Your office is Command Central, World Headquarters. Fashion your office as you would your life.

Chapter 7
Marketing and Promotion

Second to the quality of your "product" (i.e., music), but arguably the single most important factor in your success as a professional musician, is *how you market your work*. It's a horrible bit of harsh reality, but as the music industry in America stands today, it's a fact that no matter how talented you are, if no one knows about you, then you might as well have fun just playing in your room and forget about turning pro. *And*, as distasteful as it may be to some "artistes," the name of the game is still "selling." *And*, as romantic as they may be, stories about musicians who were "discovered" performing on a street corner or in some dive are few and atypical—not very good odds to play. I always say, "In order to get hit by the truck of Success, you need to play in the street of Opportunity." Metaphorically speaking, of course.

Now, until you get to a certain professional level (or have some wildly wealthy patron) to be able to hire a professional publicist, you will probably have to do this yourself. Either way, marketing and publicity are going to use up a very large part of your time and business budget. Prepare for this, and earmark money just for it. As for the actual work, if you are part of a group, one member could choose or be assigned to concentrate on this one aspect of the business. Or, if you are very lucky, have a few supportive friends, fans, or family members do it. *Just be very sure they know what they are doing*, and that they act professionally. Remember, they are representing you. A poor rep can sink an artist pretty fast, through incompetence or, even worse, a bad attitude or dishonesty.

For this chapter, let us assume that you have taken on the job yourself. Don't be afraid to blow your own horn. Remember, the first thing you need as an artist is self-confidence—belief in yourself. I was a painfully shy child and had to initially *force* myself to be assertive, or I could never have gotten onstage to face an audience. Sooner or later, *all* performing artists need to overcome shyness, or they will not be able to perform in public. Well, you can use that same performing confidence to promote yourself. It may seem immodest, but if you don't think your work is terrific, then probably no one else will, either. The more you do it, the easier it will get, eventually—just like practicing your instrument.

There are at least two areas where you want good promotion: for yourself as an act, and for "events" like individual gigs or product releases. Let's take the first one first.

Tell the world how great, unique, inspiring, etc., etc., your music is, and why. The most palatable way to do this is by using the third-person voice in your promo. No one else needs to know you don't have a great publicist and copywriter on your huge staff. Start at the very beginning of your public performing life to gather quotes from notable people. But using Sony's faux-movie-critic scandal as a warning: No fair making up quotes! Keep imaginary people as your playmates, not your reviewers!

Speaking of imaginary people, there is a cute story that renowned folksinger John McCutcheon tells regarding his promoting himself in the early years of his career: "You could do what I did for awhile. I invented this other person, Jonathan Chapman. I would answer the phone as Jonathan, and then I could talk about John McCutcheon. It was kind of wacky, but it afforded me a kind of distance that was helpful."

You do want legitimate praise from people who are authorities on music—i.e., other well-known performers, newspaper reviewers, venue owners, program directors, and so forth. If you keep your ears open after your concerts, you may also catch audience members raving about you. Don't be shy about jumping on them and asking if you may quote them, and get their names if they say yes. Make sure they are, of course, impartial listeners … although, done correctly, it is pretty funny to use a quote from your mom.

I keep a file where I throw scraps of paper on which are written quotes I received verbally from people who love my music. Others write me letters or e-mails and I save them, highlighting quotables. And I use only the very best quotes—either from highly respected folks like celebrities or well-known media types, or quotes that use only superlatives like "extraordinary" or "the best." All of us know what "damning with faint praise" is—don't use those! We want to convey *hot*, not lukewarm.

Press Kit

You will need promotional material to combine into a press kit—or to keep separate for various kinds of publicity purposes. The press kit serves as your ambassador and paper representative. It should say who you are and what you do in as eye-catching and concise a fashion as possible. One or more great photos are a must.

You should distribute it liberally, because it will be one of your main tools for selling your act. Give or send it to everyone and anyone who asks. Therefore, try and keep it economical. You don't want to wince every time you send one out because of the cost of postage or the press kit itself. It should be concise, not just for postage-weighing purposes, but also because of the fact that most people won't take the time to read through everything in a huge kit. I have a promotional brochure to send or give to anyone and that is a self-mailer. I keep a handful in my car, and more in my tote bag, which I bring to gigs and everywhere else I go. I find it more informative (and more impressive) than a business card. Then, I have modular pieces that I can add to custom tailor a kit to a venue.

Press kits should be updated as often as is necessary—if you have big changes in your look, career, contact information, and so forth. With the cost of printing so high, I try and make my general brochure fairly generic so it won't get "dated" too soon. Then I can keep it updated with the current supplemental material like press clippings, awards, credits, and so on.

It's a good idea to list a stable mailing address where people can always find you. I know so many musicians who move around so much that their addresses change constantly, and no one can find them. This is a good argument for a post office box. Likewise, a steady phone number. A wonderful, very talented singer-songwriter I know moves very frequently. She used to change her phone number each time, making it impossible and frustrating for anyone to find her—very discouraging to both fans and presenters! She solved this by using her cell phone as her permanent number.

Another good argument for keeping a separate phone number and post office box for your business is that it provides security and privacy, especially if you are a woman. Sorry to say, stalkers and other crazies do exist. Even over-zealous fans can be a problem. Early on, I got a post office box where ALL my mail goes, and that is the address I give out on all my promo. If you don't have a separate office, I urge you to use this solution. Keep a separate e-mail address as well.

It is a nice touch if all your printed materials (brochure, stationery if necessary, business card) have the same "look." You can design them yourself if you have an artistic bent, or tap a creative friend. With the terrific pre-designed business cards at office supply stores nowadays, you can make some pretty darn good-looking ones yourself if you have a decent printer and computer. They have matching stationery and specially designed paper for brochures, too.

Below, I explain the basic components of a press kit. Of course, you can get very elaborate, with glossy, die-cut, full-color portfolio covers, magnets, and special add-ons. But really, your "audition" will rise or fall on the demo. As impressive as some kits are that I've seen, if I were a presenter I would know that if the chops ain't there, I'm not going to hire someone just because they have a pretty package.

GOOD GLOSSY PHOTOS

You'll want both black-and-white and color. More and more, print media want color. Larger dimensions of 8" × 10" used to be *de rigueur*, but now many will accept smaller formats like 5" × 7" or 4" × 6". You can also submit photos via CD or e-mail, or have presenters download images from your Web site. Whatever their format, these photos are very, very important. They are the images that you present to the world, and they should convey instantly *who* you are—what instruments you play, what style, and which genre (classical piano, rock and roll, death metal, or children's music). These publicity shots should include a good headshot, as well as a full or partial body shot with your instruments; unless you are Kenny G, no one will know what kind of musician you are unless it's right there in front of their eyes.

When considering a photo for publication, papers and magazines like the dynamic or unusual shot. Hopefully, your photographer will have creative ideas of her own, to add to your thoughts on poses, settings, lighting, angles, expressions, and so forth. If your photo can grab a jaded calendar page editor, it will grab your potential audience. Remember, most times, your photo is someone's *very first* impression of you, even before they hear you play a note. Make sure it's a good one and a representative one. Also, live performance shots are very nice and extremely useful, especially if there is, say, an audience of 132,000 at the Washington Monument or 14,000 at Madison Square Garden (see photos).

It seems like it goes without saying, but please make sure the photographer you use is technically as well as artistically qualified. It's nice to save money using Aunt Bess who takes lovely vacation shots, but you forgot that in her photo albums everyone is always squinting and slightly out of focus.

Or, a friend who takes photos of cosmetic products for a living may not do as well with living beings. You don't want unimaginative, amateurish, stiff, out-of-focus shots … unless, of course, you do.

Author performing at Girl Scouts ninetieth anniversary celebration at the Washington Monument Mall, Washington, D.C.

y Stephen Fricker

Author and band at New York metro–area Girl Scouts ninetieth anniversary celebration, Madison Square Garden, New York, N.Y.

Photo by Paul Cousins

When looking over the proofs, don't immediately dismiss an interesting shot just because there may be some minor flaws. With digital technology and careful cropping, you can "tidy up" any problems. Even if one member of your group hates how he looks in a shot that everyone else likes, nowadays you can transfer parts of images very easily. Make sure everyone is happy about the final choices—you are going to use these shots for at least a year for many purposes, and the images are going to get spread around through the public far and wide. I also like to ask trusted friends and associates their opinions of the "best" shots, because I know that I can't be objective when it comes to photos of myself. A second, third, and fourth opinion gives you a wide perspective of what might grab the general public. You know you have a winner if everyone you ask loves *that one*.

To get your winning shots reproduced, you can find houses that specialize in making large runs inexpensively. Usually, the more you order, the cheaper they get per piece. Get enough made so that you aren't wincing every time you send or give one out—remember, this is one of the prices of publicity, and they are *important*.

A BROCHURE OR OTHER INFORMATIONAL FLIER

This need not be elaborate, but it should be attention-getting. Again, in a nutshell, you want it to introduce you to strangers. Basically, it should display at least one photo (your best), what you do, and how to contact you. The "style" (typeface, layout, and copy) should be in keeping with your kind of music—i.e., something dignified, traditional, or conservative for classical music, something jazzier for … oh, you know. The look should say something about you *right away*, before the person even reads it. Please proofread carefully; a pet peeve of mine, and many others, is misspelled words and bad grammar. (I know, I know, hip hop artists and rappers and hard-rock jammers do this on purpose, so there's a place for that, but choose your creative spellings wisely.) Some quotes with superlatives also add to the brochure's panache.

I like brochures that are self-mailers—i.e., don't need an envelope as they have the return address printed on them—because stuffing envelopes just adds one more step for me to do. It's a good idea to get a bulk mail permit from the post office. There are many categories of bulk mail, including nonprofit, automated, and so forth. I have the basic for-profit one. It's not expensive to set up or maintain annually, and it will save you money in postage in the long run. If you choose to bulk mail, then you will need to print the indicia directly on your self-mailing brochure in the place where the stamp would go. This also saves you the step of having to put stamps on each one. You must have a minimum of 200 pieces, and they must be identical and sorted by zip code. Go to *www.usps.com*, or type "bulk mail" into your search engine to get more information about bulk mail.

If you don't have the artistic skills to design a brochure yourself, by all means hire someone—a creative friend or relative if you are on a tight budget. I usually do the copy in Word and physically cut-and-paste a "mechanical" (a final master of the brochure) to give to the printer. I know, I know, I am from the Dark Ages and no one does it this way anymore. Nowadays, there are wonderful programs such as PageMaker and Photoshop that not only help you design every aspect of a piece, including photos, but then can store the whole thing on disc for you to take to the printer. It could be worth investing in one of these programs if you can learn to do it yourself and save a bundle on an artist. Just be sure your final product *looks professional.* You will be sending the wrong message if it looks cheap and amateurish.

POSTERS

This is a very good promotional tool to hand out liberally to presenters, to sell, or for your own use. They are not very expensive to print up, especially if you stick with black-and-white and maybe one color. They shouldn't be too big (mine is 11″ × 17″), because some venues don't want to devote more room than necessary to one artist. The same goes for store windows, bulletin boards, walls, and telephone poles in the town where you are performing.

When designing your poster, leave room to add the venue, date, time, admission, and other pertinent information for specific shows you wish to publicize. This device makes the presenters' job easier, and you more congenial in their eyes.

BUSINESS CARDS

Here is another very basic tool that is cheaper than a brochure and that you can hand out liberally (although I find people tend to keep brochures and lose business cards). The information that goes on a card is: your name or band name, your contact name if different, your mailing address, e-mail and Web site addresses, and fax and phone numbers. With all that, you may not have space for any pithy sayings or descriptions, but then again, you may.

PRESS CLIPPINGS

Sooner or later, someone is going to write something about you or your music. You can even help this along if you know someone who can write a freelance piece to send to your local paper to get published—many papers accept articles like this. At least you know it will be a favorable one this way! Once an interview, article, or review gets published, reproduce it liberally. I like to blow it up to fill an 8½" × 11" page if it's very short. Be sure to cut and paste the masthead of the paper so your recipients will know where it came from. You may or may not add the date—some people prefer not to, so it doesn't look, well, *dated*. If there was a photo, all the better.

When I photocopy a review or article, I do think it is okay to edit it, taking out anything irrelevant or, God forbid, overly negative. As long as the article is generally positive, I don't think this is dishonest. If you still have qualms about this, think of it as *excerpting*, like ads for movies do. Again, you want to put your best face forward, so as you compile these press pieces, use only the best and most recent ones from the most prominent publications.

A BIOGRAPHY

People want to know about you and your group. What sparked the love of music in you? How did you get started? Stick with the facts, of course, but don't be afraid to let your personality shine through. Using a little humor is OK if that's your style.

CREDITS

Where have you performed? Do you have albums that make up your discography? If you are a songwriter, who else performs or records your music? What media have covered or presented you (TV, radio, newspapers, magazines)? Have you opened or appeared with any "name" artists? You want to show prospective presenters that you have performed in venues like their own. Have you performed in well-known clubs, schools, libraries, hospitals, festivals, Carnegie Hall?

THE AUDIO DEMO

Voilà—*the critical piece*. No matter how slick your press kit, if you don't have a good, representative demo that someone can listen to, you won't get anywhere. *No one* hires without hearing an act. Well, almost no one. If they do, either you came highly recommended or that venue is soon to fold, having taken chances like that. If you must sink money into only one part of the promo, this is it.

People seem to prefer CDs to tapes, as they are easier to cue up and forward to the next cut. But use what you have, *as long as it is professional.* Sending a poor demo is worse than sending none. Again, remember, this is representing you and your music, more than any other piece in the press kit. Make sure it is as high-quality a piece as you can manage, right down to the packaging and label.

A demo usually consists of around three songs. Few busy folks will listen to more, and you want to give a broad sample, like Whitman's chocolates. *Put your very best song or performance first.* This is because you want to grab that very busy ear *right away* and make her want to hear more, and *really listen.* You want to show that you are right for the venue, so often I custom-make a demo to fit the venue I am courting. If you play many different styles or instruments, you might want to choose the three songs that best capture your versatility, or highlight your dazzling virtuosity.

Some places prefer live performance recordings to studio recordings. It's a good idea to have at least one sample of each, because experienced presenters know how easy it is to have a slick studio product where anyone can be made to sound good, but the act may *stink* live. If you are a really magnetic, funny, charismatic entertainer, this will come across on a live concert tape, and that charisma is a big selling point.

THE VIDEO DEMO

Another promo device that is almost mandatory once you get to a certain level is a video. We're talking about a short demo here, not a full song-length one suitable for VH1 or MTV. I know some presenters who won't even consider an act, even from an audio demo, without one. They want to see the artists in action, and if you live in Peoria and the venue is in New York, chances are, the presenter ain't traveling to come see you unless you got one heck of a terrific buzz in the industry. Some artists put their video or audio samples on their Web sites and direct presenters there instead of mailing them out—quite an economical way to do it. A professional video of a live performance is best, so the presenter can see the audience reaction, get a sense for the feel and the flow of a real concert, hear your patter (edit bloopers!), and see how dynamic you are. The audience dancing in the aisles, encores, and long standing ovations sure don't hurt. Again, if you are a terrific live act, this is to your advantage. If you're not, consider another line of work. Above all, you're supposed to be entertaining. I know that sounds obvious, but you would be amazed at how many artists think their brilliant playing or singing alone will win audiences, when they are actually stupefyingly boring and stiff onstage.

I emphasize that you should try to make a professional video if you can. These are very expensive, but worth it. A poor one—out of focus, badly edited, handheld and jittery, of poor audio quality—will actually *cost you work*. But to get a really good video, you will need to spend thousands, maybe even into the tens of thousands—much more than you would on an audio demo. This is because you will want at least two cameras (three and four are even better, especially if you are in a group, and one camera focused just on the audience is a great idea), one person just for audio, and special lighting. Video needs bright lights, unless you are purposely going for "mood"; even then, you need a strong spot or else the quality will suffer. Then you will need to edit all that footage down to about three to ten minutes.

Naturally, because of the cost, you will want to delve into making a video once you've got some experience and plenty of money under your belt. I had been performing for years—decades, even—before I could put together my simple little video. Of course, back in the Dark Ages when I first started, videos were neither an option nor as necessary as promotion. If you have a Web site (notice the smooth segue?), you can put your video and audio samples there as well.

Web Site

Another device that has become invaluable is a Web site, which is very much like a press kit and which may someday replace it altogether. This is handy to have for many reasons. You want to be easily accessible to potential presenters as well as to your millions of fans. Again, this can be either simple or as expensive as you can afford, with lots of fancy animation, video, sound clips (as a musician, you'll want these), photos, and so forth.

The annual fee to the host isn't much, considering the value to you. You should choose a logical, easy, and memorable domain name, such as your own (or your group's) name, so that people can guess the address and thus find you easily. This domain name will become your URL address. Don't try and be too clever and use something obscure—people will never remember it.

Maybe you have a talented friend (or you, yourself!) who could design your site for free or at a reduced cost. But no matter who designs and manages your site, it's a good idea to have several friends look it over when it's finished. The very talented designer who did my site, James Coffey of Blue Vision Music, says, "Web sites can look quite different depending on the computer and browser they are being viewed on. Try to have family members and friends with different types of computers (PC and Mac) as well as different browsers (Internet Explorer, Netscape, and AOL) look at your site to see how the design reacts."

Like your brochure, the site's style should represent your music. Some suggestions for Web pages you may want are:

♫ *Home page. This is your minimum. Like a brochure, you want the basic information—an introduction to yourself and your work. Here is the place for that great photo.*

♪ *Performance schedule. This is for fans to come see you live, and for presenters to preview a show. For them to see you work an audience is far better than either a video demo or a studio audition—that is, if it's a great gig!*

♫ *Reviews. Use your best quotes. You could reproduce glowing reviews or articles, but few people will take the time to read the whole thing.*

♪ *Biography. Same as in your press kit—people want to know about you!*

♫ *Audio and video samples. This takes the place of the audio or video demo tape or CD.*

♪ *Credits. Same as in your press kit.*

♫ *Products. If you have albums, bumper stickers, T-shirts, and other merchandise, devote a page to selling them! If you are reluctant to take credit cards over the Internet, you can add an order form that can be printed and then mailed to you with a check or money order, the old fashioned way. If you want to be able to take cards, but don't want the hassle or expense of setting up your own account, you can go through another party such as Amazon.com or CD baby.*

♪ *Guest book. You may want to let people write laudatory comments about you and your music, for others to see. This is a great way to get further quotable reviews. Make sure you can delete any questionable submissions.*

♫ *Contact page. You can provide a link to your email address, your P.O. box, and your business phone. Remember, if people can't find you, they can't hire you.*

♪ *What's New. Here is where you keep your fans and presenters updated about all your exciting upcoming happenings. Maybe you've won an award, your long-awaited CD is now released, you are about to embark on a month-long tour of Europe, or you are appearing on TV and want to alert the viewers. It keeps your fans current and informed about your career.*

As with my brochure, I update my site as often as necessary. Actually, my Web designer does this for me, because I don't know how to do it myself. (Learn to do it and be more independent!) Anyway, this means that the performance schedule gets updated more frequently (I have it done once a month) than, say, the products page. You want to add fresh reviews, photos, news, anything that may keep your fans interested in coming back again and again. I know some artists take photos of their fans at gigs and post them continuously on their sites, prompting their devotees to check in to see if their faces made the site!

Conferences and Showcases

There are lots of music conferences around the country that anyone who's anyone in the music biz goes to. It's not hard to find the ones whose niche you fit. Maybe you will find more than one conference—often the large national or international ones have smaller regional meetings throughout the year. These conferences can be quite expensive to attend—you need to register as a participant, pay for transportation if the conference is not in your immediate area, and maybe pop for a hotel and meals, or stay with friends. If you are lucky enough to actually get to exhibit or showcase at a conference, that is an added expense, too. At the back of the book is a list of some of these conferences and showcases, as well as other resources that will help you further.

Think of a showcase as a kind of audition that is more formal. Artists may set up their own, or they can choose from a myriad of established showcases all over the country. There are those run by agents, arts councils, and trade organizations. There are showcases for country, rock, folk, educational acts, and the wedding market. With a little research (again, you can start by checking out appendix B in the back of the book) you can find the established ones and get involved. Once again, be sure to pick appropriate types for your style of music. You don't want to be a fish among cows.

Showcases often are combined with exhibit opportunities, where artists or their reps can set up a table or booth to distribute promo material and network and schmooze with other artists, agents, and sponsors. My experience has been that showcasing, in combination with exhibiting, has been one of the very best ways to get exposure and, as a result, gigs. You get to audition for dozens or hundreds of all the right people all at once—agents, promoters, producers, presenters. If you showcase well, you will have people flocking to you or your booth to get your material, learn about you, and book ꞵ

you. The downsides of showcases are, they are usually (but not always) expensive, and you are expected to show your stuff in as little as ten minutes. Some give you a generous thirty minutes, including setup and breakdown. This is a very frenetic, nerve-wracking environment and not very conducive to doing your best work, but once you've done showcases enough times, you will relax more and get into the frantic rhythm of them. I have found that they are absolutely invaluable in my field, and most of my bookings are as a result of having showcased over the years throughout the country. Again, the rule of thumb is, do your best material, which may often have to be shortened to accommodate the time constraints. And show the breadth of what you do. Because you have just minutes to strut your stuff, you want to dazzle in any way you can.

My band and I have written and rehearsed a special "showcase set"—my best songs shortened to fit eight-, ten-, fifteen-, or twenty-minute showcases. This way, we are all comfortable and know the truncated versions very well. These sets are timed to the minute. As cruel as it may seem, some showcases will literally stop you mid-song if you go over your allotted time.

Exhibiting is a gigantic pain, in my opinion. A very fruitful one, but still a pain. Usually, a showcase is held in a huge convention hall, hotel, or other venue, and you are in a humongous room with other artists and reps who may or may not be in the same field as you. At some conferences you might be the *only* artist among people selling anything from candy to photography to wrapping paper. I find these kinds of exhibitions to be the worst.

The best ones, in my opinion, are very specifically targeted to *your* kinds of venues. Sure, it's often chaos. Everyone is trying to get the presenters' attention, the days are long, you are on your feet, and there may be hours at a stretch where no one stops at your booth. But the contacts you might make at these are really invaluable.

If you think you might want to jump into the world of showcases, conferences, and exhibitions, first go to several as a visitor to get the feel of them. Then, if you are convinced that they could be helpful, you will need to plan your booth, table, or exhibit. Hopefully, you have gotten ideas from others during your exploratory visits. Yours needs to look at least as professional. There's something very pathetic about seeing someone set up on a card table with poorly printed promo material, a mishmash of publicity photos, and so forth, among all these slick and glitzy big-time agency booths. You want to stand out, but not that way! You might need help from someone who is very good at displays, because you are playing in the Big Time. You don't want to look amateurish.

Most conferences and showcases will provide exhibitors with a table or a booth—for a fee, of course. You may want to get the biggest and best space you can afford. You want to look confident, successful, professional. Here is where you will be meeting all those important contacts you came to meet. Here is where you will disseminate your promo and talk up your act. Your agent or manager can rep you here, but I find no one can talk about my act better than me. So, even if my agent is there, I like to hang around the booth in case there are questions only I can answer. Plus, presenters often like to meet the artists in person. In any case, whether you are repping yourself or just making an appearance, dress professionally and, most importantly, comfortably. You may be schmoozing with presenters, record companies, agents, radio, and TV people, and you want to impress but also be able to last through the day. Pace yourself, don't overindulge in either food or questionable substances, and get plenty of sleep. You will need your stamina. It's tempting to stay up late at these things, talking with all the folks you'll be meeting, going from showcase to showcase and checking out all the venues and other artists. But remember why you came—you need to be alert, coherent, and, again, professional.

You may have to provide your own lighting at your table or booth. You may have to pay extra just to get electricity. It's worth it for the lighting and also if you have a TV, laptop, or CD player to play your demos. By the way, many exhibit halls require these to be used only with headphones so that the noise doesn't intrude on your neighbors' booths. In appendix A I have included my showcase checklist. It's very helpful to make one for yourself—it's very easy to leave something behind, and very frustrating when you do.

I have found that at conferences and showcases, if I don't get a showcase spot, it is often fruitless to just exhibit, *unless* it's in a region where I am already well known. I have regretted it almost every time I've gone against this policy. So I forego the expense and trouble of *just* exhibiting, except for the half-dozen showcases I do regularly and where I have a reputation. But things may be different for you; you might want to try just exhibiting. I have also heard of the magic number three—that presenters need to see you or hear about you at least three times before they will book you. This might be an argument to exhibit even if you don't showcase.

Competitions and Contests

A good way to get exposure, notice, and gigs is to enter contests and competitions. If you are confident about your songwriting, playing, singing, or whatever, why not try your hand at putting your best up against the best of others? Normally, I really hate competition in general, especially in the music biz. I think there's just too much of it in life anyway, and how can you be *objective* about something so *subjective* as art and music? But, on the other hand, you have nothing to lose in testing yourself, other than a little of your ego and maybe an entry fee. And on the bright side, if you place well, you might just get some notice from the powers that be. The more prestigious the competition, the bigger the buzz you'll get if you do well. Of course, it will also be harder to win, place, or show. If for nothing else, an award or win looks great in your promo.

I believe that one of the things that helped launch Emmylou Harris's career was winning the "Best of the Hoots" competition at the old Cellar Door Club in Washington, D.C. This club was the premiere venue for live acts in the area, for many different kinds of music genres. When she won, people took real notice of her gifts and doors opened. It is of some comfort to me (and looks good on my promo) that my singing partner and I came in as first runners-up in that very same competition. I am not ashamed of losing to Emmylou!

Now that we've covered promotion for your act, let's talk about another major way to gain exposure—promotion and publicity for a specific event like a gig or new product release.

Event Promotion

Shameless self-promotion. Yep, it's the same name for a different part of the game; not too much different here from promoting yourself in general, except that we go from the general to the specific. Let's say you've done all of the above and you are getting the gigs. Now you want folks to come out, because what good is being in the performing arts if you have no one to perform to? We performers do what we do for many reasons, but one thing is common— we must be heard. And seen, if at all possible. We need an audience.

USING YOUR FAN MAILING LIST

One thing that you can do very simply and inexpensively (for free, in fact) is, at every gig, put out a mailing list for people to sign. Many performers use the one-page format—you know, stick a piece of paper on a table by the door for people to use as they arrive or leave. I don't care for this method myself, because it leaves all kinds of room for problems—illegible writing, incomplete information, crowding at the table, and bottlenecking at the door. What I find works better is smaller cards or pieces of paper that folks can pick up and fill in at any time and drop off in a conveniently placed box. This eliminates the crowding and bottlenecks, and it lets people fill in the blanks at their convenience, maybe during intermission.

On these slips of paper or cardstock, I preprint areas for their name, street address, city, state, and zip code, allowing spacing for the four-digit suffix if they know it. Also, I have a space for an e-mail address and phone number. I've rarely had to use the phone number, but occasionally, I can't read someone's writing or someone wants information that I can give more easily by phone. Fans' email addresses are invaluable, since the cost of snail mail—even at bulk rate—is getting very high. At the very bottom I leave a space for comments—another cheap and easy way to get good quotes. Some people also leave me questions or ideas for other venues to contact who may want to hire me. This method makes it easier to get all the complete information you want. I also put *my* contact information on the slip of paper, so if they want to reach me, they can tear off that part and keep it before they drop their info in the box for me. So this serves a dual function.

These are people who liked your music enough to bother signing the list, and who want to hear from you about more gigs in their area, CD releases, and upcoming news. They may come to another gig and bring their friends. Record companies, managers, booking agents—all want to know what and where your fan base is. Is it local, regional, national or international? Does it number in the hundreds, thousands, or tens of thousands?

People tend to move much more frequently than institutions and businesses—thus, your fan mailing list will be more difficult to manage than your presenter list. Yet, it is equally vital that you keep both current. Here is where that user-friendly database software comes in handy—refer back to chapter 6 for suggestions. You don't want to keep sending out mail to dead addresses.

Divide your fans up into geographic groups—say, around major cities or local regions. This can be done in your database by referencing zip codes. Then, you can send out notices of your upcoming gigs in each group's area. I know it gets pretty costly to send fliers, but you can print up a postcard with your whole local itinerary on it rather than single gigs—postcard postage is much cheaper even than bulk rate, and you don't need to sort them by zip code. This can be done at regular intervals (monthly, quarterly, etc.) or as the gigs occur in a given area. As I mentioned, e-mail notification is even better, quicker, and cheaper. If you are good at graphics, you can even e-mail some pretty snazzy-looking "fliers."

You may think it goes without saying, but you want to be sure you include all pertinent information on these notices. This includes: your name or your group's name; the name and address of the venue where you're playing (some people like to include directions); the date and time of your show; a contact phone number for further information (this could be yours or the venue's, though yours is probably better); the admission or cover charge, including discounts for students, seniors, or others, plus any other charges like drink minimums. Also, if the gig is an album release party or a benefit, or if there are other artists on the bill, you should provide these pertinent details in your notice. Remember, you are trying to build a fan base—be good to them and they will be loyal to you (we hope!).

MEDIA MAILING LIST

You need to also develop a *media mailing list*. You can send press releases to all media in the area of the gig. Because personnel changes so much, unless I know of a specific person to write to who I also know is still there, I usually send a press release to "events editor" or "calendar editor."

For print media you should also include a photo—more and more, color shots are appreciated and favored. Photos in a newspaper or magazine attract more attention than just a listing on a calendar of events or even a blurb, especially if the shot is dynamic or eye-catching. Be aware of publication deadlines, and send your releases in time. Monthly periodicals have much earlier deadlines than weeklies or dailies, so you really need to think ahead. It's also a great idea to contact reporters and writers for these publications and ask to get an article, review, or interview about your work. Most want an unusual angle—after all, why should they give you precious space in their publication over someone else? Maybe you are a hometown kid who's "made good," or maybe this is a fundraiser for a local charity that's been in the news. *What's the hook?*

For broadcast media (radio and TV), first send out a press release addressed to the calendar editor. It's a great idea, too, if you can include your CD with specific cuts marked for airplay. If you know of a particular DJ who plays your kind of music at the local radio station, address it to her, but keep this mailing list current, as DJs move on and shows change. Then, follow up with a call or e-mail offering to do a live interview and mini-concert as a teaser to your show. Broadcast media have so many hours of airtime to fill. If you are good, interesting, funny, or have some other redeeming value, you would be surprised how welcomed you will be on these shows. You can research not only shows that feature your kind of music, but also special-interest shows on local TV channels or ones that highlight your specialty—maybe it's the environment, or humorous songs, or whatever. You may want to do a call-in contest or offer free CDs or tickets to your show on the air. The idea is, you want to generate interest in your music and in your gig. See chapter 13 for more.

Other Creative Publicity Channels

The last idea I'd like to offer you is the "teaser concert." This is a little mini-concert, like what you'd do on a radio or TV show, but it's in a different venue and in front of a live audience. For example, some friends and I were producing a benefit concert for our local food bank, to be held at a theatre that showed mainly art and foreign films. We figured that the type of audience that would like these kinds of films would be open to supporting something like the food bank. They were used to coming to this cinema often anyway, so why not sing a few songs at the same venue where the concert was to be held? Since there were several acts involved, each one of us volunteered to sing a song or two on a different day during the two weeks leading up to the benefit. Not only were we able to draw a few more people to the benefit who wouldn't normally have known about a concert like this, but we were also able to add to our own individual fan lists.

So there it is, marketing and promotion in a nutshell. There are many more ideas to get your name and music out there—all you have to do is be your creative self to think up more. All boiled down, the trick is to get your name out there as *often* as possible, to as *many* people as possible. Music needs an audience, and you have to build yours. Creating a "buzz" is so important in this business—in some ways it's as important as creating the music itself.

Chapter 8
Managers and Agents

For those artists gifted with a business head, it would be unthinkable to give up control to another. It's been said that the late, great Harry Chapin was "unmanageable" in that he felt very strongly about the directions and choices he wanted in his career, regardless of what his manager would advise.

Other artists need direction, someone else's business head, or even just an objective third party to give feedback. Some musicians may be perfectly competent enough to run their own careers but simply would prefer not to—they'd rather concentrate on solely making their art. These folks will want to seek out a rep. This chapter will tell you what, how, and why.

Definitions, Roles, and Responsibilities

What's the difference between a manager and an agent? Either can act as both, especially in the beginning of an artist's career, but each serves a different general function.

Besides the cost—a manager usually gets somewhere between 10 and 20 percent off the top of everything made by the act, while agents can claim only a percentage of the *bookings* they themselves set up for you—there are many factors to consider when you decide to hire an agent, a manager, or both.

WHAT MANAGERS DO

A manager oversees *all* aspects of the artist's career. This means anything from career and business direction to tour supervision. In short, it is the manager's responsibility to, well, *manage* your professional (and sometimes it gets personal) life. Once an act reaches a certain level, the manager's responsibilities may get spread to other personnel, such as a business manager (most likely an accountant), attorney, road manager, publicist, and so forth. These support personnel will be covered under another chapter.

A manager guides the act through the myriad of details that go into a performing life: choosing what clothes to wear onstage, finding appropriate venues, recommending and researching voice coaches and choreographers, coordinating interviews with media, overseeing photo shoots, and so forth. She is a hand-holder, a shoulder to cry on, a cheerleader, a sage. She is the one who stays calm and rational when the entire band is on the verge of chaos. She butts into the personal life of an artist when bad habits threaten the professional life. It is the manager's job to keep the career on track and to get the artist to the next level.

You can expect a good manager to guide you through the jungle of the music industry, steering you away from pitfalls and towards opportunity. A good manager has your best interests at heart—after all, if you rise to the top, hopefully you will take everyone who helped you get there with you. A good manager has contacts in the industry and may be able to get you on TV, and in touch with record companies, quality venues, a good attorney, accountant, and publicist. She will be aggressive on your behalf, but not be a pit bull that will alienate people whom you need to be on your side. She will have good people skills and be a savvy and tireless advocate and mentor. She will help get you on the right path and up to the level where you belong, and knock on doors that aren't available to you by yourself. Ideally, she will have good business sense and know the music biz inside and out.

WHAT AGENTS DO

An agent, on the other hand, is someone whose main function is to find the artist work. Again, the manager could fill this role, especially at the start, when income doesn't warrant a larger staff. An agent promotes the artist through the mail, the phone, and at showcases; negotiates fees, with the low limit set by you; writes the contracts; makes up schedules and tour routing; and follows up on any problems that may arise. A good agent will smooth the way for most aspects of a booking, from making sure all your needs are known to the producer to getting directions to the gig and arranging hospitality and lodging. (A road manager, once you have one, may take over some of these areas.) A good agent will have a list of, and solicit, appropriate venues for you, and hopefully think of other unusual or creative venues that you may not have thought of.

Working with an agent or agency certainly can be a big plus for any artist. Many venues will not even consider booking an artist who doesn't have an agent. They don't want to have to deal on that level. Having an agent is perceived as being more professional and genuine, and an agent often has more clout. It leaves the artist free to work on his art instead of running that part of the business. Fred Wolinsky, executive director of the New York agency Encore Performing Arts, Inc., repping children's and family artists, says, "The relationship between the artist and the agency should be mutually beneficial and symbiotic; neither should feel taken advantage of. Also, the continuity of the relationship is important, so sponsors will always know where to find the talent." Lastly, Fred maintains that even if the artist has an agent, the artist still needs to help with the promotion, through showcasing, compiling and sharing a mailing list, and so forth.

An agent could work alone, or as part of the staff of a larger agency. He could work solely for the one act, or could represent a "stable," or roster, of artists. There are advantages and disadvantages to all of these scenarios. The solo agent will likely work on a smaller scale, maybe at a lower level than one who is part of a bigger agency. This may mean that he is hungrier and may work harder as the sole proprietor of his own business. He may have more flexibility or be easier to contact and hold responsible for all the details of getting the booking, both good and bad. On the other hand, he may not have the support and resources of an agent within a larger organization.

This is the same good/bad situation as with an agent who reps just one act as opposed to having a roster. If you are the only act an agent reps, you will get all the attention, time, resources, and energy. Of course, that means you'd better be working enough to support that agent, unless he is doing it part time or as a favor to you. On the other hand (there are a lot of hands, as you can see), if you are part of a "stable," you won't get as much personal attention, and you will have to share showcasing opportunities with your fellow agency-mates … but the burden of working enough to support an agent is shared too. You get the idea. Some other advantages to being part of a roster of artists are, if you have a good agency with a stellar reputation, work regularly comes to that agency, and its reputation and those of your fellow stablemates will also shine on you.

Sometimes these multiple-artist agencies (usually smaller ones) will want only one of each kind of act—one country artist, one singer-songwriter—so the acts don't compete or conflict with each other. Larger agencies might prefer to specialize in a style, like all rap or country artists, repping several in the same genre so that they can recommend an alternative if the one requested isn't available. And because all acts in an agency are pre-screened for quality, the sponsor who has worked with and likes the agency will feel comfortable and assured of what she will be getting in the future. So when a sponsor, upon learning that her first choice isn't available, asks, "What else have you got?" you might benefit from a recommendation from the agency—even though your name is initially unfamiliar to the sponsor.

Beginning the Search and Making the Selection

You can hire a manager and agent, or you could rep yourself, if you have a realistic grasp of your business abilities. But let's first assume you don't have the head for business, or you don't want to go it alone because you want to totally concentrate on the art. How, then, do you go about finding a manager, agent, publicist, and so on?

First off, ask yourself, "Do I *need* a manager? Is my career at a level where I can afford to give away a hefty percentage?" If the answers are *yes*, then you can start looking.

FINDING A REP: PEERS, FRIENDS, FAMILY, AND THE KINDNESS OF STRANGERS

Do you know other artists and acts who are similar to you and who have a support team? Maybe you could approach their manager or agent to convince her to take you on as well. You could give her a demo, but eventually you'll need to invite her to a live gig so she can see for herself what an amazing live act you are. Don't be too discouraged if, after a half-dozen or so invitations, the rep still hasn't shown up. Usually an established manager or agent will only consider a new act if: (1) the act already has a fairly large following, an established reputation, and a "buzz"; (2) the act is willing to tour and otherwise work its butt off; (3) the act is earning enough money to make her percentage worthwhile; *or* (4) the act is *so* fantastic and has so much potential that the rep can't say no and she wants to get in on the ground floor with the artists. If number one is the case, you may have managers and agents approaching *you* and beating your door down anyway. If number four is the case, the manager or agent will definitely want a long-term relationship. She is not going to want to devote hundreds of hours and days of work on an unknown, untried act and get it to a certain level of success, only to have it bail on her. In fact, this is true at any level. That is why contracts are important, to protect both sides. (Contracts and other legal matters will be discussed in chapter 15.)

But getting back to finding a manager or agent: If you don't know similar acts who have someone working for them that you like, then you have to start casting around. A good source, especially for those starting out, is friends and family. I always prefer working with people I know, or who are recommended by someone I know who can vouch for them, over perfect strangers—unless they have a sterling reputation. You are going to be working very closely with your manager and agent and you need to be able to trust them. Honesty and trust, needless to say, are probably the most important parts of this business relationship. In many ways, it's just like a personal relationship; if you don't feel you can trust your entire professional life with someone, I say, *don't continue with it*. Be cautious—get to know each other.

If you are at the beginning of your career, do you have a friend or family member who has a good business sense and whom you trust? Of course, it doesn't hurt if they know the music biz, too. I know many acts who are managed by a wife, husband, sibling, good friend—someone who believes strongly in what the act is trying to achieve, and who loves its music. People like this will learn as they go, and you know (or hope) that they will stick by you and vice versa. The caveat here is, if you start off being managed or repped by a friend or family member, try not to lose sight of the fact that you care about this person and that you *first and foremost* have that personal relationship. If you can keep the business and the personal stuff separate, that is 100 percent the best way to go. Don't let the business relationship sour the personal, or you may lose that loved one. Divorces have happened when a spouse is the manager; terrible lawsuits and lifetime rifts have occurred when a parent is the manager. Professional breaks hurt much more and do untold damage when they occur with a close friend or family member.

But after you get to a certain level, you will want professional management. And you will certainly need it if you don't have a friend or family member willing or able to take on these tasks. Then, ultimately, you may need to turn to strangers. Look in the phone book and trade magazines, go to conferences, and network, network, network. Start with the smaller agencies and management companies, who may be hungrier and more willing to gamble on an unknown, until you make a name for yourself. Research the reputation, the history, and the roster of the agencies you are interested in. Once you have narrowed down the most likely ones with the best fit to your kind of act, invite them to your gigs and showcases. Again, don't be discouraged if few or none of the managers or agents you have invited show up.

Keep plugging away, keep inviting them. Once they see your name enough and if you can create a "buzz," sooner or later they will come. The law of averages is with you if you keep at it.

CHOOSING THE BEST MATCH FOR YOUR NEEDS

Once you start getting offers, sift through each one and pick the one with the best deal and with whom you feel you can foster the best relationship. Your research will come in very handy at this point. Also, do not be discouraged if you can't get an agent interested. There are so many excellent musicians and not enough agents in the industry, so don't take it too personally.

I started my professional career at age fifteen, simply by phoning every record company listed in the Yellow Pages in Washington, D.C. My naïveté actually worked in my favor—I simply didn't know this was the most unorthodox way of going about getting a manager. My singing partner and I just knew we wanted to make a record. Not surprisingly, not one company gave this young duo the time of day, until I reached the very end of the list. The head of this small company, perhaps intrigued by our youthful audacity, granted us an audition. He must have seen something he liked in its raw state in us, because soon he signed us to *both* a record and management deal. We ended up signing a two-and-half year contract (without using a lawyer, I should add—a practice I heartily *do not* recommend). This was negotiated down from a five-year contract by my smart mother, who is blessed with fore-sight and thus looked out beyond our tender age, thinking that we might want to go to college instead of continuing this career. At any rate, this launched us professionally. He nurtured and developed our talent and stage presence, hired a voice and drama coach, and shaped our attitudes as professionals.

Securing the Deal

Once you find someone capable (and that certainly is *the big* criteria), you will need to negotiate terms. Remember, a manager usually gets somewhere between 10 and 20 percent off the top of everything made by the act. Although the managerial agreement between Colonel Parker and Elvis was for 25 percent, he actually eventually got closer to a *whopping 50 percent*, insisting on getting his name on as co-writer of Elvis's own songs and con-trolling the rights to Elvis merchandise. Brian Epstein also took 25 percent of everything from the Beatles—ultimately making more than twice the amount each Beatle himself got. The group had only agreed to it because they did not know any better. They had no legal advice—or recourse—on the matter. And remember, the gross includes everything—gigs, sales of product, royalties, residuals, *everything*. Music attorney Howard Leib believes that 25 percent is incredibly high for a manager. So you want to make sure she is very good and can really produce results to warrant that. See chapter 15 for the details on legal matters.

Agents take anywhere from 10 to 35 percent of the fees from the bookings they actually get you. Their percentage, also negotiable, hurts a lot less because they get paid only when they get you work. Also, their efforts have more apparent, tangible, and immediate results than a manager's. For those that charge at the higher end of the scale, you will have to determine how good the agent must be to be worth that (based on the volume and fees of the work he gets you); how much you can afford to give up out of your fee; how badly you want to work with the specific agent; what services you are getting; the quality and locations of the gigs he can get that you couldn't get yourself; and how hungry you are to work, period.

Also, make sure you ask about "charge backs," which are any expenses that the agency incurs on the artist's behalf that it then turns around and charges the artist. Some follow this policy; some don't. In order to assess the agency, you will need to look at the *total fee*, not just the commission.

Later, when you're a big star, you might want to renegotiate your contract down to a lower percentage. The agent may consent to this because since your fees will be higher, he'll still make more money, and he won't want to lose you as a valuable client. Ensure your option to do this by keeping the length of your contract fixed. Many agency contracts start off with a one- to three-year term, as it takes some time and a lot of work to launch a new act. After that, it may be reduced to one-year extensions.

Managers will want an exclusive contract; agents may not. An exclusive simply means that you will work only with the agent or manager, in a specified capacity. There are deals where one agent will rep you throughout a region, so that you can be repped in another region by someone else. Or you may have an agent who wants to rep you exclusively, nationally and internationally. This agent had better get you enough work so that you won't need to turn elsewhere. Or the agent might have an exclusive with you only in one market—e.g., the educational scene—and you are free to work with others in the public arena. Joseph Giardina of the New Jersey agency Arts Horizons feels the advantage to an exclusive is that your agent will hopefully rep you to the fullest. Conversely, he believes that if you are nonexclusive (working with two or more agencies), there's a chance you might get more work, but each agent may not work as hard for you, or you may get forgotten. In my own career, I have repped myself for so many years that I prefer nonexclusivity when it comes to agents. At the moment, I rep myself as well as work with two agencies, with completely different deals in different parts of the country. When one agent doesn't get enough work, I have found that the more agents working on your behalf (up to a point, of course), the better. But in these cases, it is imperative that there is constant, precise communication between the agents and the artist, so there are no accidental double bookings. Fred Wolinsky of Encore agrees and also adds:

> When an artist works with several agents as well as reps him- or herself, he or she must avoid conflicts and overlaps. It can be disastrous if two agents (or an agent and the artist) are both promoting and bidding on the same job, and competing with each other. Whoever puts the time in and does not get the work will be very upset, and it can hurt the relationship. It can undermine the credibility of the agent with the sponsor, and also confuse the sponsor. So no one benefits from that scenario. If you work exclusively with an agent, this will never happen.

Self-Managing and Booking versus Hiring Someone

Of course, there is an alternative to all of the above—you can manage and rep yourself, or you can hire an assistant to take over some of the duties that both a manager and an agent would normally do. This is the route that many, many artists go at the beginning of their career. In fact, I know many very successful acts who have been doing this throughout their entire career. The advantages of this approach are: You have *total* control of your own career—it rises (*and* falls) because of your decisions alone; there's no one else to take credit (or a percentage) and no one else to blame; you learn the "business" side of the business; you know your act the best, and therefore you may be the one who can represent what you do the best; and you will be quite appealing to sponsors who believe that, whether it's true or not, if they book an artist through an agency they are paying a higher fee because of the commission. If the contract was done properly however, this last concern shouldn't be the case. Usually, the price is the same whether booking through the artist or through an agency. This, of course, means that the artist takes the hit when booked through an agency.

One of the disadvantages of self-managing and booking is that there is no reality mirror—no one to tell you when you might be heading in the wrong direction or making a bad decision. Another is, two heads (or three or four) really are better than one. Another person gives a different perspective, may think of things you wouldn't yourself, and may tell you things you don't want but need to hear. An artist alone can't possibly know all the available opportunities that a seasoned agent would know.

The most important thing for an act who chooses to self-manage or book is that *someone* needs to have a head for business. And this is where many artists don't cut the mustard. It's one thing to be a brilliant singer or musician, and quite another to be a good businessperson. And that is why so many artists end up hiring someone else—because they would unintentionally tank their own career in a heartbeat! After all, it's not called "show *play*"; it's called "show *business*" for a good reason. Sad to say, many artists are total flakes when it comes to running their own careers.

So the choice comes down to this: Are you, as an artist, willing and able to steer your professional life yourself? If you have a good business head, if you want to maintain total control (not to mention all of your income), if you are willing to devote *at least* 75 percent of your time performing the duties of booking, bookkeeping, publicizing—in short, running a small business—then this is the way to go. You can avoid the corporate world and keep all the profits yourself.

Ani DiFranco is a perfect example of this, and hers is the best success story of this type. I saw her at the beginning of her career at a showcase and booking conference. She stood out head and shoulders above all the other acts because she was so unique, and so good. I immediately knew she was going to be big. Apparently, so did every record company and booking agent there and across the country. But she chose to form her own company, manage, record and book herself, and stay completely independent. She did everything, in the beginning, by herself. After many years of going it alone, she is now in the position of devoting most of her time to creating and performing, and has hired a staff to take care of the business end. But she didn't start off that way, of course, and she still oversees every operation. Her company, Righteous Babe, has grown to employ many people, and is at the time of press recording other acts under her label. She probably is a self-made millionaire, and she calls all the shots. But—and this is the key—she has a very shrewd head, as well as the virtue of being an incredible artist. Uncompromising in her values as a businessperson and as an artist, she believes in treating everyone well and fairly. That combination is quite rare in this business.

Holly Near, one of the "mothers" of the women's music movement, is another fine example, starting and running Redwood Records in California. She and DiFranco are just two of many shining role models and success stories. Maybe you could do it, too.

During my long career, I've had it every way possible—had good and bad managers and agents, managed and repped myself completely, and had a mixture of all of the above. I've come to the conclusion, at least at this stage in my career, that I am happiest managing myself. But when it comes to booking, I like working with a variety of regional and national agents to supplement what I do for myself. This mix works best for me because although I make more money booking myself, my agents get me gigs I couldn't necessarily get myself, so they are worth the percentage they ask. I work best when I am in control. I hire an assistant to do some of the drudge work I hate, like direct mailings, phone calls, clerical tasks, and data entry stuff. (Chapter 9 touches on much of this.) So in this way, I walk the same path as Ani DiFranco, Tom Chapin, and many other highly-regarded, independent, self-managed artists who also work with agents. Frankly, if you are good with the business end, the only down side that I see to this is, once again, that you give up time and energy to do your creative stuff. But I feel the trade-offs are worth it.

Whatever route is chosen, *it is imperative that an artist never lose sight of his career*—financially or otherwise. The music business is littered with the bodies of artists who left all the business matters in others' hands, only to be ripped off or mismanaged. One constantly reads and hears about acts losing fortunes through dishonest or incompetent management. So acquiring some knowledge of bookkeeping, contracts, and other aspects of the biz is crucial for every performing artist, whether or not you choose to hand over the reins.

Chapter 9
Support Personnel

Unless you plan on being a complete loner, a traveling minstrel driving your-self from gig to gig, setting up everything from the bookings to your own sound system, writing and negotiating your own contracts, etc., etc., etc., you will sooner or later be working with what I will call support personnel. We've already covered managers and agents, so let's look at other vital people who, sooner or later, may play a part in your career.

Accompanists

Many singers and musicians play with others, be it in an orchestra, rock band, opera, or whatever. Even a diehard soloist might sometimes play with an accompanist. Music is a gregarious sort of art form. This is one of the reasons why, in my opinion, the playing of music is so joyful. Since this chapter deals with *support personnel*, I am going to address the issue of accompanists rather than a "peer" situation like an orchestra or band, as was discussed in chapter 3, where presumably all the members are on a *somewhat* equal footing with regards to billing, status, pay, and so forth.

How does one find and keep great accompanists? Of course, the first place to look is right in your own community. Like any other group, you will be needing to gather frequently for rehearsals, business meetings, and so forth, and it sure makes it more convenient if everyone lives within easy driving distance from each other. I have worked with accompanists who, although I loved their playing and we got along famously, became "geographically undesirable" simply because it was such a hassle to get together to rehearse. One or more of us had to travel over an hour to get together, and for a time I worked with an accompanist who didn't even own a car and wasn't a confident driver. It made even getting to gigs a real strain, and he was often late. Either I had to pick him and his gear up and drive him home, or he took public transportation, and boy, did that get old, since he played electric bass and guitar and had to schlep an amp!

But of course, if you really have something special and can get past geographical obstacles, it may be worth the extra effort. My present bass player/guitarist used to drive five hundred miles interstate round trip once a week for rehearsals and gigs when we first started … but now, it's not nearly so bad. To put him out of his misery (or maybe add to it?), I married him. His commute is much better now.

I met my present drummer when his group and mine were on the same bill at a local outdoor festival. My bass player was very taken with this guy, who was the percussionist for another trio. We asked if he could do some recording with us, and then some gigging. Well, we "stole" him away from the other group, as they weren't gigging much, and we were. For a while he worked with both groups, but eventually it came down to the bucks—we were paying him vastly more *and* giving him much more work than the other group. And it was a big plus that he lived in our town, not two minutes from us.

As further example of this other side of the coin, we all know of rock bands whose members even live in different countries, and they manage. For me however, convenience counts for a lot, and probably if you look and ask around, there are many fine musicians living near you. Go out and listen to all kinds of music, live. Just because you play bluegrass, for example, doesn't mean that that hot jazz bass player you saw at the local club couldn't also work with you. But I think the *most important criteria* are musical and personal compatibility over every other factor. Playing music with others should be fun and inspiring, not a chore!

ADDRESSING LOGISTICS BEFORE YOU PLAY

What arrangements you make for billing and pay will, naturally, be up to you. If you are a "solo" act but you have accompanists, your name is out front, but you may want to put theirs smaller under yours. Or not. You know Rod Stewart doesn't add his band members' names to the bill, but *somewhere* they get acknowledged. Factors like pay, how the act will be billed, decision-making, and so forth should be discussed and agreed upon *up front*, once again so there are no misunderstandings. Once, when I was younger, my duo had a drummer and bass player who, after playing with us for only a few months, decided they wanted equal pay and equal decision-making, since we were "a group." My partner and I disagreed with them, considering them "accompanists" to our duo, and we finally parted ways amicably. But if all had been understood from the beginning, no such "mutiny" would have occurred.

Another matter of concern is if your accompanist doesn't play with just you, but has one or more gigs going concurrently. Until you get to a place where you can give him enough work to support him full time, this in fact will probably be the case. It should be made very clear what arrangements will be made when there are competing interests and scheduling problems involving your accompanists. At any rate, it's an extremely good idea to have at least one sub for each of your accompanists, in case of illness or other commitments. Of course, this means more rehearsals for you, but in the long run it's in your best interest.

I think it's crucial that your dealings with every human being you come into contact with during the course of your career should be equally honorable and respectful. You would think this goes without saying, but you would be surprised at how many musicians are smiling and pleasant Nice Guys and Gals in public, but treat their staff, accompanists, and techs like dirt. Remember, your accompanist is your rock—he is there to support you and make you sound great. Also, your good name is easily besmirched by disgruntled employees and associates.

PAY

There are industry standards for pay for musicians (e.g., studio musicians and Broadway pit musicians), but if you don't belong to a union, you are free to pay your accompanists whatever everyone agrees on. As usual, the market comes into play here. When it comes to accompanists, my philosophy stays the same as for setting my own fees: *I believe musicians should be paid well.* As your fees rise throughout your career (these I'll discuss in chapter 14), so should your accompanists'. Pay should be agreed upon well in advance of rehearsals and gigging, of course, and you may or may not want a contract with them, depending on how close you are, or how much you trust each other. But it goes without saying that you must be fair. Especially in the beginning, many novice and even semi-pro musicians will play for free, just to get the experience, exposure, and maybe "prestige" of playing with someone better-known—or just to be gigging. But there will be hard feelings if the accompanist is paid grossly less than the artist. I would never ask a musician to play for free unless I am, too, as in a benefit or fundraiser. Even if the pay in a dinky coffeehouse is $50, split it equitably. There have even been times when I have not been paid, but I paid my accompanists out of my pocket anyway, for their time, talent, and travel.

Also, wherever possible, I like to have the venue pay all the musicians separately. This is because I don't want my gross distorted by their fees, I don't want to have to hassle with the bookkeeping and 1099s that go along with my paying them, and I also don't want to be responsible for late payment. In fact, in the cases where the venue insisted on paying me everyone's fee, and the check was late to boot, I would either pay my accompanists right after the gig out of my pocket anyway, or reach an agreement in which everyone would be paid as soon as the check came.

Not all front musicians may subscribe to this method of separate checks, and some may actually prefer only one check for the whole act. Furthermore, many venues don't want the hassle of separate checks and will only pay the leader one check for everyone—as in the situation I just described. There are, of course, more complicated bookkeeping issues with this method.

Road Manager and Crew

Most musicians starting out, and even some longtime professionals, don't have roadies. For most, roadies are a costly luxury, but they may become a necessity if: (1) you have lots of heavy equipment and can't or don't want to do the lifting, setting up, breaking down, and such, or (2) you are touring a lot and don't have a good head for details such as directions, hotels, lighting, and fog machines.

The road manager's job is to take care of *everything* the musician needs on the road. He is responsible for making sure that all necessary personnel and equipment make it to the gigs in one piece and in good shape. He books hotels and arranges for ground and air transportation, greeters, hospitality, and much more. He inventories instruments, equipment, and the product to sell before and after every gig, and maintains meticulous records against loss or theft. He oversees the roadies, whose job it is to physically move the equipment, set it up, break down, fine-tune, maintain, and repair everything so that all is ready for the musicians to work.

Needless to say, all this requires a big budget, and you won't need to worry about this at the beginning. Again, there may be union wages to pay if you go that way. But many bands just starting out have friends who are more than glad to help out as a favor, or for drinks or other perks. Sometimes you can find novices wanting to learn about the music biz who just want to tag along and be helpful. But beware: Chances are, your equipment and instruments are not cheap, and the people you use as roadies should know not a little something about them, and be reliable and careful. You get what you pay for, and for free, well, they may just be less than careful or trustworthy. My life rule about treating people well applies everywhere. If you can, pay your roadies at least *something*, even if they offer to work for free.

But what if you can't afford, or don't really need, all this? Great! Learn how to do all the necessary tasks yourself and save a bundle. Learn every aspect of servicing and running your instruments and equipment (see chapter 4). This is a good idea, even if you have support personnel, because you don't want to be helpless and at the total mercy of your equipment or an unfamiliar sound guy. Also, there are hundreds of stories of musicians who thought that the venue would supply a sound system. When they got there, the system was nonexistent, nonfunctioning, or inadequate. You have to be extremely specific about your needs. You might have a tech rider on your contract—don't assume that, because you asked for five mics, you will also get five mic stands! Don't laugh, it's happened. For more information that should go into a contract and riders, see chapter 15.

Another caveat is that moving equipment, even acoustic instruments, can take its toll on the body. We know musicians who have had several hernia operations from too much heavy lifting, and who are probably destined for others if more care is not taken.

Being your own road manager is even more complicated than being your own roadie, and setting up and maintaining a tour on your own will be covered in its own chapter.

Tech Crew

Your tech crew may also be your roadies, but this crew should be particularly knowledgeable and capable within each area of expertise. You surely don't want your sound tech to be hanging rigging for the giant statue that will descend to the stage at the right moment, nor do you want your guitar tech to be messing with your pyrotechnics. I don't want to get too deep into the fancy stuff, because chances are, until you reach the pinnacle of your art form, you won't be needing explosive experts or animal trainers. Let's concentrate instead on possibly the most crucial member of your team, your sound tech.

Your sound system can make you sound glorious or horrible. Many times you will be at the mercy of the house PA, which in most clubs is uniformly terrible, and the club's sound tech, who one would hope would be good but may not be. Because of my years of experiencing bad sound systems and techs, I try not to rely on the venue's. On my very first tour, my manager was smart enough to insist that we invest in and travel with our own PA, as the places we played in were so variable in their acoustics, and some didn't even have any sound system at all. To this day, I invest in excellent equipment, the best I can afford. Please refer to chapter 4 for more on this.

Since I mostly travel with my own sound system, and at the moment don't have any other roadies other than my accompanists, each of us in the band has become very proficient in sound teching and very familiar with the system. If the venue has its own great tech and system, or if you can afford to travel with a specialist, more power to you. Treat your sound person like a god, because he can make or break your act. Your own sound tech will also know your show's cues, like when to hit the accompanying CD or special effects. Ask him to pay special attention not only to the house mix but also to the monitor mixes for each musician. The ideal situation has each person getting his or her own monitor with separate mix. Personally, I think individual monitors are crucial (so that each musician can hear his own part and whomever else he wants to hear clearly), but others seem to manage without *anything*.

Be sure to leave plenty of time for sound check—there's nothing worse than going onstage with little or no sound check, and having to work out the kinks during the show. The bigger the group, the longer the time you'll need. For my trio, we assign an hour and a half for load in, setup, tuning, and sound check. By the way, it's a very good idea to pack lots of duct tape for securing wires and cords down across the stage. It's cheaper than a lawsuit! Anyway, this hour and a half leaves us relaxed and gives us time to run songs if we need to, fix appearances, change into stage clothes, and so on. Always thank your sound tech from the stage publicly at the end, or sometime during the show. If he is not your own tech, it's also a nice gesture to give him free albums or some other goodie.

Clerical Help

After you reach a certain level, you can kick back on the clerical duties and assign them to an assistant. This is assuming you are self-managing and self-booking—otherwise the managers and agents you've hired will alleviate your paperwork pains for you. How do you find competent help? The same way you find anyone you want to surround and support you—by asking, keeping your ears and eyes open, and relying on friends and family to either be that person or recommend someone else. Clerical work is pretty easy, so you might try the local high school. Teens are always looking for work, and you can offer, if not the highest hourly rate, at least the perk of learning the music biz, getting to hang around really cool people, and maybe flexible hours. Many will jump at the chance. Of course, if you pick someone green, you need to train him. He should at least have the basic skills of typing, filing, and phone decorum. You can start him as simply clerical help, then gradually train him to rep you and even give him a chance to book you. If you put him on phone duty, make sure he is articulate and mature sounding. You want a professional image, and that's hard to maintain if your assistant answers the phone, "Yo, dude!" Unless, of course, that *is* your image ...

Even if you don't choose to hire an assistant, at least consider training someone—your husband, your teenage daughter, your baby son's sitter—to handle office work while you're on tour. I do a lot of business on the phone when on the road, but that's a big hassle. I inevitably leave something important at home, and it's great to have someone to deal with things like the mail and other details of your life and business.

PAY

My policy on wages is to find out what the range is in my area for clerical workers at this level, and to pay as high in that range as I am able. This not only is the right thing to do, but also hopefully will foster loyalty with someone who is intelligent and more than competent. And you also hope that that person will become part of your family of true believers in you and your music—not a likely result of underpaying the guy chained to your desk. Remember, you are in this for the long haul, and you want friends, not flunkies, and certainly not enemies.

In return for good compensation, you should expect conscientious work from your employees. What you don't want is to invest a lot of time and training into someone who doesn't care about you or your business, and who will leave you at the first opportunity. Also remember that this person will have access to a lot of private and sensitive information, and if you alienate him— or if you hire someone who is untrustworthy from the start—you just never know how that will come back to haunt you. Some celebrities make their assistants sign confidentiality contracts. You probably don't need to go that far, but the point is, be fair and scrupulous in all your dealings and then hope no one will write a tell-all book about you someday!

If you pay someone more than $600 per year, you have to file a 1099 on him as an independent contractor. Once you start adding more full-time staff, you will need a lot more advice than this book can offer, as you will need to do the whole income-tax withholding thing and more. At this point, consult your accountant. (You do have one, right? No? See more on this later.)

And another thing: I always do things completely above-board, like reporting income and hiring help. It's just so much hassle to do anything "under the counter"—you just never know when something (or someone) is going to come around and bite you in the butt! When you are rich and famous, you don't need the scandal; heck, even when you are poor and struggling, you don't want it. Even with something as legitimate as bartering, there are tax ramifications. Again, consult an accountant.

Attorneys

Sooner or later, once you go professional, you will need an attorney to guide you through the mire of contracts you'll encounter. Partnerships, performance, recording, managers, agents, publishing, trademarks, copyrighting—all need contracts or some other form of legal guidance. You *could* use Uncle Harry, who's a real estate attorney, for the cut-and-dried, simple contracts, but it's far better to use one who is conversant in the music industry, which has its own peculiarities. A lawyer who is a general practitioner may not know everything that's pertinent, such as statutory rates for mechanical licenses. Furthermore, it's an added perk that lawyers who specialize in the music business may also be very well-placed. They may know influential people in the industry who could possibly aid you in your climb to the top.

I would not advise negotiating, much less signing, a contract without having an attorney at least review it first. If you are interested in incorporating (see the section titled "Business Managers and Accountants" below), you may also need an attorney. You need an attorney whenever you create something that needs protecting; when you begin any business association, such as a partnership (which is what a band is); and when you are dealing with possible infringement issues. Please see chapter 15 for a more in-depth look.

As I mentioned in chapter 8, when I first began my career at the tender age of fifteen, I didn't use a lawyer for my first recording and managerial contracts, contrary to my own advice above. This was years ago, when the business was simpler and perhaps less cutthroat. My parents, and my music partner's parents, accompanied us to meetings with the manager; they reviewed the contracts, and they negotiated. We were lucky that time—I have a very shrewd mom! I wouldn't do it again without an attorney. Though they charge by the hour and it can get costly, believe me, they are worth it.

A bad contract will come back to haunt you and be even more costly than the bucks you will spend on a good music attorney. Some attorneys may want to charge you a percentage of any deal they negotiate on your behalf, much like a manager might, instead of taking an hourly rate. This may or may not be to your benefit. Look at your situation: If you are just starting out and don't have much money to begin with, this might work for you. But if you hit big, it's definitely to the attorney's benefit and not to yours!

How to find one? Well, there's always the trusty Yellow Pages. But even better are music industry resources like guilds, conferences, unions, trade magazines, and so forth. Best of all, are recommendations from other musicians. If you live in a major music center like New York, L.A., or Nashville, you practically fall over music attorneys in the street, they are so numerous! But if, don't live in one of these cities, then you will need to do some research. Entertainment attorney Howard Leib cautions, "Remember, *any* lawyer can call themselves a music lawyer. Ask about their background and experience." And interview several before you commit. See whom you feel most comfortable with, who seems most knowledgeable about the biz, who comes with trustworthy references. Ask for the names of their other artist clients, then call them up and ask them questions, too. As with a manager or agent, do your homework and you probably won't get burned. I like to trust my gut with people—but that is fallible, as we all know.

Public Relations

Once again, you will start off doing all the PR and marketing yourself. There is a separate chapter on this DIY approach. But let's say you have risen to the level where you are now prepared to hire someone, at least part time. The trick to finding a good PR person is the same for all other support personnel—ask others! Again, it's better to find someone who has expertise in the entertainment field. A person may be a wiz at promoting widgets, but it's very different promoting an act. Even try and find someone who is knowledgeable about *your* kind of music, because that expert will know the best ways and in which media to present you. For an obvious example, a classical pianist will be promoted quite differently than a rap group.

Many PR firms will take a retainer and monthly fee, some will do it project by project. You will sit down and discuss what works best for you and your budget. I recommend that every musician performing professionally set aside some amount of money for PR. You could be the most amazing musician in the world, but if no one hears you or about you, you might as well go dig ditches for all your playing will get you. Don't underestimate the power of industry "buzz"—once some powerful people start lauding you, doors open, and things can move very fast. A good PR person is worth her weight in gold. If she is a good one, she can have your name and face everywhere, and that helps create "the buzz." Of course, you can have a great buzz and not live up to it, too, but that's another story.

Business Managers and Accountants

Your overall manager may also be your business manager, or you may use a separate accountant. This person will oversee incoming and outgoing royalties, taxes, tour budgets … anything behind a dollar sign. Unlike in other areas, finding an accountant familiar with the music biz isn't as crucial, but it's nice and, of course, preferable. More so than in any other area, it's an extremely good idea to familiarize yourself with basic bookkeeping, accounting, taxes, and insurance. Chapters 14 and 18 both cover these topics more in depth. There are hundreds, if not thousands, of stories of artists getting ripped off by either dishonest or incompetent staff, and poor accounting of your income and outgo can hurt you the most. Even as a young teen starting out in the biz, I knew enough to pay attention to *income*—exactly how much we got paid for every gig—and where, how, and in what names the money got held. Unfortunately, also being very naïve and not having a separate business manager or accountant, I didn't watch all the *outgo*—the expenses for recording, marketing, and so forth—and just trusted our manager. As a result, after our two-and-a-half-year contract expired, we didn't have much in our bank account to show for all our hard work. Now I do my own bookkeeping but hire an accountant for all the other stuff. I see where every penny I make goes—I control the checkbook, and then I meet with my accountant maybe two to four times per year.

Do shop around—fees vary wildly. I like to ask other musicians whom they would recommend, because it's helpful, though probably not necessary, that the accountant know something about your particular business. Also, a personal recommendation goes a long way in establishing trust. If someone you know and respect trusts this person to oversee his finances, then that says a lot. If there is any doubt about trust (and again, *keep your own eye on things!*) you could hire an auditor to check your books or whatever else you may feel suspicious about. Auditors cost money, but if you are truly worried, it may be worth the expense.

Teachers, Coaches, and Therapists

No matter which field of music you are in, you will probably need to hire coaches or teachers. I would think most artists want a long career, and having good technique will help prolong your professional health. The best way to find any teacher is to ask around, even calling music schools. Once again, a personal recommendation is worth a lot. When you find a teacher, "audition" him first. See if you feel comfortable and compatible musically as well as personally. You won't keep up your lessons if the teacher is impatient, bullying, uninterested, or incompetent—or an egomaniac, who spends most of your lesson showing off or talking about himself. If you can, audition several teachers to see which is the best fit for you and your style of music. And of course, once you find one, don't sell yourself short or waste money and time by not practicing what he teaches. This goes without saying—you shouldn't be aspiring to make a living in music if you aren't willing to practice!

Some singers (myself included, a long time ago) think they don't need teachers or coaches—after all, what could be more natural than singing? But poor technique will not only inhibit what sound you *could* be getting, but it could also actually hurt your muscles and shorten your career. Ron Meixsell, opera singer and voice teacher, says,

> *Good technique creates more general awareness and sensitivity. The singer will know when something is wrong because it doesn't feel right, or it actually hurts. The young singers that I teach have heard those warnings that a voice teacher will take away your natural sound, and not respect your individuality. That is true in some cases, but ultimately it is the singer's responsibility not to allow that to happen. Find the right teacher if you feel you are being disrespected.*

I cringe when I hear Bruce Springsteen screaming, but he has made his whole career on that style. He just won't have a voice left in his old age! If Janis Joplin were alive today, her voice would probably be destroyed by now. Pete Seeger is another example of what an untrained voice can suffer. He can barely sing any more—he leads singalongs now, but that's the extent of his concerts. Most singers' voices—Bonnie Raitt's, Joan Baez's, and Joni Mitchell's immediately spring to my mind—lower with age. Joan went back later in her career for some vocal instruction, which actually did change the sound quality of her voice but has probably prolonged her career. Joni Mitchell has lost her highest register through age but most likely through heavy smoking.

Especially if you are in a very demanding field, such as opera or musical theatre, you will definitely need voice teachers, coaches, *and* therapists, which are all different animals. A *voice teacher* will take your natural gift and instrument (your vocal cords, diaphragm, facial muscles) and help you achieve your full potential without hurting yourself, by working on proper technique. He will work on resonance, timbre, vibrato, phrasing, placement, pitch, posture, register, breath control, enunciation, pronunciation, and more—in other words, teach you to sing correctly. Ron Meixsell says, "Singers ideally need to find a balance between their 'chest' voice and their 'head' voice." Voice teachers help singers find that balance.

A *vocal coach*, on the other hand, works on repertoire. She will also help you with the dramatic interpretations of a song. Usually, a coach is a pianist with a strong background in the various genres of music. Singers in musical theatre, cabaret, and opera all come to mind here as needing a vocal coach. Ron says, "Although coaches can teach—and conversely teachers can coach—it can be problematic and even dangerous if it's not their area of expertise."

A *voice therapist* is trained in the mechanics of the voice and works on vocal dysfunction. This is an important member of your vocal health team, along with your teacher, coach, and ear, nose, and throat doctor. She evaluates and treats voice problems by working on voice conservation and vocal hygiene, as well as advising you on how to control contributing factors to vocal disorders, such as acid reflux and dehydration. She not only works with you to avoid "phonotrauma" (vocal abuses) but also helps you with the three most important aspects of a healthy voice: relaxing muscle tension, developing tone placement, and breath control. I hired one when, having stopped seeing my teacher, I got into trouble with chronic laryngitis, a singer's nightmare. (I also saw an ear, nose and throat specialist, who looked for polyps and nodes on my cords—a most unpleasant experience, I can tell you.) For more on vocal therapy, read chapter 17.

Like singers, instrumentalists also may want coaches or teachers to help extend their playing life with good technique. Sadly, I am self-taught on all my instruments and so have some very bad habits that are nearly impossible for me to break. Starting off with a good teacher would have set me on the right path, and I'd be a much better musician today. I would have gotten to a certain level faster, and with more precision and correct technique. If I had to do it all over again, I would have learned how to read music better as well as play my instruments correctly. Again, the value of a good teacher or coach is immeasurable. Although there is a certain charm in being untrained (grunge and punk musicians revel in their raw, untrained talents), don't let your rock-and-roll friends convince you that you don't need training. Often, "the persona of many rock musicians is 'I did it my way,' and so younger musicians want to emulate that rebellious life style," opines Ron Meixsell. There will always be some self-taught musical geniuses, but why keep reinventing the wheel? You'll get there faster with help. Of course, in some fields of music, ongoing formal training, preferably started when you are young, is absolutely mandatory.

Another very important, though less measurable, value in having a teacher is the trust that develops between a mentor and a student. Over time, while working closely together, a relationship forms where the teacher gets to know the student's patterns of thought and behavior. A thoughtful and concerned teacher can thus help guide the student not only musically but also personally, gently showing the most productive way to his goals and perhaps steering him away from harmful practices.

So, there are your core support people. As acts grow, they can start adding all kinds of hangers-on until they have a huge entourage. There are wardrobe keepers, dressers, set designers, makeup artists, hair stylists, gofers, and on and on. Just remember, the more people you add on, the less of your income you get to keep—or, conversely, the more you have to work to maintain this stable of folks. By the time you get there, you certainly won't need this book any more!

Chapter 10
Technical Matters

Your agent has just booked you a cool gig—or maybe you've arranged it yourself. Your accompanists are going to meet you at the site at the time you've designated, and your administrative assistant will be at your office to take phone calls while you're gone. Now that your focus is on the venue itself, what issues will you need to address in order to ensure that you'll be able to do your very best job?

First of all, call the venue in advance to find out what you may be grappling with upon arrival. You should know everything you can about certain physical components of the performance space and the audience seating. Not only will you need to know of possible obstacles to loading in your equipment; you'll want to know specifics about the stage, the sound system, the audience, and the lights. Discussed below are the details to consider when you speak with the presenter about the venue.

The day of the gig, try and get to the venue well in advance of the concert in order to load-in, set up, tune up, sound check, change clothes if necessary, and chill a little bit before hitting the stage. Again, you may want to call the venue in advance to see if there are any challenges to load-in. We once performed on (and had to schlep all our stuff up to!) the fourth floor of a building that had no elevators. Know these things in advance, arrive earlier than usual, and be prepared.

Even if you are a totally acoustic act who doesn't need anything like a sound system or lights, you will still need to know *something* about the technical side of a performance, as there is more to staging a live concert than just your music. It's a good idea to know the rudiments so you will not be totally clueless, vulnerable, and at the mercy of the venue. Remember, how you *think* you look and sound in your own head is *not* how you look and sound to the audience, especially if your show is filtered through fancy lights and a PA.

Stage Details

The stages on which you will be performing can vary from nonexistent to—may you be so lucky—Carnegie Hall. That is to say, from abysmal to perfect. They may range from a four-foot by eight-foot piece of plywood over mud to a state-of-the-art, acoustically designed space with velvet curtains, scrims, and lights. This is your platform, your pedestal, if you will. You want to present your music, both aurally and visually, as well as you can, and that includes your stage.

SIZE, SHAPE, AND SURFACE MATERIAL

You may want to ask: Will you have enough room to move around if that's part of your act? Is the space sufficient to hold all your instruments and equipment? Stage ceiling height is also relevant because it affects the sound onstage and also what gets sent out to the audience. Or, if you are Christine Lavin, you need to know how high you can throw that baton! You want to know how *deep* the stage is (the distance from front to back) and, if there is a proscenium (area in front of the front curtain), how deep that is, too. You might want to know how *high* the stage itself is, and how far away the first row of chairs is. Is it a fixed stage, or is it comprised of portable modular risers that fit together? If it's the latter, you want to make absolutely sure it is well-balanced and sturdy so that there will be no unfortunate accidents. Is the stage round? U-shaped?

The surface of the stage is important because you may be moving around quite a bit on it, and you want to know how acoustically "live" it is. I have been on stages that are carpeted—these are pretty dead acoustically. Wooden stages are great—I love them. They are forgiving and feel good if you are standing on them for a long time, and they are resonant. Wooden stages also have plenty of "give" to them—which can be bad if you and your instruments are sharing that stage with sixty tap dancers. Your precious instruments on their stands may just jump around, too, like popcorn popping in a pan. Certain stages resonate more than others, so you should be aware of that if you tend to tap or stomp your feet! This can work for or against you.

What you definitely don't want is something rickety, slippery, sticky, or uneven. I've sung on stages that have actual *holes*, either through damage or because of an electrical outlet set into it. These are annoying at best and treacherous at the worst, so forewarned is forearmed. If you see a problem surface (try and walk the stage before the audience comes in) that can't be fixed immediately, make a mental note about its nature and location so that it won't accidentally trip you up.

Another thing to ask is if the stage is "raked." This means tilted from upstage (back) to downstage (front). Some stages that present theatrical productions are. Thankfully, most are not, but you never know. This could wreak havoc if your act involves roller skates. Some stages are lower than the audience, who themselves are on raked seats (going progressively higher as they go back, like bleachers). The advantage to this is that everyone can see better than if they were all seated on a flat surface. The only disadvantage I can see is if you are getting people from the audience up onstage, sometimes they get so excited they might tumble down the raised or stepped aisles! In any case, when using steps onto the stage, it's a very good idea to have someone there to help prevent falls or tripping. My drummer, who serves this role for me, once saved a little kid from tumbling off the steps and into a recessed area directly in front of the stage, which brings us to the next point of discussion …

STEPS

Are there any steps leading from the stage down into the audience area? This is useful if you are getting audience members up onstage and if you want to step down into the audience. Some stages have doors, on one or both ends of the stage, that lead to hidden stairs to the stage. I don't like this arrangement, however, because whoever is coming off or onstage disappears for a few seconds before reemerging in sight. In this situation I ask if portable stairs are available to put in front of the stage.

CURTAINS

Are there any, and where are they? At the front, sides, back? Sometimes, on bigger stages, there are several curtains that can divide the stage lengthwise; these are good for hiding people or equipment for use later. It's also an ideal situation if there are multiple acts, because one can be quietly setting up behind a middle curtain while the first act goes on in front. Then, when it's the second act's turn, the first act removes their stuff and the second act is already set up and ready to go. This works particularly well during showcases, when there is very little time between acts for set-up and break-down. At a particularly well-run showcase I attend, three curtains are used. The showcase organizers arrange the order so that smaller acts can work on the apron in front of the front curtain while two other acts are setting up—the second artists are stationed between the front curtain and the middle curtain, and the third one's stuff is stashed between the middle curtain and the back, ready to move forward when it's time. After the third act is done, the front curtains close and the whole cycle starts again. This is an extremely efficient method and use of stage curtains. Of course, it mandates that each subsequent act is respectful and quiet during setup, and that acts going off move as quickly and quietly as possible.

If there aren't curtains, what is the stage's back wall surface? You might need this information if you wish to hang any sort of decoration or banner for your act. First, ascertain whether the presenters will allow you to hang something as a backdrop. Then, if there is a curtain, you can use large pins. But if it's cinderblock or some other hard surface, should you use duct tape or some other material? Be sure to ask the venue, because certain adhesives can leave marks.

OUTDOOR STAGES

Outdoor stages have their own particular peccadilloes. Some are uncovered, leaving you at the mercy of the weather. Either you are melting in the hot sun or getting soaked in a misty rain. Unprotected outdoor stages are also susceptible to wind, which can knock over instruments and music stands, blow away sheet music, and ruffle clothes and hair. At times like these, it's a good idea to use the heavier kind of music stands and make sure your instruments are secure onstage. There are great music clips to hold music to stands—my group likes to use the long ones that look kind of like giant clothes pins except that one rod is made of clear, colorless plastic so that you can see right through it to your music. And women, don't wear short loose dresses or skirts that can accidentally catch the wind unless it's part of your act to emulate Marilyn Monroe! On windy days, those with long hair may want to clip it back—it's very annoying to have hair flying in your face and into your mouth when you are trying to perform.

In any case, performing outdoors presents its own challenges, not the least of which is that *everything* gets dissipated—the sound you are putting out, and the audience reactions you get back. That all-important mutual energy is tougher to muster, sustain, or discern because there are no walls or ceiling to contain it.

Also, performers should refuse to play if it's rainy or misty and the stage is wet or can get wet. You just don't want to mess around with electricity and water, nor do you want your precious instruments to get damp (not to mention your own bad self!). See chapter 15 for tips on including this condition in your contract.

Seating Arrangements of the House

It may sound silly and gratuitous, but you might want to know the seating arrangement for the audience. Will they be completely surrounding the stage ("in the round"), in which case you'd better hope that stage revolves?! Will they be seated three-quarters of the way around you? Will they be seated on the grass, the floor, on bleachers, tables, and chairs? Will there be any aisles?

If I have any say over the seating arrangements, I always ask for at least one center aisle, for safety reasons. Plus, often I will come down from the stage to mingle with the audience during the show, and an aisle facilitates this.

As an aside, when performing for a family audience, I usually request that the children and the parents sit *together*. Although it can sometimes make it harder for very little ones to see over the heads of adults seated in front of them if the seating isn't raked, I have very good reasons for requesting this. Sometimes venues like to have a separate seating area for the kids, usually right down in front on the floor or on cushions or carpet, and then they will stick the parents in the back on chairs. I don't like this arrangement, because: (1) the children tend to act up and run around more without their parents right next to them, (2) the parents tend to sit in the back and either talk to each other or read (*Yes! That happens! People—this is not television! We can see you!*), and (3) we really want the concert to be a family sharing experience, with the parents and children making music and having fun *together*. So I strongly discourage any other seating arrangements at these kinds of gigs.

Backstage

Backstage areas, when they exist, can be even more varied than the stages themselves. There may be a gorgeous area with multiple air-conditioned dressing rooms, lighted mirrors, showers, sofas, TVs and more; or you might have to pee in a Porta-Potty in a field. It's a very good idea, when you are booking the concert, to ask about these amenities.

> 𝅘𝅥𝅮 *Dressing Rooms. Are there any? If so, how many? This becomes particularly important if your group is coed. As chummy as you may all be, you probably want your privacy when changing into your performance duds. Does it have mirrors? If so, are they lighted? Applying makeup is a real drag in bad light. Are there any full-length ones so you can check out your total look before heading onstage? Sometimes, I've gone on with my shirt buttoned incorrectly or something hanging out. (Not a bad idea to ask someone else to check out your look if there is no full-length mirror, just in case.) Does it have accessible electrical outlets for hairdryers, curling irons, coffeepots, and so forth? Is there a place to hang your street clothes and stash other stuff?*

♪ *Restrooms. Is there a bathroom solely for the artists' use or will you have to share one in the lobby or restaurant with the audience members? Are there showers, towels, soap, and other toiletries for your use before or after the concert?*

♫ *Security. Is backstage secure enough to leave your stuff there? Who will be responsible for this security? Are there lockers? Will there be a stage manager?*

♪ *Air-conditioning. In warmer climates, I also ask if the dressing/backstage area is air-conditioned. The reason for this is that I have performed on outdoor stages in the summer where the dressing room is air-conditioned but the stage, of course, is not. If you tune your instruments backstage in the cooler, dryer air, chances are, once you hit the heat and the humidity, your instruments will go bonkers. The same is true conversely—if the stage and house are air-conditioned but the dressing area is not. (Unlikely, but it happens).*

Of course, for those gigs where there are less-than-adequate facilities (or none at all!), you will have to adjust. Hopefully, you have planned ahead, asked the presenter for whatever needs you cannot live without, and brought whatever the facility lacked. For example, I always bring my own hand wash gel, as often there is no soap in the restrooms. Also, I bring a small mirror with my makeup, because I like to do last-minute touch-ups backstage, and there often is no mirror there. The ultimate example of preparedness comes in the form of my friend Janice Buckner, who travels in her own air-conditioned RV. She rescued me once when we both were performing in a field, where the nearest bathroom was at least a half-mile walk away!

Sound

Oooooh, now here is a *very* important section, maybe one of the most important in this whole book. After all, the presentation of your music is what it's all about, isn't it? In this chapter we will assume that you don't carry around your own PA system. If you do, refer to chapter 4. But if you don't, you will want to be familiar with what is available to you at the venue. Even if you are an acoustic act and won't be using *any* sound reinforcement, you will still want to know what the acoustic situation is where you will be performing. It's very disorienting and frustrating to walk into a venue expecting one thing and getting something altogether different.

First question—indoors or out? Sound works very differently in either situation. If you are acoustic and outdoors, you might want to situate yourself in front of a wall or some other surface that will reflect the sound to the front. Otherwise, the sound waves will float away all around you. As mentioned above, outdoor gigs are more diffused both in sound and in other forms of energy. Even playing in a tent is acoustically better than playing in the great wide open. Otherwise, unless you are playing brass, percussion, or some other louder instrument, you may as well resign yourself to being "background" music because you won't be heard all that well. If you are indoors and acoustic, again try and surround your area with something that will reflect sound. Of course, the more members in the group and the louder the music you play, the less trouble you will have holding your audience's attention. Bluegrass bands have *no* trouble filling a big barn with no amplification.

If your act needs electricity outdoors—namely, for amps for instruments or a PA system—you, of course, need to ask the venue to supply it beforehand. One exception to this is if you are busking (performing on the streets for passing tips). In these cases you will be supplying your own system. I have seen small, battery-operated amps work admirably—expect to spend a small fortune in batteries, then. If there is electricity supplied for an outdoor concert, make sure it's adequate for the job. I hate using generators because they are notoriously noisy, and may not put out proper amperage or wattage. Use a surge protector just in case.

If you need a sound system but don't supply your own, make absolutely sure that the venue has what you need, down to the mic stands! Don't take anything for granted. I've heard many, many horror stories of acts getting to the concert site after being assured there was a sound system. Yes, there were amps, speakers, and mics, *but someone forgot to mention there were no mic stands!* (There have been some very creative last-minute jerry-rigging of broomsticks and so forth.) Some artists actually can demand specific types of mics, amps, speakers, and other equipment. Once you get to a certain level, you, too, can have this kind of clout. They know they sound the best through these particular kinds of equipment, and they want their sound to be optimum. There are other singers who, if they don't travel with a full PA system, do bring their own mics. Many singers don't like to use a stranger's mic for hygienic reasons, or they want to be assured that they will get the sound they want with a familiar mic.

Sound Check at the Venue

If there is more than one act on the bill, sound check becomes more complicated, and you will probably also need to arrive earlier than usual. We like to send one of our group out into the audience during sound check (which is a very good reason to be wireless), unless there is a sound technician or someone else that you trust doing the checking for you. We know best how we sound, so who better to judge?

Get the house sound (EQ and volume of each instrument, then the balance between instruments) down as you like it. Test the full range of your set—be sure you sound check when playing your softest number and your loudest one. If you have multiple instruments, each one needs to be balanced with all others playing with it in each piece. If you have the "luxury" (I consider it a necessity) of each musician's having his or her own monitor, after the house mix is set, you will want to do monitor mixes for each person. Usually, each member of the group will want a separate mix, highlighting her own instrument over the others. If you don't have separate monitors, don't have the capability to have separate mixes, or have no monitors at all, you will have to make do with relying on the house speakers. This is really a bad idea, but often all you get.

If you are on a bill with one or more other acts, the best order for sound check has the *opening act* performers sound checking *last*. This just makes sense, so that after the last sound check, all the settings can be left in place, then changed back for subsequent acts. It goes without saying that the sound tech should take meticulous notes about the settings for each act after their sound check, since everything will be changed throughout the night and you want to get as close to the settings made during sound check as possible. A good sound tech knows this, and yet is constantly tweaking settings during your set to make you sound as glorious as you can.

LIGHTING

Lights are yet another aspect of stage work. Again, if you are at the level where you are hiring and touring with your own light crew, you are not reading this book! If you are starting out, do not underestimate the value of lights onstage. Depending on the venue, you may not have any choice—what's there is there, and can't be twiddled with. But in concert halls, good clubs, and other venues they know that lighting creates a mood that can enhance the music. If you are fortunate enough to play in these kinds of halls, talk with the light techs and give them a copy of your set with detailed notes on how you want the lighting on such-and-such a song. Without a whole lot of rehearsal, good luck on getting half of what you want—but at least there was thought and discussion.

WHAT TO REQUEST

At the *very least*, ask for *some* stage lighting, even in a small bar situation. It's horrible not being seen, and worse when you yourself are not able to see! Low lights in the place might be romantic, but it's hard on the musicians—just in case, you might want to carry your own music stand with lights attached, or other fixtures. And you may wish to voice your feelings about spotlights aimed at musicians from a darkened house; such lighting creates a certain separation, which you may or may not like. I find it distracting to have bright spots blinding me, keeping me from seeing faces in the audience. Rather, I prefer to see my audiences in low light. I want to see their reactions, and my performance feeds off their responses.

Some venues have very sophisticated lighting with several techs to staff them. Follow-spots, fancy colored or cutout gels, and moving lights can all add to (or distract from) your music. Make sure you know the lighting situation well in advance so you can either coordinate lights to fit with certain songs, request a simpler setup, or specify whatever you feel enhances your music the best. It certainly is a good idea to listen to what the lighting techs or designers have to say—they are, of course, the professionals here, and they just might help transform an ordinary concert into something truly magical.

Some acts like to travel with their own simple setup, having been "burned" too often in places with very poor lighting. Be sure the venue can handle the extra juice draw, because powerful lights suck up a lot of electricity, and you don't want to be blowing any circuits in the middle of your set. If you are going to bring your own and you don't have a lighting designer or an electrical engineering degree, consult with someone who does or who is equally knowledgeable. Some big music store chains have lighting departments, specializing in stage lights, with helpful sales clerks. Pick their brains about setup, maintenance, and so forth. Again, unless you really know what you are doing, maybe leave the repair jobs to someone qualified. Venues usually frown on artists setting fires in their buildings …

So there you have some of what to look out for and to address, besides simply making great music. The whole atmosphere that your music creates—whether it's one of peace, excitement, spirituality, or rebellion—will be affected by whether or not you pay attention to the details of the *technical* end of a show. That's part of the beauty of live performance.

Chapter 11
Product Sales

Because you are a working musician out there sharing your art with the world, sooner or later, someone will ask you, "Do you have a recording I can buy?" This is the greatest compliment and a wonderful morale booster. You will want to say, "Of course! How many of which one?" Selling your CDs can be a very nice supplement to your income, and many artists go beyond selling CDs and add other products. But let's start with the most obvious and what will probably be your biggest seller.

Recordings
We will not get into the technical aspects of making a recording, but rather the marketing and sales, both at the gig and elsewhere. There are many other books that will lead you through the technical details of actually recording (see Recommended Reading in appendix B).

Recordings are the most logical and most wanted commodity a musician can sell. People who have seen you play live and who love your music will naturally want to take a reminder home with them. It's such a nice thing to realize that you are in people's lives, hearts, and CD collections because they appreciate and admire your art. You want them to have a little permanent piece of you, just as you gave ephemerally when performing live for them.

Nowadays, it's so easy for anyone to make his own CDs. Recording equipment is easy to learn, relatively inexpensive to buy, and the quality of the end product is usually quite high. There are now digital recorders and burners so that you can make your own CDs right in your own home. Add to this nice graphic arts software and a color printer for the inserts, and you are in business. You can either invest in your own recording system, cajole a friend who owns one, or hire a professional recording studio to make your recording. In any case, you want to make a recording that is the very best quality and is the most representative of your music as possible. Heck, with the magic of a recording studio, you can really go to town and sound *better* than you do live! If you are going to be selling it, it had better be good, or you will disappoint or possibly anger and alienate your fans. There is no excuse for putting out something of poor or marginal quality these days.

When designing the cover, remember to put in all important information: your name, title of album, record company name and album number, track titles and numbers, and song lengths in minutes and seconds (helpful for radio airplay). If you want retail stores to carry your CD (and if you want *Billboard* to chart your sales), you need to add a UPC bar code symbol. This entails sending away for a code number by supplying pertinent information (see appendix B). You also want to make sure relevant info is on the spine of the CD. Some like to add the sticker with the artist's name and CD title on the top, over the shrink wrap. Don't forget the copyright notice either (see chapter 19).

Some artists like to have their albums available in two formats: CDs and cassettes. I have found that CDs outsell cassettes by about two to one; other artists have other ratios. People like to have the choice. I think it's a smart marketing move to have each title in at least two formats. Believe it or not, my first two recordings came out in vinyl! And some people *still* buy vinyl.

Whenever and wherever you gig, take along some of your albums. Even at gigs where you might not be able to sell to the audience (libraries and municipalities are notorious for this prohibition), you might get approached in the parking lot by a new fan. I also design and print up order forms to hand out to anyone who asks. You want to make it as easy as possible for someone to purchase your albums.

One caveat at the gig: Try not to be obnoxious about pitching your wares. No one likes commercials or feeling like he is being solicited. The best approach I have seen is a gentle and humorous sentence or two just before intermission or at the end of your show. Likewise, your product table or display should be attractive, tasteful, and low-key so that the audience doesn't feel like they are watching the Home Shopping Channel. As for the display, I like to put out a few of each album. If you put out too many, it's hard to keep track of them, and they might "walk away." On the other hand, if you put out too few, there won't be enough for lots of people to look over.

Folks like to handle the merchandise, read the cover, see what songs might be on the album and choose between two or more. I have cardboard display stands that can hold seven CDs and eight cassette tapes together. This way, I can show that I have both formats, with fifteen copies of each album out for handling, all displayed upright, neatly, and compactly. I prefer this to laying them down on the table, where they cannot be seen as clearly. I have one display stand for each of my albums, plus a blown-up color copy of each cover, laminated and with an easel back for easy display. Some artists like to list the songs on each album prominently, making it easier for the buyers to find the songs they want.

It's also a very good idea to display the prices of each product on one very readable sign. It's easier that way for everyone to get the prices, rather than someone having to say over and over, "CDs are $15, cassettes $10." Some venues, like festivals, require you to put price stickers on all your product, or insist that all artists' products be uniformly priced so that it's easier for their vendors. If you take checks and want them made payable a specific way, you can put that on the sign as well. Likewise with credit cards. If you want to take cards, you have to apply to each company (Mastercard, Visa, Discover, etc.) or go through a "broker" (some banks can do this) and pay a fee. The company will then set you up with all the supplies you will need, give you a vendor number, and so forth. Taking credit cards is a good idea when people want to use mail order or get albums over the Internet, or even in person at gigs. The downside is that there is a monthly fee to pay, plus a small percentage of each sale. This complicates your record keeping a bit with more paperwork, but it may be worth it.

If you have help at the product table, make very certain that your helpers know the prices of everything. With a lot of different products, it can get very confusing to your sellers. If, as I suggest in chapter 14, you keep everything at round numbers—which includes any sales tax—no one has to deal with small change. Don't forget that you are *collecting*, not keeping, whatever sales tax is necessary, and don't forget to pay it when due! The law says you need a vendor's license for every state you sell in, and you must collect that municipality's sales tax (it might be just state, or it might have county and other local taxes added). You will need to keep track of all this.

On top of this, have handy a wallet or box with plenty of small bills for changing cash. Keep track of the amount you start with—it's handy if it's consistent every time. If you take checks, you might ask the buyer to write his phone number on it in case of a problem. In all my years, I've never been burned by a bad check, but you never know. Half a dozen pens for your fans to write checks, as well as a handy-dandy CD and cassette opener, are also useful and make things flow easier and faster. After big concerts, when there's a huge mob at the album table, I have helpers take the money, remove the shrink wrap, and get the CD and cassette inserts out and ready for me to autograph. I'm at the next table schmoozing and signing. It's very fast and efficient this way. You might also want to put out your mailing list cards for folks to sign.

I keep a product inventory form with my stuff so that I know how many of what sold (see appendix A for a sample Product Inventory Form). This is pretty important for bookkeeping and for inventory, so that you know what your bestseller is. My form has the performance venue and date at the top, followed by several columns. The first lists the names of each one of my products, with a blank space in front of each to fill in the quantity that I bring. The next column is what remains after the concert, the third is the number sold (column one minus column two), the fourth is the price per unit (to make the math easier), and the last column is the subtotal for each product (column three times column four). At the bottom is the grand total of all product sold and how much money I *should have* taken in. I say "should have" because sometimes change is made incorrectly, product gets lost or "walks away," or whatever. At the end of the night, when I count up the cash box and then subtract whatever sum I started with to make change, I *should* end up with that "should have" amount. What I end up with has never been *vastly* different from the "should have" sum. If it is, something's very wrong and you might want to investigate. Later, before the next gig, I use this inventory form to restock whatever I've sold.

Be sure to bring enough product so that you don't run out—it's disappointing to your fans, as well as to your pocketbook! In the rare instances where you do run out, offer them an order form so they can order it by mail later, or direct them to your Web site to order. Better still, promise to send them the product as soon as you get back to your home or office if they will pay you right then and there. Give them a receipt (I carry a receipt book in my product box) and your contact information. Most purchases at concerts are impulse buys, and it's better not to lose the sale. Make sure you take a legible name, address, and phone number from them, and ask if they want it autographed. In exchange for their trust, you pay for all packing and postage costs, which is maybe a dollar or two at the most. When you send the product, enclose a nice note plus another order form to make their next purchase easy, and you will make fans and maybe even friends.

Other Product

The possibilities are endless, only limited by your imagination and chutzpah. I know many artists sell posters, books, bumper stickers, T-shirts, mugs, key chains, you name it. Some have a veritable boutique set up at their concerts! If you wish to go that route, it's fairly easy to find manufacturers who will custom print anything on just about anything. Usually, if you order in large quantities, you can get lower wholesale prices. It might be wise to first start with a lower quantity just to see what sells—otherwise, you may get stuck with ten thousand neon lanyards! But once you determine your hot sellers, order a lot. Your profit will be higher (or you can lower your price for your audience), and you won't have to be constantly re-ordering. By the way, you can mark up your price to whatever you wish, but when pricing your wares (including recordings), keep in mind what the market will bear and stay in line—no gouging, please.

Also, some artists don't sell full-length albums (twelve to sixteen songs), but rather EPs (extended plays of four to six cuts) or demos (one or two songs), for whatever reasons. In these cases, price proportionately. It's also nice to have some free giveaways, like stickers or—believe or not, I've seen this—emery boards …

You might want your name, logo, album cover, song lyric, or face plastered everywhere. In this branding-conscious society of ours, it's a form of advertising. Or, on the other hand, you might want to raise your "hip" quotient by putting out something really cool and obscure just because it will raise eyebrows or curiosity. The more clever or beautiful the design, the more you will sell. Whatever your motive, it's amazing what people will buy just because they like you and your music. As I said before, product sales make for a nice supplement to your gigging fees. Some artists make more from the sale of product than they do from their performance fee!

I did find one interesting phenomenon while I was experimenting with what to sell. In my family show, I often use inflatable toy guitars as props for kid volunteers from the audience to pretend they are rock stars playing along with us onstage. After the show, I would sell them (the guitars, not the kids), along with the cool black sunglasses that completed the look. They sold like hotcakes! Unfortunately, I found that they cut into my album sales. Kids would beg their parents to buy them *something*, and the guitar-sunglasses set was cheaper than the albums. Now, the upside to this was that no one had to go home empty-handed if they wanted some kind of souvenir of the show but didn't have enough money for an album. The downside was that I would have preferred that they went home with my music! In any case, I would autograph the guitars and the albums as a memento of the show, and everyone was happy.

Since I am an author, I also sell my books at shows. Again, I look at all other product sales as a little more sauce to the gravy of the album sales. Of course, you can get carried away and add all kinds of stuff to your product table—just remember, you're a musician and *the music is what's important!*

Distribution

Back in the old days, an artist absolutely needed a distributor to help get the product out into the world, because selling product was impossible any other way other than selling at concerts. Distributors ordered a quantity from the record company (or from the artists themselves if they were their own record company) at wholesale cost, then distributed them to stores for retail sale to customers. They, of course, added their percentage, as did the stores. If you were an independent label, you could still sign with a smaller distributor to get your stuff into the stores. Nowadays, things have changed quite a bit with the advent of the Internet, and some smaller distributors have gone out of business. Paul Foley, General Manager of Rounder Records, informs me that there are still several national indie distributors as well as some good regional ones in existence as of this writing. He advises, "If an artist is going to tour outside their home market, they need distribution to ensure product in stores."

The larger distributors, of course, are still functioning—that is how Madonna's recordings get into Tower Records. But unless you have a record deal with a major label or a large independent, or are well-known, you will not have access to any distributors, large or small. They are simply not equipped for, nor interested in, distributing the smaller quantities that up-and-coming artists will be selling.

Of course, you can always go to your local mom-and-pop music stores and ask if they carry local artists. If they do, they might buy a small quantity outright. More often than not, though, they will take your recordings on consignment, meaning you leave them a few copies to sell. If they do sell, they pay you; if not, they return them to you after a predetermined length of time. Some small- and medium-sized chains also have consignment programs. Even Tower Records will do this for local artists. You might also try some related stores, like baby and toy stores if you do children's music, or stores that specialize in Irish products if you play Celtic music. Some gift and home design stores also sell instrumental New Age music. You just never know until you try. Think of where you like to shop, approach the owner or manager, and give it a try. Give them a free demo copy to play during store hours. Sometimes customers like the music they are hearing while shopping and ask for it.

Lucky for us DIYers, there is still another way to get our music into the hands of buyers all over the world.

The Internet

Now, artists can cut out the middlemen and still have access to listeners and fans worldwide. Check out the chapter on "Marketing and Promotion" for tips on setting up a Web site, where you can be your own retail store. The Net is also a great place for "broadcasting" your music. You can be your own little empire. Simply by making it easy for anyone to find you, you are making yourself and your music available internationally. You will want to link your site to as many other related sites as possible, so that someone browsing those sites can easily find you. Likewise, you want yours to be easy to find through search engines, so your keywords need to be thoughtfully planned. For example, I use "children's music," "folk music," "family music," "singer-songwriter," and so forth.

If you are interested in selling your product over the Net, you have to decide whether or not to take credit cards. This is the easiest way for folks to order your stuff, but it's more costly to you. So far, I have resisted the temptation because I don't like the administrative and bookkeeping hassles, and personally, as a consumer, I am leery of giving my credit card info over the Net unless I am *absolutely sure* the site is secure. With artists' sites, consumers might be hesitant for that same reason. So one alternative is to have a mail order form that can be printed out and mailed to you with a check or money order. Another is to use an online service that *does* take credit cards. The advantage of this is you can direct those fans to this service who want to use cards rather than a check. You don't make as much money, but it's a convenience you offer your fans. You don't want to lose a sale just because you don't take credit cards.

Here is a route you can go if you don't have a Web site, or in addition to it. As of this writing, some examples of online sales services are CDBaby, BN.com (Barnes & Noble), Buy.com, and Amazon.com. All these online services take a pretty hefty slice of the retail price, similar to a regular store's cut, because that is basically what they are. Right now, Amazon calls its system the "Advantage Program." You can contact whatever service you wish to go with, and its personnel will let you know what the criteria are to be accepted. Once they have agreed to carry your work, then you send a few copies of the accepted recordings to them (as of this writing, Amazon only takes CDs, no cassettes, but other services may take more formats), and then they warehouse them. When customers contact them about your product, they take care of the order, the billing, and the shipping. Periodically, they give you statements about your account—how many you sold of which product— and send you a check. When they start to run low on your inventory, they contact you, and you send them more. As of this writing, Amazon.com is trying a new system, called Amazon Marketplace, which handles the order forms and the billing but contacts the artist to do the mailing. Amazon Marketplace will take a much smaller commission of the retail price than it would if it had to ship, thereby passing more of the profit on to the artist. This theory works well for everyone: Amazon doesn't have to warehouse thousands of artists' CDs, and the artist gets to keep more of the money and doesn't have the hassle of taking credit cards himself.

Remember to use a business mailing address, especially when dealing over the Internet. There are some crazies out there, and you might not want them to know where you live. This is a good idea for all your promo, even if you are not on the Net.

Mail Order

As an independent artist, you will need to get your product to your fans beyond selling them directly at your concerts. You can increase the quantity sold pretty dramatically if you offer product through the mail. Whenever you do a mailing to your fans—to notify them of a specific gig or a tour, to update them on your career, or whatever—you can also add a catalog of your products along with a mail order form, making it easy for them to buy your stuff. Also, if you are performing at a venue that prohibits the sale of product, most will allow you to leave a stack of your order forms in some conspicuous place. I hand and send these forms out liberally. They cost next to nothing to print, and you might make lots of sales.

You will need to investigate the laws in your state regarding selling through the mail. Usually, you will not have to charge and collect sales tax if the buyer is outside of your state, but again, check your state's laws. Also investigate the requirements for notification of delivery times. Some states require you state on the order form how many days the consumer should expect for delivery.

On my order form, I like to use photos of each product. Remember, a picture is worth a thousand words. Your fans might not remember the name of your album when they saw you in concert, but maybe they saw it on your sales table and remember the cover. Or maybe they have one of your recordings already and want to buy a different one, but maybe don't remember the title but do remember what theirs looks like. In addition to the photos, of course, you should put the title of each album. I also add the names of the songs on each album, because the buyer might be trying to find a specific song that he heard over the radio or enjoyed at your concert. If you want, you can put a short description of each recording or any other comments or reviews you think might be helpful or pertinent. You should put the item numbers (all your recordings should have a particular number issued by the record company, distinguishing it from others on the same label), what formats each recording comes in (CD, cassette, vinyl, DVD), and the unit price. I like to give my fans a small price break off the usual retail price when they mail order, because they have the added expense of shipping.

On the part of the form they tear off and send to you should be the following information: quantity ordered, item number, description (title and format), unit price, and subtotal (quantity times unit price). If you want to offer to have it autographed, put a place where they can indicate they want this—usually a place for a checkmark. At the bottom of the subtotal column should be another subtotal of all the items. Under that, designate a space for any sales tax required. Shipping and handling charges come after that. You can charge whatever you want, but be reasonable. Figure out how much the packaging and postage cost you, and then add a little bit more for the labor of wrapping and shipping it off via the U.S. Post Office or some other carrier. Be aware that some shippers will not deliver to a post office box. If you choose to use one of these shippers, note that restriction on your mail order form. You want to figure out how much one item costs to ship, then two or more. Each additional ounce does not add that much more postage—I charge an additional $1 per item after the first one. Of course, if you are shipping in large quantities to the same address, say, ten or more (for example, sometimes I ship quantities to schools), $1 per item is too much and you can refigure the shipping costs. Packaging is pretty cheap, especially if you buy in quantity. I like the bubble envelopes because they are light, inexpensive, and easy to use. I use the kind that can hold up to two cassettes or CDs. Other artists might like small cardboard mailers, padded envelopes, or even boxes.

If you sell products other than recordings, you will need appropriate mailers. You will want a fairly large quantity of these if you expect to do a brisk business through the mail.

The last line item is the grand total of all the sums above. Make sure you put an easy-to-use space where customers can print their name, address with zip code, and phone number. This last bit of information is so you can call them if there is a problem or if you have questions—maybe you are unsure of a digit of their address, or something else is illegible. If you want the check or money order made payable a certain way, put that on the form, along with your mailing address, phone number, and any other contact information you want them to have. Be sure to specify delivery times if required by law, and be sure to fulfill the orders promptly within those times.

I also like to make it easy for fans to order my albums as gifts. I give them the option of sending me their recipients' addresses so that I can mail directly to them. I also offer a gift note with a personalized greeting from them if they wish.

I keep all these fulfilled orders in a file. I have never had a problem with damage or loss (knock on wood). These order forms are also useful if you want to add the names and addresses to your fan mailing list. I don't think people object to this—in fact, many expect that when they order something through the mail, they will automatically be added to a list. It's a great way to build up your fan list, because you know they at least like your music enough to buy it. They've proven they are fans, and probably will appreciate getting notices about upcoming gigs in their area or new recordings.

Happy selling—it's wonderful to earn extra *passive* income!

Chapter 12
Touring

If you are a live performance musician, chances are, sooner or later, you may be called upon to tour. If you want a regional, national, or international career, then you *must* tour, or else become so famous you don't need to because people will know you through your recorded work. But even celebrity artists probably started off touring, or toured *sometime* during their careers. Touring just seems to come with the occupation. Of course, there are some musicians who have very successful and happy careers and never have to leave their home area. They might be studio musicians or teachers, or live in an area with enough of their types of venues to support them. More power to them—they can have a semblance of a "normal" life! But if you choose the life of a gigging musician, you may have to start packing your bags.

To Tour or Not to Tour

There are many considerations when the need or desire to tour arises. If you're in a band or group, can everyone free himself from other obligations? Will you need subs, or will you go out as a condensed version of your group. What will being away from home do to families, friendships, and day jobs? What will being together so much do to the group dynamic? Does everyone get along well enough to spend hour after hour, day after day, with each other? How will the finances work? Does your career depend on touring?

There are, of course, compelling reasons *not* to tour. People who have never done it may look at it as romantic, exciting, and glamorous. But although it may be all that in part, in reality, most of it is hard, boring, exhausting, and usually not very profitable, if at all. If you have a family—a partner or children, I'm talking here—extended touring is extremely hard on everyone, especially kids. There's a true story behind Harry Chapin's song "Cats in the Cradle." You may be familiar with that song; the lyrics were written by his wife Sandy to wake Harry up to the damage that being away from his family inflicted. Country superstar Garth Brooks concurs:

> *It was a tough decision (to stop touring), but my children are my top priority now. I started in the music business without children, but when I brought them into the world, I committed myself. I can't tour anymore and be a father.*[1]

One obvious obstacle is finding childcare, which becomes a real issue for touring musicians who have kids and no partner, or for musicians whose partner works full time. But the biggest reason against touring if you have kids is the toll exacted by extended separation. Even if you only have a significant other and no kids, it can be the kiss of death to a relationship. Life on the road has its temptations, and absence sometimes makes hearts grow apart. The partner left behind goes on with her life at home, often making new friends and experiencing new things that the touring artist is not a part of. The same is true for the one who is traveling. Jealousies and alienation are not uncommon. If tours are extensive, people grow apart. There's that human toll to consider.

When my daughter arrived, I made a conscious decision not do any more extensive touring while she was young. Moving into children's music after performing exclusively for adults was perfect for me for a number of reasons. Of course, I love children, and I soon began writing a lot for kids because I was so enamored of my baby and wanted good music for her and others. I also discovered that there was a vast treasure trove of venues within one or two driving hours of where I live. I could make a wonderful living and *never* have to tour! Even now that my daughter is a teenager, when I tour, I set it up so that I'm only gone *at the most* a week at a time, maybe five times per year.

Another reason not to tour is the dollar cost of touring. It's pretty astronomical, even if you plan to drive yourself in your own car, sleep in strangers' living rooms, and eat very cheaply. Still, I know solo singer-songwriters who are *constantly* on the road, depending on the kindness of their hosts and doing just fine. They might have to battle loneliness—and have humongous cell phone bills. They don't come home with a lot of money, but they do sell albums and make *some* kind of profit—or else they have a working spouse who carries most of the bills!

[1]Dotson Rader, "Why He's Coming Home," *Parade*, 16 December 2001, p. 6.

One cost that is not often considered is what constant travel and work can do to your health. Pop singer Janet Jackson says, "Touring is very grueling. It's very taxing on the body … living out of your suitcase, going from city to city, night after night. It's a tough job."[2] And this is from someone who travels first class and stays in deluxe accommodations! Unless you are very vigilant, your sleep, diet, and exercise regiment may suffer while you're on the road. And what if you get sick while on the road? Is your insurance, if you even have any, adequate?

The reasons *for* touring are equally compelling: You are supporting a newly released album; you want to extend your fan base beyond your home area; it is a good part of your income, or you have wanderlust and enjoy life on the road. It can be fun to go to new places and to meet all sorts of new people, turning them on to your music and making new fans far and wide. Spending lots of time alone or with your band, without the distractions of home, can also be a creative time, allowing you to concentrate on just writing or playing. Usually, bands come home really tight with each other, both musically and personally.

Booking a Tour

Give yourself *at least* three to six months to plan a mini tour; six to twelve months is even better. The longer you plan to be out, the more advance time you'll need. Also, the longer you have to plan, the more advantages you'll have in terms of making good choices. Venues have to be contacted, promo sent, terms negotiated, dates settled. If you plan far enough in advance, changes won't be so costly to make, and venues can be more flexible. You won't be pushed to the wall when it comes to finding lodging and other resources. When you're planning the itinerary, it goes without saying that it makes the most amount of sense, in terms of gas and time, to plan it *geographically*. Granted, sometimes it doesn't work out so smoothly and you might find yourself crisscrossing north and south, east and west, but sometimes it has to be done.

It is very expensive to mount and sustain a tour, so you have to consider everything very carefully *before* you go out. Start with a budget of estimated costs—hotel, food, gas, tolls, any car or equipment rental, unexpected expenses such as repairs, percentages to agents and managers, payments to support personnel, and so forth. Estimate how much you will make in performance fees

[2]Janet Jackson, "Quotable," *Newsday*, 10 February 2002, D3.

and product sales. You just may be dismayed at the bottom line. Again, it's a rare tour that actually *makes* money, so be aware from the start that the dollar sign might not be the best reason to tour.

When planning a tour, I usually start with my sponsor mailing list. This is one of your most valuable resources for your career. I do a big annual mailing to all presenters and venues on my mailing list, just to keep my face and name in front of them. I send my general brochure, then add maybe a short cover letter and some further promo I want them to have, such as current reviews.

When I know the time of year I will be in their area, I will contact them again, as far in advance as possible. If you try to book too close to the time of the tour, chances are their calendars will be full already or you won't be able to get your first-choice dates. On the other hand, if you try to book too far in advance, *they* may not be ready. Each venue will be different, and you might want to keep notes about how far in advance they book.

So, I'll call each venue, asking for the person who books. If I've been there before, I'll have made a note of the person's name, but, of course, there is always turnover. In this business, it can be quite rapid! Here is where your phone skills come into play. If it's a cold call, they've never heard of you and you want to convince them that you'd be great in their place. Tell them the dates of when you expect to be in their area. Mention how rarely—or how often!—you get to their area, so this would be a good opportunity for them to treat their audiences. Mention your successes in similar venues elsewhere that they may have heard of. Offer to send them your promo—do all the schmoozing I mentioned in chapter 2, except now you are calling long distance. Along with the demo, press kit, and so forth, I will send another cover letter stating the dates I expect to be in their area, so they'll have it in black and white in front of them. Most people will not remember what you told them on the phone. Don't forget to keep detailed notes of all conversations. This is extremely helpful when you make your follow-up calls. And do make them, about two weeks after you've sent your promo. See if they've had a chance to review your material, and if they haven't, urge them to soon, as you are building a tour, your time there is very limited, and you wouldn't want them to miss out on your wonderful concert. If they have reviewed it and they are interested, proceed as you would any other gig call, and if they are not interested, thank them politely and ask them to keep your material on file for the future when you are back in their area again.

If you have played in their area, mention the venues and the glowing response and reviews (only if they were truly positive, of course; if they were negative, you may not want to show your face in that town again!). Here is where your performance logs and meticulous record-keeping in your database come in handy. You will already be forearmed with all this information when you are making these calls. Tell them how you wowed the crowd, how you sold tons of product, and how people were clamoring to have you come back. Won't they be the lucky sponsor to reap the benefits of your swelling fan base? When booking an area, be sure that you are not overlapping territory too much. You don't want to be stepping on anyone's toes. Some venues want a radius restriction, meaning you won't be able to play anywhere else within *x* miles from them for *y* months after their booking. You can understand this— you don't want to play the club's competitors so soon after you've played them.

Get excellent directions for each booking. Ask them to send you *written* ones along with a local map if they can. Some bookers may refuse, and then you are on your own. It's a good idea in these cases to map out *to the street* where you are going well before you leave. You may be treading in unfamiliar territory, and you don't want to get lost or be late. I also ask the sponsor to write the directions out themselves rather than using online ones like MapQuest.

Scheduling

Let's say now you have nailed down a few gigs in the area. How much you want to work is up to you, of course, but consider this: Book concerts too closely together (i.e., every day), and you will get pretty worn out pretty quickly from the work itself, not to mention from the travel; book them too far apart and you won't make very much money with all the down time. Remember, every day that you don't work, you don't make money but are still having to pay lodging, food, and gas. Pacing yourself is an art when booking a tour. Make sure to leave rest days spaced sensibly about, as well as enough time to get from one booking to the next without having to speed, break your neck, or be too stressed out before a gig. I like to have a central base where I can stay put for a few days at a time, that is close to all the gigs in the area. This might not work for everyone, especially those doing one-night stands in a different city each night. But if it is possible, the advantages to this method are that you don't have to keep packing all your stuff up every day, your lodging feels more like "home," sometimes you can get discounts on lodging with multiple nights, and it's just less stressful overall. It can be really disorienting being in a different location day after day. You may have heard of groups starting their show off with "Hellloooooo, Pittsburgh!" when they're really in Detroit ...

How long you want to tour is up to you too, but again, consider your (and your bandmates') stamina, situations, and homesickness quotient. As I mentioned, I don't like to be gone longer than a week, but I have a daughter still at home. Perhaps when she grows up and moves out, I'll be willing to tour for longer. I love to travel, but I also love being home. I find it a hassle to find house sitters for plants and pets, and I don't like the mounds of mail and other business I have to deal with, even with an assistant, when I get home after being gone for long.

Transportation

Transportation is a major factor in touring. How will you get from gig to gig? Will it be a road trip in a van or a bus, or are you flying? If using a road vehicle, whose will it be—your personal one, your band's, or a rental? If flying, how will you get from airport to gig to lodging and back to airport?

HOW MANY SETS OF WHEELS?

In our group's case, if it's not too far and we aren't going to be gone too long, we will take *two* vans for the three of us. If we took only one, we would be pretty much tied together all the time, and we'd be very crowded with all our equipment and personal stuff. With two vehicles going, our expenses are higher but we have more flexibility, and we can haul more stuff. Of course, if you have a big van, a bus, or semi, this won't be a problem. Oftentimes, our tours are tied in to showcases in the area where we are gigging, so we bring not only our instruments, PA system, equipment cases, props, personal suitcases, and boxes of product, but also loads of showcase material, including my display and a hand truck. We've got packing and loading down to a science, and we rely on checklists a lot. Our drummer brings his own van and carries all his own stuff, so he's free to take off on his own when we're not performing. That independence means a lot to all of us.

WINGS

Of course, when we fly, we pare down our equipment needs drastically. The venue might supply the PA system and drum kit, then we just bring our instruments, our wireless system, product, and our personal suitcases. The venue also may supply ground transportation. Still, we have seen acts that board commercial airlines with a *huge* amount of stuff. It all goes into baggage, and they have to pay extra, then rent a vehicle at the airport. Naturally, all this extra expense jacks up their fees quite a bit.

Here's a tip I can share that won't work for everyone. We tour the San Francisco Bay area regularly, plus have family and friends who live there. Because we fly there so often (once or twice every year), we decided to buy duplicate equipment and just stash it there at some willing person's home, rather than schlep our stuff or rent each time, which we did for years. This second PA system and used amps are not as high-quality as the stuff we use every day, but they certainly work fine for what we need. We brought some of our lesser-quality instruments and extra mic stands to leave there permanently. The cost of buying used stuff was, in the long run, cheaper than renting a PA and instruments every time—not to mention the peace of mind of not having our more valuable instruments traveling in the cargo of the plane. Now, every time we gig there, we don't have to bring anything more than mics, cables, and our wireless system, which fits into one small suitcase. Quite a difference, and much easier to travel with every time. Of course, this presupposes that you have similar circumstances—a long-term, free, and safe place to store your stuff, and some duplicate equipment and instruments.

Flying with instruments is always a joy (sarcasm dripping from every syllable). I have several instruments of varying value and so far haven't flown with my very best ones, but other musicians do. If they are really valuable, it's wise to buy them their own seats if they are too large to carry on and store in the overheads. It used to be standard for musicians to carry them on and the airlines would put them *somewhere* in the cabin; nowadays, it's darn near impossible to bring them on board unless it's a flute or something just as small. Of course, drums, keyboards, amps, and the like must be put into baggage. Then, it's imperative to have really travel-worthy, waterproof, heavy-duty cases. These are enormously expensive, but if you will be flying a lot, they are worth every penny. By the way, I don't like to use instrument cases that have the brand of the expensive instrument emblazoned on it. It's just advertising, "Steal me!"

If you check your equipment and instruments, it doesn't mean they will ultimately end up in the same place as you if you are changing planes or have any sort of layover. For this reason, *try and book nonstop flights whenever you can.* Once, we had a nightmare flight from New York to Winnipeg, Canada. Because of bad weather, we were delayed on takeoff, which put us into our layover city late, and we consequently missed our connecting flight. Our bags and instruments went on to Canada, but the airline put us up in a hotel in the States overnight, with nothing but the clothes on our backs. It all had a happy ending, as we were finally reunited with our stuff and went on to have a wonderful time. Another time, we were flying to a show in Texas and we got there fine, but our instruments did not. At least, they weren't on the same flight with us. After a few tense hours, we finally did retrieve them in another terminal, but it was harrowing. All this to say that flying is iffy enough without trying to get all your stuff there in one piece too.

Be sure to *clearly* mark all your bags and instruments with some distinguishing tags, lock everything, and make doubly sure cases don't pop open—we wrap duct tape around them just to be safe. Locks and even hinges have been known to break with the rough handling, and it's heartbreaking to lose your precious instrument—not to mention inconvenient to have to rent something!

When budget is a factor (and when isn't it?), check the schedule for an off-peak flight—it may be cheaper and less crowded. Very early morning flights are good ones. Even a red-eye might be the best option if you can afford the time to arrive the next morning. If you can sleep on planes, you hopefully will arrive refreshed and have the day to relax and get ready for the gig.

It goes without saying that you want to find a flight that will get you there in plenty of time to get your stuff, settle in, rest and wash up, and maybe eat and chill out a bit before the gig. It's too much to ask to dash in from some airport, set up, and then do a spectacular concert with frayed nerves. Don't forget the effects of jetlag, too. Ask if your airline offers e-tickets (electronic tickets). The convenience of not having to carry or worry about losing them means a lot. Just make sure everyone carries photo IDs. If anyone in your party requires a special diet, be sure to order it in advance. Major airlines are becoming very accommodating to almost every taste and dietary requirement.

Lodging

Lodging needs for all those traveling must be worked out in advance. It's just too risky to blow into a town and expect to find enough available rooms that are a convenient distance from the gig and safe, clean and reasonably priced. You may or may not even require commercial lodging. If you are lucky enough to know people in the places where you will be gigging, there's nothing like staying in a home with personal hospitality, amenities, and home cooking. The benefits are that the expense is much less, the accommodations may be more homey and comfortable, and you (hopefully) like your hosts. If you have time to kill, your hosts may also act as tour guides to tell you about or show you around their town. If you are a solo act traveling the country, you may welcome the company. If the hosts are unfamiliar to you, you might make new friends.

But there are also disadvantages to staying in people's homes. Maybe you will have to sleep on their floor or sofa or in some other uncomfortable arrangement. Privacy might be an issue, and you may find yourself looking for means of escape from your friendly hosts. However, you *should* socialize at least a bit with your hosts, even if you don't feel like it. You may be incompatible, not like their food, or be allergic to their pets or their smoking. But if you do choose to accept a person's hospitality, try to always be gracious and a good guest. No matter how the gig went, what hassles you went through to get there, or what your mood is, your hosts are doing you a big favor by welcoming you into their home. Find out their preferences on your smoking, shower schedules, and noisy and quiet times. Play with their kids and dog. It's a nice touch to send a thank-you afterward and maybe give them an album to remember you by.

Only you can determine what situation is best for you. However, it's not likely you'll be staying in private homes when on tour. And some people might prefer to stay in a hotel or motel. Use the Internet or a travel agent if you need help in locating and booking something. The bigger chains have toll-free numbers that hook you up with a central booking office that can possibly help you reserve rooms all along your tour. Other advantages to chains are: You can be pretty sure they are consistent in the quality of their facilities and service (so you know what to expect), they have many sites in all the major cities and in many smaller towns, and their rates are somewhat standardized to help with your budgeting.

Remember your budget—the more money you spend on the road, the less goes into your pocket at the end. Having considered this, you still may feel it's worth it to be comfortable and have luxury digs in order to feel spoiled while on the road. If you are on an extended tour, you might just like to have a Jacuzzi and cable TV with a hundred channels, just like at home, or a pool or gym to keep up the exercise routine. If you are going to be doing business while on the road, you might need a port for your computer modem, access to a fax machine, or whatever else for your traveling office. My husband just needs a coffeemaker in the room. Remember, they'll get you at the minibar and refrigerator stocked with snacks! It's cheaper to hit a store and stash food in your room.

Some bands like to have adjacent rooms or even suites. Some prefer the solitude and quiet of a room far away from their group. Whatever the situation, remember that you are sharing the lodging with other guests. There is nothing more obnoxious than a bunch of rowdy musicians carrying on loudly at all hours of the night in a hotel. This behavior is what gives musicians a bad name!

Again, be very wary about your instruments and equipment at hotels and motels. Some places are notorious targets for thieves. We *always unload completely* and never leave anything of value in our vehicles in these parking lots. Many places have safes for smaller valuables. Keep doors locked at all times, even if you are just going from room to room.

Meals

This is a controllable expense, almost more so than any other factor in touring. You can choose to eat elaborate, expensive meals three or more times a day in fancy restaurants; pick cheaper, simpler places; do takeout or delivery or fast food; or even bring your own comestibles, especially if you have certain dietary restrictions. It may be hard to maintain a macrobiotic diet, for instance. Some musicians bring a coffeepot, hot plate, even a microwave on the road with them to save money or for the convenience. Some acts have riders in their contracts that require the venues to supply or pay for meals. In any case, food is another factor to consider when planning your budget. But the most important part of all this, to my mind at least, is that you are eating nutritiously and sensibly while on the road. When you are away from home, it's easier to fall into bad eating habits. You might not be able to get the fresh produce you could before, or you may be stressed, in a hurry, or unable to find a decent restaurant. If you are not touring for an extended time, it probably won't matter if you skip a few meals or eat poorly for awhile. But if you *are* on a long tour, you want to watch your health. Getting adequate sleep, healthy food, and enough exercise should be a priority because touring is so stressful. Plus, if you get sick while on the road, it's a real pain to find a doctor, not to mention the strain of losing income. Check out chapter 17 for more on this.

Touring Abroad

If you are going to be touring abroad, you may need to get visas. Each musician certainly will also need a passport. Getting one requires a long lead time between filling out and filing the application and actually receiving it.

Well in advance, check on what papers you will need—some countries require specific working papers. If you belong to the union, it can facilitate visas; otherwise, you can ask travel agents or go online for information. Also, you may need inoculations in some developing countries. Be sure to check out health concerns.

One caveat when abroad, whether working or as a tourist: Foreign customs vary wildly. Some gestures, manner of dress, and behavior that seem innocent to us may be offensive or mean something totally different abroad. It's a good idea to familiarize yourself with the customs of the countries where you will be traveling. Needless to say, you are a guest in their country and somewhat of an ambassador of ours. I try and learn at least "please" and "thank you" in their language. And common sense dictates not bringing or carrying illegal substances. Foreign jails and legal hassles can be *really* bad.

When touring abroad, it is even more important than when touring in your own country that you work with contracts. This will hopefully insure that payment will be forthcoming and that amenities like lodging, travel, sound systems or anything else the booker is supposed to provide indeed will be. If you think it's a hassle trying to chase down fees or get a PA when you're home, just imagine the nightmare when you're thousands of miles away in another land.

Chapter 13

The Importance of Radio and TV

If you are a recording artist—becoming one is advisable if you have the opportunity—you will want radio airplay. There is nothing that compares to the exposure radio can give an artist—all the touring in the world will still only reach the numbers you can accommodate in a concert setting. Radio and TV expose you to thousands of ears that otherwise might never have the opportunity to experience your music live. Also, nothing will boost an artist up the ladder of success more quickly than lots of airplay. On the other hand, many, many artists go through their entire careers without ever getting airplay, or even making a recording.

Radio

You may have had the experience of turning on the radio, hearing a new act for the first time, and getting floored by its music. It makes you want to buy the CD, go to the concerts, find out more about the act. If most of the act's music hits you this way, then you become a fan, hopefully for the life of the act. This is what many musicians dream about and strive for. How else can a new act break into the consciousness of the public beyond its touring?

How do you go about getting stations to play your CD? That's a tough tackle, one that stymies many artists. *You* know your CD is stupendous—well-recorded, with terrific material that people love. The dozens, hundreds, or thousands of fans who have bought your recording also know this. Why can't the program directors at your favorite radio stations and those like it see this?

Let's start at the beginning. You need to research which programs on which stations play your kind of music. There's no point in pitching your country record to a Top 40 station. There are publications, Web sites, and trade organizations that have lists of these. John Platt, DJ at WFUV in New York, recommends *Billboard, Radio and Records*, and the *Broadcasting and Cable Magazine Yearbook*, available in bookstores and libraries. He likens the radio world to an inverted pyramid, with the largest portion at the top being the commercial stations. These tend to be owned by conglomerates and often have an aversion to risk, meaning they usually don't play unknown artists. Under these are the public radio stations, unfortunately very few of which are formatted for music. But the ones that are *do* tend to be in the major markets and are more open to exposing new artists. They don't need to rely on the hits because they do not have the same profit imperatives. Finally, at the small bottom end are the individual programs that stations run, often on the weekends. The hosts have more freedom to play what they want. John suggests checking out those programs' playlists (posted on the station's Web site) to see if you fit, then e-mailing the host. Be patient and persistent, but not pesky—there's a fine line, John warns.

Once you have determined which programs and stations to target, you *could* do the "shotgun" approach—you know, spend hundreds of dollars sending out CD after CD, addressed to this DJ or program director, cold. But truthfully, that's like throwing money into the gutter. Stations get dozens of recordings a day, hundreds in a week. How are they going to distinguish yours from all the others? *Why* should they pick yours out? No one has time to wade through all of them, hoping to find the one that jumps out with that "hit song" or that breaks a new exciting artist or group. It is *extremely* unlikely that *anyone* unknown would get airplay this way, or even get listened to by the station. Don't waste your money with this approach.

Likewise, don't even think of bribing someone at a station to play your music. It's hugely illegal (known as "payola"), not that it doesn't still go on.

There are services that you can hire to promote your recordings to program directors. These companies have established a relationship with stations. Program directors and DJs know that if one of these companies introduces someone new, it's worth giving it a listen. Of course, this means that the company has to like your recording or otherwise think it worthy of promotion. Just offering these companies money won't necessarily entice them to risk their reputation with the stations. There may be some unscrupulous businesses that may offer to do this regardless of the quality of the work, but you know where that will get you. For the big commercial stations (and even the public radio ones), John suggests e-mailing the music director (who is usually easier to reach than the program director) and asking if there are any independent promotion people that they trust. Then contact that promoter to see if he will take you on.

Managers and attorneys who are well placed in the music business have some clout and can sometimes get airplay for their artists. This might be the best way to approach it. Otherwise, it's a rare artist who gets heard by someone in radio and then gets support. One station won't be enough, or it will be a very slow climb to get nationwide exposure. Again, an industry "buzz" can work wonders, so take advantage of this if you've been able to create one for yourself. For instance, one thing you can do is, when you are gigging in a new town, contact the local radio stations and offer a live, on-air interview and request they play your newest CD, which you have thoughtfully sent them in advance. Smaller stations and college stations are more likely to give you a shot, and they are good places to start. If you have built a following, have your fans call and write their local stations requesting to hear your CD. The more this happens, the better your chances of airplay are.

Another tack, albeit a rather unorthodox one, is to actually hand a DJ or program director your CD at a place outside of her work, like at a concert, a party, or even her home. An article in *Newsday* written by Jon Lane about original rock bands on Long Island cites how Keith "Fingers" Steele, the afternoon-drive DJ for WBAB/102.3 FM, came upon local group Majesty. "I don't know how they found out where I lived, but these kids handed me a tape. I played it, absolutely loved it, and showcased them on my show." Not long after that airing, the band changed its name to Dream Theater, now the well-known progressive rock band. Likewise, my folk duo long ago got a break on a well-known radio station because our drummer at the time also had the temerity to go to the DJ's house, ring his doorbell, and ask him to listen to our record. Just be careful that you are not "stalking" these people! That is *definitely* a no-no. Be polite, not pushy, and respect their privacy.

Nowadays, there is radio on the Internet, and lots of niche "stations." It takes quite a bit of investigation to get your music on air this way, and I haven't done it, but I bet some of you already have. It's a great way to circumvent the traditional commercial stations and get worldwide exposure.

Television

Getting on TV is even harder, but there are such things as public access channels that are easier to get booked on. Of course, their viewing audience usually is quite small, but it's a very good way to learn your way around the peculiarities of TV appearances. You can gain valuable experience and make your mistakes there before David Letterman comes calling. Performing in a studio in front of just one to three cameras and one host is so incredibly different than performing before a live audience. If there is a director and she wants you to "play to the camera" and there are several cameras, you have to keep watching for the one with the red light and play to it without getting distracted and missing a beat. There's no audience reaction, no applause at the end. If you have any control or say over the matter, see if you can bring in your own small audience so that you can play to them instead of the cold camera lens. It will feel and look more like a real concert to you, and perhaps you will feel more comfortable. Many talk shows already have a studio audience—that's a big plus.

Years ago, there used to be variety shows on TV that musical acts could break into. You didn't have to be a big star yet to get booked, but you did need to have some public interest or else be so different that *something* made you stand out. Nowadays, most TV shows don't risk their precious airtime on unknowns, because ratings matter more than anything. If you have your heart set on a big TV show, you might try to pitch what makes you unusual or really different, if you don't have a name or reputation. There have been shows geared expressly toward showcasing unknowns and give them a shot, like *Star Search*, *Pop Stars*, and *American Idol*, but they are extremely competitive and really are looking for a certain kind of talent to fit their molds. Again, try your local station and pitch yourself as a human interest story—maybe you are playing at a worthy benefit?

If you are a songwriter or composer, you may write music for TV or movies. This, too, can be a very lucrative business when you take into account syndication and videos. Then you get into licensing deals. (Please see chapter 19 for more information.)

Lastly, if you have a music video, you can try and get it onto a channel like MTV or VH1, but good luck with that. You already need to be a "player" in order to get into rotation. But if you are going to try and make it in rock, pop, R&B or some other more commercial genre, you will need a full-length video sooner or later. More on video was covered in chapter 7.

PART II

Part II: Taking Care of Business—Your Dollars, Your Papers, and Your Health

Chapter 14
Money Matters

This is a sticky subject to get into in a book, because it's so personal and individual. There are some guidelines for setting fees, for instance, but amounts mostly run the way anything else is priced—supply and demand. Considering that the "supply" is huge—everyone wants to be a musician, and some want it so badly they'll play for peanuts or for free—"demand" is the operative word here. The more "in demand" your act is, the more money you can command.

If you want to make your living as a musician, your income from royalties must be steady and numerous, your recordings should sell well, your performance fees must be suitably high, and you must be gigging often ... all so that you can earn enough to live from music alone. "Enough" is relative, of course, depending on your level of need and comfort, the cost of living in your region of the country, and so forth. If, however, you just want to have fun with some friends, you are more flexible to charge whatever you wish, or even to play for free (though if you do too much of that, don't quit your day job!).

How Much to Charge for Each Gig?
In certain markets, there are price ranges in which most acts will fall. For example, in my field, the children's educational market, there is a range of fees for singles, duos, trios, and so forth. Furthermore, there are discounts for block bookings, since many venues will hire an act for two or more concerts on the same day. This is quite different from the bar or club scene, where you are expected to play up to five sets per night, and you are paid by the night. Research your market, make friends with veterans in that market, and pick their brains.

WHAT YOUR PEERS MAKE

One of the first things to consider is what other acts similar to yours charge. What is the market out there? Are you going to be playing bars and clubs, listening rooms, weddings, or festivals? Fees for playing weddings are usually pretty high in the scheme of things because people feel okay about splurging on their special day; in bars and clubs, on the other hand, you may be lucky to be working for a pittance above tips. Ask around—don't just ask the owner or manager at the venues, but also ask other artists. Venues may try to low-ball what they pay, knowing that you are just starting out and are somewhat naïve and eager to play. So rather than trusting them to set the fee, ask the musicians who regularly play there. Offer to buy them a drink at the gig, or ask them if you might contact them at a later date to pick their brains. If you meet other pro musicians at conferences, showcases, networks, clubs and so forth, do the same. It seems whenever and wherever musicians gather, we tend to talk "shop," and that means chatting about venues, press kits, fees, and more, so you'd fit right in. You might say, "So, how much does the Happy Times Bar and Bowling Alley usually pay for a Saturday night?" It's much more diplomatic than, "So, how much are they paying you tonight, anyway?"

Some may be reluctant to tell you for various reasons. They may want people to think they are getting more than they really are, or they may indeed have a special deal with the venue and are getting more than other acts appearing there. If they have built up a following and can bring in business for the venue, their appearance will be more valuable and they therefore can command higher fees. Or maybe they just don't want to tell you. This is particularly true if you don't know the artists personally—after all, why should they give such personal information to a stranger? Don't let a sour reply dissuade you—many performers remember how it felt to be starting out, how they depended on the goodwill of others who came before them, and they may be happy to help you out.

THE QUALITY OF YOUR ACT

Once you've gotten an idea of the range of fees in your market, you also have to take into consideration where you fit into that market. If you are just starting out and have no following, you certainly would charge at the lower end of the range. In fact, you might have to start out playing for free, just to get your foot into doors and build a following. We call this "paying your dues." As you build a reputation and amass fans, you can start commanding higher fees within the same venues, as you are drawing your *own* audience and thus making money for the venue. Longevity and reputation mean a lot in this business, simply because most musicians find it so hard to hang in there. It's not an easy way to make a living, and if you can persist, you may be rewarded in the long run.

Likewise, you have to realistically assess your talents and all that you have to offer compared to other artists in your market. What makes you unique, and would someone pay big bucks for it? Maybe you are a truly remarkable instrumentalist, with a style all your own. That makes you special and you will stand out from the crowd, so perhaps you could charge more than the average professional musician in your field. Maybe you write hysterically funny songs that you deliver in your own quirky way. Be honest with yourself as to where you fit in the grand flood of artists out there. I have one friend who sets his fees using this reasoning: "We have been out there in the market for ten years, and we are in the top 5 percent of artists in our field [in bookings]; therefore, we should price ourselves *above* what most of the others are charging." I say, if you can do that and the number of bookings doesn't decrease as you raise your price, more power to you. Personally, I raise my fees cautiously, as we are already at the top of our market and we do want to keep up a full performance schedule. As the number of our gigs per year remains steady or increases, and as the *quality* of the gigs improves (meaning larger, better-known venues), only then do I feel more comfortable raising our fees. Beware of pricing yourself out of the market.

Of course, the more people you have in your group, the more you'll have to charge and probably the less each member will be paid. You have to weigh the advantages of a bigger, perhaps better, sound versus the disadvantages of making less per person. I get around this dilemma by offering a variety of options to the venues. Because I no longer perform solo (which is the option most affordable to the venue, as well as paying the most per person!), my lowest fee is for my duo, with proportionately higher fees for the trio and quartet. Since I am "the act" and the other musicians in the group are my accompanists, we do not get paid equally. How you choose to structure a similar group is up to you, but generally I like to pay my accompanists well—see chapters 3 and 9.

HOW FAR YOU HAVE TO TRAVEL

If you have to travel a good distance to get to the gig, that extra time, gas, and so forth should figure into the fee. I have several tiers of fees, which are determined in part by the driving distance. Up to a one-hour drive is included in the base fee, one to two and a half hours is higher, and anything farther than that constitutes a "tour" because I may need to stay overnight. Touring fees depend on a whole lot of additional factors—for instance, if I am going to be in one area for two or more days, I will give the sponsors a lower fee than if I have to go to a different region every day. I also consider whether lodging and meals will be paid for by the sponsor or will come out of my pocket, and whether I stay with friends and family. See the sample fee schedule in the appendix A.

PLAYING FOR FREE? PAY YOUR SUPPORT CREW ANYWAY!

Sometimes, when there is not much money involved and it's a gig I really want to play (a benefit, fundraiser, or rally, for example), then I won't take any fee but will ask for a small one for my accompanists. Don't, however, forget to take into consideration other support members such as roadies, agent, manager, and so forth when negotiating fees.

THE ART OF NEGOTIATION

Speaking of negotiating, remember that it's always easier to come *down* in your fee than it is to go *up*. If you start too low, you can't ask for more, but if you start with your highest fee, the venue is ever so grateful when you start coming down! In these cases, I like to let the venues know what my usual fee is, to show them what a favor I'm doing for them by reducing my fee so much. If you are reducing your fee, try and get something in return, like the approval to sell product, a promise to hire you again for a higher fee if the gig goes well, or some other perk.

On the other hand, I have heard expert negotiators say, "Never mention a number first—let *them* offer first and you counter-offer." This works where fees are not standard and could possibly be higher than your normal fee, such as for TV and special events. There have been times when I have kicked myself because the event had such a high budget that I could have gotten much more than my normal fee, had I not "offered" first. This kind of savvy—knowing when to show your cards after they've shown theirs—only comes with experience.

You may want to keep your fees flexible depending on the venue and even the time of year. For instance, libraries are wonderful venues as listening rooms, but they generally have small budgets, and some prohibit the selling of product. I don't ever refuse a gig just because I'm not allowed to sell my product. I figure you never know who will be in the audience, who might lead you to other gigs, or who at the very least might become your new fans. As for seasonal slumps, lower your fees to stimulate business (our seasonal slump is always summer). It keeps us working and, again, has led to higher-paying gigs later on.

So there is something to the "but you'll be getting exposure" argument. Just remember that musicians have died from exposure! Don't sell yourself too short.

Recordkeeping

If you own your own business (and self-employed musicians do), the good news is that you can write off most of your expenses on your taxes. Consult with your accountant about this. You will need meticulous records of gas and mileage spent going to and from rehearsals and gigs, as well as receipts for meals on the road, strings, sheet music, tolls, performance clothes, haircuts, makeup, instrument repairs, concert tickets, CDs ... *anything and everything music-related or used for your business*. I jokingly ask all my accompanists to get a receipt even if they buy a cup of coffee at a gig!

I keep all receipts in a file by year, just in case of an audit. I instruct my accountant to be conservative when doing my taxes—I don't want to trigger an audit with any red flags, so I report every dime I make, especially since some of my income from sales of CDs is in cash. But you are still allowed to take all legitimate expenses—just make sure that they are legit and you keep receipts.

As I mentioned earlier in this book, you will want to have a reliable spreadsheet program, which will make your bookkeeping easier, more accurate, and quicker than doing it by hand. (Who does anything by hand any more if you have a computer?) I use Microsoft Excel, but you can find a spreadsheet program that fits you best. CPA Jeff Seader recommends Quicken or Quick Books, which make things even easier than Excel, as they write all your checks on the computer and categorize them for you automatically.

Monthly records (see appendix A for a sample page) are kept with one set for income (credit) and one for expenses (debit), each on a separate page for each month. Again, you want to keep all income from music separate from all other income, to make doing your taxes easier. You can customize your spreadsheet for expenses according to your own circumstances, adding or deleting categories as necessary. As for paying *yourself*, consult your accountant for the best way to handle this for your circumstances. Some acts give themselves a salary; some take money as needed.

The main goal here is to get your bottom line for income, and to record legitimate business expenses for deductions for tax purposes. It is also important information for you, anyway, to see where your hard-earned dollars are going. For example, you may find that you spend *way* too much on phone bills and can cut back by switching phone companies or calling during off-peak hours, taking advantage of time zone differences across the country. By analyzing your books, you can make effective changes—to your pocketbook's benefit. No matter how busy I am at the beginning of every month (unless I am on tour), I make time to record the expenses and income from the previous month. I keep an envelope of cash receipts and pay myself back by check monthly as petty cash expense. Likewise, I am meticulous with my checking accounts, reconciling every time I write a check and again, once a month, when the statements come. You would be surprised at how many mistakes I have found, made by both me *and* the bank. If I don't have this discipline—this monthly ritual, if you will—I find that I fall behind and really get swamped with the bookkeeping after only a few months. Things get lost, you forget things. Make it a habit and this chore won't seem so onerous. I find that it's much easier to make the task small by keeping up with it monthly than to have to deal with a huge task less often. This is a real secret to time and money management.

Here's another tip I have found to be useful in many ways. I use a charge card that gives me frequent flyer miles on a major airline. I use this credit card for *everything*, from gas to groceries to haircuts—both major and minor purchases. What this does is helps me keep a record of *all* expenditures, both personal and business, as well as letting me and my family fly free for vacations every so often. This does entail more record-keeping, but again, I manage by keeping the task small by doing it regularly. At the end of every day, whenever I use the card, I gather all the receipts and enter them into a separate spreadsheet just for this card. This record is spread with all my bank accounts across the top, including personal, savings, and business. I enter each of that day's expenses under the proper column, depending on which account it should come out of. Then, at the end of the credit card reporting period each month, everything has been recorded clearly, and I can just pull my business expenses from this sheet onto my books.

Another kind of record keeping that you will need to do if you sell product is the collecting, recording, and paying of sales tax as it applies in your state. In New York, for instance, if you sell product only in small quantities, you will need to file and pay only once a year. If you sell lots of product and thus owe a lot of sales tax, you need to do this quarterly. Regulations and forms for this can be obtained through your state's Department of Taxation and Finance. In any event, you will need to obtain a license or resale certificate in order to sell product. Although you can do this yourself, without an attorney, you might want to consult with your accountant or lawyer about how to get the paperwork you will need. When you set up your license to sell, the tax agency will automatically send you forms to fill out and send in with your payments. Once you start selling product, make sure you keep a separate record of the sales tax you have collected so that it will be easy to figure out how much you periodically owe. Of course, once you start touring, it becomes quite complicated. You will need to obtain a vendor's license (some states grant temporary ones) for *each state* you sell in. The sales tax you collect is therefore determined by each location, and you need to keep track of this. Once sales tax is collected in each place, you must send it to that state's tax department. This is a big headache if you tour extensively—a good reason to turn it over to your business manager or accountant!

I like to use round figures with tax included when selling my product ($10 for cassettes, $15 for CDs, etc.) because most people pay with cash and I don't like to deal with small change. So, I have figured out how much of that is tax due, and how much I get to keep. The formula for this is: The collected cost (a) equals the cost of the product (b) plus sales tax (c) (a = b + c). To arrive at these figures, I start with an estimate. For instance, let's say you collect $10 per tape, and you have a 7 percent sales tax rate for that particular district. I am *guessing* that about $9.30 will be the cost of the product. Multiply it by 7 percent to get $.65 sales tax. But that doesn't add up to $10, so the price is a little too low; in this case, give yourself a little bit more—say, $9.35. Seven percent of that is still $.65, and that *does* add up to $10. Or, if you have a calculator handy, add 1 to the sales tax percentage and divide the collected cost by that number: $10 ÷ 1.07 = $9.35

Sales tax percentages will vary from state to state, as will laws regarding sales tax for mail orders. Be sure you are up to date with this information.

Another thing you might like to do is keep year-by-year overall accounting charts to see if your business is growing. If it's not, why not? What can you do to turn things around? Where can you cut back on expenses? What other marketing can you do? It's useful information to learn where your financial peaks and valleys are. They might be seasonal; if so, you can adjust your marketing strategy to beef up the slow periods. A veteran agent I know says his business usually "sawtooths" (goes up and down in small increments) from year to year, but in general he expects the trend to be upward. Something is wrong if it's downward!

Retirement and Looking to the Future

Many, many musicians I know don't think about retirement or even the near future. We tend to be a happy-go-lucky group of people, concerned with the here-and-now of our art. Most young people in *any* field usually don't think ahead. This is a big mistake, especially in our line of work. I think it is safe to say that most professional musicians do not have a pension plan, have not saved a lot, and have not put much into social security. As with health and life insurance, it is up to *us alone* to take care of our needs now and in the future. We can't afford to buy into the flaky musician image, because if we don't take care of ourselves, who will? Okay, maybe a spouse, your grown children, or a manager if you're lucky enough to have a savvy one. But the big rub here is that most professional musicians barely make enough to live, much less to plan and put aside for the future. *We have to stop thinking of music as a poverty profession*, and start thinking of it as a small business that must provide for its owner.

If you have an accountant—and once you are at a certain level you certainly should—he can guide you. Better still is an investment advisor who is trained in retirement and investment matters. Even if you can only save a tiny amount per month, *do it*. I once attended a seminar where the leader showed "the magic of compounded interest." I was astounded at what could be gained if you start early enough and are faithful and consistent with your savings plan. It's never too early or too late to start squirreling away money for a rainy day or for retirement. Some vehicles you can consider are IRAs in all forms and life insurance policies (covered in chapter 18). Since we are considered self-employed, a wonderful vehicle as of this writing is the SEP IRA, which allows you to put aside more of your income than in a traditional IRA. Of course, this presupposes that you *have* extra income to sock away. Even at my lowest level, I tightened my belt and tried to save *something* every year. What we are trying to avoid here is the sad prospect of a poverty-stricken old musician with nothing. We've all heard *those* tales.

Whatever plan you choose, make sure you know all of its limitations and specifications. Your eligibility for certain plans may be affected by minute details that can change from day to day and year to year. CPA Jeff Seader cautions, "Be careful if you have any employees who work for you over a certain number of hours, usually more than twenty hours per week. If you plan to have a SEP IRA, your ability to contribute may be limited, or you may have to include your employees in your plan. Speak to a tax advisor before setting one up." Another avenue is to join a musician's union (see chapter 16). But besides this, you still need to prepare *yourself* and plan ahead. Chapter 20 gives you ideas if you want to stay in the music industry or related fields, but no longer want to perform.

Chapter 15
Legal Matters

You're going to need an attorney someday. Probably. Definitely. If for no other reason than to protect your interests when you sign that big recording contract with Sony Records. If you're going to be a music professional, then you are going to be running into many kinds of contracts—managerial, recording, gig-related, and so forth. Plus, you may want to incorporate. I've turned to longtime entertainment attorney Howard Leib for his expertise in this chapter.

Trademarks
Howard cautions that with a band, the most important aspect of the trademark is the band name. The first issue is, can they own it? At the beginning, this may not be too important, but somewhere along the way, especially if the band about to get a recording contract, they are going to need to look at trademarking the name. This entails first making sure that the name is available so that they are not infringing upon anyone else, and then filing their own application for registration. A trademark or entertainment attorney should do this so that it's done right. Another issue is: Within the band, who owns the name? This is discussed in greater detail below, in the section on band contracts. (Always make sure, when you are reviewing managerial and recording contracts, that the trademark will not be taken and owned by the other party.) The costs for trademarking will vary from attorney to attorney, but the fees paid directly to the Trademark Office will run between $300 and $400, as of this writing.

The name of a show could also be trademarked if it's crucial to someone's act. Again, in the beginning of a career, this is not as important.

Incorporation

We discuss *why* we might want to incorporate in the chapters on Support Personnel and Insurance. Here, we will discuss *how*. If you really feel the need or want to incorporate (and you should investigate this carefully), call your accountant to discuss the tax implications. Then either she or your lawyer will file the application with the appropriate state governmental department. There are filing fees that vary from state to state.

Your most tax-friendly option is the S corporation. According to Lawrence C. Ré, attorney with the New York firm Munley, Meade, Nielsen and Ré, an S corporation protects whatever personal assets you may have from what may occur within the business. If you have a house, a nice car, an art collection, or whatever that you want to keep separate in case of a lawsuit, it might be worth looking into incorporating. The downside is that you need a lawyer or an accountant to incorporate, and in some states there are small filing fees that you must pay every year.

Jeffrey Seader, CPA of Santolli and Seader, advises, "Check with your state tax authority to see if subchapter S corporations are permissible where you live. Certain localities such as New York City do not recognize S corps, so you may have to pay some additional tax on your earnings." Your accounting gets more complicated and therefore more expensive. Your corp books and bank accounts must be kept separate from your personal ones.

The upside is, of course, the protection against personal liability. I incorporated when I first started out as a solo artist. This was because, until I made my living fully as a musician, I supported myself also as a visual artist in the medium of glass. I needed the liability protection that an S corporation gave me in case one of my pieces broke and hurt someone. Now that I am a full-time musician, I still keep the S corp because one never knows if some unforeseeable accident might happen to an audience member or some other innocent soul. I own a house, which would be untouchable in case of a lawsuit against my corporation.

Contracts

Contracts are legally binding agreements between two or more parties. I would venture to say that no one should sign anything without the advice and input of an attorney. The messes you can get into, the fortunes that can be lost, and so on make the cost of a good entertainment attorney well worth it.

BAND CONTRACTS

At the point when a group or band is serious about getting out there touring, trying to shop a record deal, and so on, Howard Leib strongly recommends that a formal agreement be drawn up within the band. "It's always easier," he says, "for people to be understanding and giving and easy when it's imaginary dollars than when it's for real." If you can iron out the nitty-gritty details of the practical matters of working together, you can get through anything. Howard also notes:

> *I've seen more bands break up over the concept of putting together the partnership agreement than over anything else. How is the money to be divided? This is a big issue, especially when it's about the songwriting provisions. If everybody writes, then how do you split that up, considering both the writers' and publishers' shares? How are decisions in the band going to be made? What happens if somebody wants to leave the band? How do you replace somebody who wants to leave? How do you get rid of someone if the other members want that?*

Also, who owns the name of the group (the trademark)—the band as a whole, each member, the most senior member—and who gets to use it under what circumstances? All these considerations and more need to be worked out in advance. You will save yourself much heartache, money, and legal hassle if you can anticipate the issues. This is one of the many reasons why an experienced music attorney is necessary—he will know the concerns that need to be addressed in the contract.

I would think that all members of the band would want to meet with the attorney in order to discuss and protect their own interests. Here is where you may find out each other's "true colors"! Of course, everyone can save money by having the heavy discussions and reaching some decisions *before* meeting with the attorney, rather than hashing these things out on his expensive time clock.

MANAGER AND AGENT CONTRACTS

The first assumption here is that the artist has done the homework and thoroughly researched the background, history, and reputation of any manager or agency she is considering hooking up with. You do not want to sign *anything* with *anyone* without investigating the candidate first.

For both manager and agent agreements, the initial draft of the contract will most likely be supplied by *them*, not the artist. The reason for this is that the band gets only one manager contract, but the manager may have lots of band contracts. The agreement should be negotiable. As a real basic start, Howard cautions that

> *if any manager wants to charge you a fee to manage you, rather than get paid a percentage of your income,* **run from the room.** *You will find people who like to call themselves managers, who will try and charge you to evaluate a project to see if there is something there, or something similar to that. Managers or agents get paid* **when** *you make money—they do not charge you a fee up front.*

This is different from "charge-backs," which are legitimate expenses that a manager might pay out of his own pocket (or his company's pocket) on your behalf. And I use the word "legitimate" emphatically here; such expenses might be posters, photographers … anything that you need to further your career. Questionable expenses are first-class, 'round-the-world air jaunts or season tickets to the Yankees! You get the idea. It's not unreasonable to place a limit on both individual expenses and gross monthly expenses.

Of course, the contract should spell out the commission the manager or agent gets. When negotiating the manager's percentage, try to make sure it's based on the monies that *you get to keep*, not money that just passes through your business, such as fees paid by you to accompanists and sound and light techs, as well as fees paid from record companies which go toward record production. Also, it is very common (but still negotiable) for fees to be paid to the manager or agent directly, who then distributes the third-party and artist fees and keeps his own commission. Naturally, as an artist, I prefer that the fees are paid to me and then I pay the commissions. Howard says, "Whoever is holding the money is in a better bargaining position if there's a dispute." You might try and negotiate for this.

These contracts should state the duration of the terms. Be sure that there is a time limit for receiving commissions on deals negotiated by the manager which continue after your contract with that manager has expired. (These are called "after term rights.") Howard says, "Most first drafts of management contracts say the commission on their deals goes on forever. *It doesn't have to.* You can limit it—three years, five years, seven years. You can try to take it out altogether." For instance, if you have a long-running gig that goes on for years after you've parted ways from that first manager, make sure there is a clear time limit for him to collect from that gig. Likewise with a record deal. Your new manager might also want a percentage from these, but it's only fair that the person who got that gig in the first place benefits from it—but for how long? This is a point to negotiate. From the manager's side, many years and initially money from his own pocket will go into developing that artist, and he should be fairly compensated for this investment. Unless the act is already well-established, it's a gamble for both parties.

One thing that you'll never see in a first-draft management contract, and which very few attorneys ask for, is something that Howard thinks is very important and calls "the out-clauses and mile-markers":

> *The manager's job is to help you improve your career. I see no reason why there should not be something in the contract that says if you, the artist, do not earn 'x' dollars by 'y' date (both factors are negotiable), then you have the right to terminate the agreement. Most managers will agree to this, as long as you put in fairly reasonable numbers, because it's logical that a manager will not want you around if you're not producing. If I am representing the artist, I want to make sure their career isn't stagnating with a manager who isn't able to help them.*

Your manager and agent are two of the most important people on your professional team. It's imperative that you have mutual trust, think long-term, and try to anticipate various scenarios where you could run into trouble. It's better to have vision and try to catch potential problems early than to have lawsuits, hard feelings, and financial disasters rear their ugly heads later.

RECORDING CONTRACTS

With recording contracts it is crucial, more so than with any other aspect of this business, that you have a competent music attorney to negotiate, review, and guide. There are so many pitfalls and points that the artists themselves (or even with a manager advising) cannot know about. For instance, certain concessions are not offered at first but are very easy to get because the companies don't care that much about them, but artists themselves wouldn't know to ask for them. Also, there are points in a contract that may sound horrible to the artist, but are actually standard in the industry and *no one* can get them changed.

The first thing Howard advises is to make sure you are getting a *recording* contract, not a *shopping for a recording deal* agreement. This latter kind of contract may or may not be a good thing, as it ties you up for a certain length of time without really gaining you anything.

The first record deal a new artist or band gets, unless the group is highly in demand, will not be a terrific one (in your favor) because a newcomer has no bargaining power. It will, most likely, be heavily in the record company's favor. While artists who achieve success will frequently be able to renegotiate the terms of this initial contract, Howard points out that this is by no means a sure thing, so when you sign a contract, be sure you can live with *all* its terms. As a general rule, the more pages the contract runs, the worse it is for the artist. Each time the record company has a problem, it adds a clause or paragraph to solve that problem. There are so many fine points to a recording contract that an attorney *really* needs to go over, but here are some points the artists can watch for:

♬ *Product commitment. Make sure you know how much product you are being called on to make—i.e., how many recordings (and what kind— singles or albums?) over what period of time, and how many options the agreement calls for.*

♪ *Options. "Options are not good things," opines Howard, "because it's never the* artists' *options, it's always the* company's. *An agreement with an initial period and six options is actually just an agreement for the initial period, with the record company having the right, but not the obligation, to keep the artist under contract for more periods. This is a fact of life in this industry—you won't be able to change this, but you should understand it. When they say it's a seven-record deal, it may mean it's for a single with option for others." The artist* must *stick with the company if it chooses to extend these options, even if she is unhappy there, or else risk a breach of contract lawsuit.*

There is one concession that you might be able to get with regards to options, which is similar to the point we mentioned with the managerial contract. You can try to specify that if the record doesn't sell x number of copies or doesn't generate y dollars in royalties, then you can get out of that contract. Howard's worst fear for his clients is that they will be tied to a contract that's not going anywhere, and therefore the artists won't be able to do anything with their talents.

♬ *Length of the agreement. Longer is not necessarily better. Standard record contracts are for seven years. You may not want to be tied up that long, especially if the company is not working hard for you. One safety net being considered now in some states is legislation that may set a limit on the maximum term of the recording contract.*

♪ *Money. What is your royalty? What is it based on—suggested retail price, or wholesale? What about the advance? Will there be a fund that the company gives you which, if you don't use it all to make the record, you can keep? Or is it going to be a budget, where all bills get sent to the company within a limit? With new artists, it probably will be a budget.* "Remember," Howard cautions, "every dollar you're spending on the recording is your money *as part of your advance. You won't see a royalty check until all the advance is recouped. So act frugally.*"

♫ *Music publishing. If you are the writer of some or all of the works on the recording, some companies may want a piece of your publishing rights, or a discount on your mechanical royalties. This is because* they have to pay you *these mechanicals, and if they have this clause, then their expense is less. This is, of course, not a good deal for the writer, who should try and strike this from the contract if it's included.*

♪ *Free goods. This is what the record company gives away for promotional or other purposes. The artist is not paid on these, so try and put a limit on them.*

♫ *Delivery. There will be a time limit as well as format considerations for the delivery of your recording to the company.*

♪ *Approval. What does the record company have the power of approval over? The cover, song selection, title, and more may fall under here.*

♫ *Video. Will there be one, and what are all the issues concerning it?*

♪ *Re-record restrictions. This comes into play at the end of the contract's term. How long must the artists wait until they can re-record a song originally released under this contract? What counts as a recording and what doesn't?*

The various drafts of the contract will travel back and forth between the legal department of the record company and your lawyer for review, negotiations, and changes. No revisions may be made on the contract without the consent of all parties. Once a final draft has been agreed upon, your attorney receives the hard copy for you to sign—then *voilà*, you've got yourself a recording contract.

PERFORMANCE CONTRACTS

In the appendix A at the back of the book is a sample contract for perform-ances. I try never to perform in a venue—even a simple house concert or a freebie—without one. More than anything, it spells out the agreement you and the booker have made, where and when the performance is to take place, what you will provide, and what they will provide. There really is no standard performance contract—you can customize your own for your own needs. But for example, let's go over my sample. Most of the points are self-explanatory, but I'll elaborate on some:

🎵 *Contact Information. At the top you might want all* your *contact information, including mailing address, phone and fax numbers, and e-mail and Web site addresses. Make it easy for anyone to get a hold of you— information should be everywhere, on everything you put out.*

♪ *Gig-specific information. After that, fill in all pertinent information about the gig. If you filled out an intake/inquiry form when booking the gig, you can lift all the facts right off it for your contract (see chapter 2).*

🎵 *Fee. Somewhere in the contract, you might want some kind of indication of when* you *expect to be paid—right after the show or a week later? Some venues don't pay for weeks or even* months, *like municipalities. Here, too, you might want to mention if you want separate checks for each member of the band. I put this in, then write "Please see separate cover letter." I put their names, amounts, and social security numbers on this document instead of the contract, just to keep it looking "cleaner." You may do differently.*

♪ *Deposits. Although maybe I should do it as a matter of course, I only ask for deposits during my very busiest season, which happens to be December. We offer a very popular multicultural holiday show, and because there are really only about three to four weeks that I can book this show for, each date during that time is at a premium. I do ask for a 50 percent nonrefundable deposit, because I have had the unfortunate experience of having someone cancel a prime date at the last minute, leaving me unable to book someone else to fill in, and thus losing income. Think of what a financial disaster it would be if many people cancelled during your busiest time, with you unable to rebook those dates.*

🎵 *Cancellations and Rescheduling. You need to establish some kind of policy about cancellations. During my peak season, I always take great pains to explain to the booker that I sell out every single day during this time, and therefore cannot offer a rescheduled holiday show in case of snow or my illness. I do offer them any other of my shows at any mutually convenient date over the next six months. In any case, I try to get presenters to agree to not cancel a gig outright, but rather reschedule so I don't lose the income. This is in effect no matter who cancels for whatever reason. I do not return deposits, as I stipulate that they are non-refundable but can be applied toward a new concert.*

♪ **What is the presenter providing?** *Here, you want to list everything you can possibly imagine. Don't take it for granted that there will be a stage or sound system. Do you need water onstage and backstage? Will they provide help with the unloading of your equipment or the selling of your products? What about sound and light techs? Will you need driving, parking, and unloading directions? Try and anticipate all your needs here. Very complicated requirements may need contract riders, such as technical directions or a stage layout. More on this later.*

As for directions to the venue, always ask for these in writing, because it makes the presenter have to sit down and really think about how people would get to the place, either using public transportation or their own vehicles. Many professional venues know this and have preprinted directions to give to anyone who asks. What I don't like are those Internet-generated directions, where you type in the starting point and destination. They are often wrong and vague and don't account for things like construction, exits that don't exist any more, and so forth. Therefore, you might to inform the sponsor that you prefer he give you directions in his own words.

♫ **Contract rider.** *What may go on a contract rider? Any other specific technical or gig needs, such as hospitality—are they putting you up in someone's house, providing hotel rooms, meals, backstage food and drink? Unless we are on tour, my band's needs are simple—we just ask for electricity (don't assume!), a table for the selling of product, and bottled water for onstage. You wouldn't believe how this last item baffles some presenters! If and when a presenter balks at your needs, explain that at least water is necessary—you will be working hard and probably sweating up a storm. I ask for bottled, because cups onstage spill, and you never know the quality of the water if it's from a tap. Point out that it's a very small accommodation, it's part of hospitality, and hey, some acts' riders are several pages long and include booze, fresh sushi and fruit, specific kinds of coffee ... and the famous black jelly beans. Not to mention hair stylists and makeup artists and masseuses ... You can remind them that musicians on the road really* *need to feel comfortable and well-taken care of, and like to watch their nutritional needs. It's a part of their welcome to you, their guest.*

Technical riders should include all sound and light needs, plus any equipment or instruments they are providing, such as a piano (make sure it's recently tuned and in good playing condition!) or set of drums. Some venues ask for a stage plot, marked where each member of the group will be situated along with amps, monitors, mics, and so on. This makes the stagehands' and stage manager's jobs easier. Be specific if you need a particular kind of mic, amplifier, direct box, music stand, stool, whatever. There is a story about a well-known singer who was quite particular in the specifications of his stool onstage: It had to be a certain height, with a certain number of rungs, made of a certain material. The venue couldn't find such a stool and so actually had one custom-made. When the artist got there and went onstage to perform, he didn't sit on the stool once. He did, however, use it to hold his water glass.

♪ *What the performer is providing. Here is where the promo that the venue requests should be listed, plus anything else you agree to provide, such as a sound system. When booking the gig, be sure to ask exactly what the venue's PR people need to promote your show. Give them any and all they ask for. After all, it's to everyone's benefit when there is good publicity. Have fabulous quotes from top media or famous people they can use in press releases. Send photos liberally—as I said earlier, a good shot in a newspaper is worth much more than simply a blurb or a calendar listing.*

I make two copies of this contract, sign, date, and send both to the presenter for her signature, requesting that one of the copies be sent back to me with driving directions attached.

Wills

Here is another oddball topic in a book like this. But like life insurance, it is something boringly, painfully practical that you may want to consider. Maybe you don't have much to pass on, but if you have a family, you want to make sure your desires are known and followed. It is particularly important if you have children that you make provisions for their custody, or guardianship, and care. We often don't look that far down the road of our lives, especially when we are young and carefree musicians; we expect to live long and don't even want to confront the possibility of our death. But if you're in the music business, there are specific factors to consider, such as:

🎵 *Royalties. Who will receive them after your death? If one of your compositions becomes a hit or if your recordings suddenly become popular after you die, it could mean a lot of money for your heirs.*

♪ *Copyrights. Who will own your compositions after you are gone? If no provisions are made, they could revert to a relative you hate.*

🎵 *Investments. Forget about your fortunes—what about your precious, beloved, and valuable instruments? Without a will, your $4,000 vintage Gibson guitar may go to your fourteen-year-old nephew who's in a garage punk band and likes to carve graffiti into whatever is handy…*

If you are part of a band, what happens to your rights upon your death? Other band members might buy out your part and take out insurance to cover this or make other arrangements. This should be covered in the band contracts, because dying is another way to leave your band!

An attorney can not only draw up your will but also do a living will (what to do in case you are comatose and unresponsive and someone needs to make medical decisions for you), a health proxy, and more. Because we are on the road so much and sometimes working in questionable places like bars, an untimely death is not so terribly far-fetched. Sorry to have to bring up such a grim topic, but be prepared for any eventuality, I say.

Chapter 16

Unions

Unions have changed a lot over the years. When I was first starting my professional career, I considered joining the AFM (American Federation of Musicians) because, well, that's what professional musicians did. But what scared me back then were all the restrictions. I had heard that if you were a union musician, you could not play in non-union halls, nor could you play with non-union musicians. Based on those two things alone, I decided not to join. The union was sort of looked on as "the job police," preventing musicians from working in situations that didn't meet their rules. Members had to sneak around and work under assumed names to avoid getting penalized.

However, while doing my research for this book, I turned to a friend, John McCutcheon, a fellow folk musician who also happens to be the current president of Local 1000, a chapter of the AFM. He gave me some insight into the considerable changes the AFM has gone through over the past fifteen or twenty years (and continues to go through), as well as considerable information about Local 1000, which may be of help to those of you who are traveling musicians. The union is now much more democratic than ever, and it certainly addresses many of the issues covered in this book—insurance needs such as health, disability, life, accident, liability, and instrument and equipment; pensions; contracts; credit; loans; and more.

The American Federation of Musicians of the United States and Canada

The AFM is the largest entertainment union in the world. If you are going to be a session player or studio musician, you must join the AFM in order to work. You might be able to get away with doing one or two gigs without joining, but if you are going to be playing a lot as a session musician, you need to join. Beyond that important factor, John McCutcheon feels one of the best reasons to join *any* union is, "They enable individuals to accomplish in groups what they cannot do all by themselves." The union's sole purpose is to advocate for the betterment and rights of musicians. It makes sure artists get paid what they are due and that they are treated fairly. As a group, musicians can enter into collective bargaining agreements, get group insurance policies, and so forth. A while back, these advantages made sense mainly to session players or members of big ensembles like orchestras or big bands, which were covered by salaried contracts. But now, John feels that the only downside—for anyone—of joining the union would be if musicians did not avail themselves of its benefits. Even the old bugaboo of the union's forbidding its members to play in non-union halls or with non-union musicians is now, by and large, ignored and unenforced for single engagements.

The entire continent of North America is carved into geographic AFM jurisdictions, which have their own local chapters. There is one chapter, however, which is determined not by geography but rather by the kind of work the members do.

LOCAL 1000: THE NORTH AMERICAN TRAVELING MUSICIANS UNION

Sometime around 1995, some itinerant acoustic musicians felt the AFM didn't quite meet their needs, and so investigated how they could start their own chapter tailored to their particular circumstances—i.e., typically playing one-night stands and traveling from venue to venue. These tended to be folk musicians, singer-songwriters, children's artists, blues and bluegrass artists, and other folk- and roots-based artists.

Nowadays, Local 1000 is exclusively for folk and acoustic musicians: Rock, R&B, symphonic, jazz, or other genres cannot join this local. If you are not sure whether your situation would fit into Local 1000 or the chapter in your area, John encourages contacting either office, and your case will be determined individually.

John explains the distinguishing characteristic of the Local 1000 chapter:

> *The unique thing about Local 1000 is that it is* **nongeographic,** *as opposed to other local chapters, which are* **based on a geographic area.** *Local 1000's jurisdiction is wherever its members play, for the length of time that they play there. For example, if I am playing at*

> *the XYZ club—which is not a union venue—for the length of time
> that I am onstage, working under that contract,* it is in fact a union
> venue. *As soon as I step offstage, it ceases to be a union venue.*

Regarding contracts, you can use *your own*—the one you've always used and
designed for your needs—as the union contract, as long as you put the union
masthead (which you own as a member) at the top. Also, you need to add
paragraph number six from *the union's* standard contract: a clause that states
that the performance cannot be recorded without permission. Another option
is the contract available through Local 1000 or other locals that enables a
musician to get contributions into his pension fund and that can make provisions for a health care plan.

The union has set a promulgated scale for fees, which are the *minimum*
that can be paid for a particular kind of gig. (A member cannot play for less
than the specified fee under a union contract, but she *can* perform for her own
designated fee if she is using her own non-union contract.) There are two reasons for setting this scale: (1) It establishes a floor that takes into account the
economics of the community where the gig is, and (2) it tries to set a standard
so that people get the idea that musicians should be paid as professionals. "It's
as much a matter of dignity as it is of economics," John says. Some examples
of these fees for a solo act are (as of the time this book was written):

- 🎵 *Concert: $200*
- ♪ *Club or small concert: $100*
- 🎵 *Opening Act: $60*
- ♪ *Festival: $200 per day*
- 🎵 *School (K–12): $200 per performance*
- ♪ *Higher education: $300 per performance*

Ensembles add 50 percent of the solo rate for each additional member.

You can check out Local 1000's Web site at *www.local1000.com* for extensive information. Some of the information below is not exclusive to the 1000,
but may also apply to your local chapter. Basically, here is what Local 1000 is
all about:

- 🎵 *Dues. Annual dues are $120 per year as of this writing. This can be
  paid in one lump sum or in quarterly installments. New members pay a*

one-time initiation fee of $100. If they already belong to another AFM local, they pay only $35. Beyond that, there are work dues for every gig played under a union contract of 2 percent of scale (your actual fee stated on the contract), with a maximum payment of $20.

♪ **Group pension plan.** This plan is AFM-wide, not just particular to Local 1000. It is a trustee-run, third-party plan, not owned by the AFM. The biggest contributors to the fund are the large record companies, which pay 10 percent of all recording performers' scale to the pension fund. This money is assigned to the performer's name and Social Security number. Once the performer becomes "vested" (works for five consecutive calendar years under union contracts), the money will be paid out to her under this fixed formula: When she turns sixty-five, for every $100 in the pension plan in the performer's name, she will receive $4.65 per month for the rest of her life. For example, if the artist accrues $100,000 in the plan over the life of her career—not terribly hard to do—on her sixty-fifth birthday the plan will begin paying $4,650 per month to the artist until she dies. After that, if the artist has named a beneficiary, that person would receive 50 percent of the pension amount until his death. This plan does not prohibit the artist from having any other personal retirement plan, such as an IRA, although there may be some limits.

♫ **Pro bono lawyers.** Artists can get help incorporating, auditing their record company, or any other fairly simple legal maneuvers for free. The union lawyers are not meant to take the place of your own music attorney, who will review or negotiate contracts and take care of other, bigger legal business. The union lawyers can answer questions or give direction over the simpler issues.

♪ **Health insurance.** Local 1000 offers a health plan that pays for all medical expenses up to $50,000 total, excluding direct hospitalization charges. It comes at no cost to members but is financed by employer contributions on gigs under the terms of collective bargaining agreements by Local 1000. The chapter also has a discount prescription plan.

♫ **Contract support.** If you use the union contract (or your own with the union's heading; see above) and file it with the union, its personnel will enforce the terms either through a phone call or, if necessary, legal action.

♪ **Twenty-four-hour emergency assistance.** Using the toll-free number (800) ROADGIG, you can get legal assistance, on-site support, a cash advance, money collection assistance, and more. You must have a contract on file with the union to access this service when you call.

♫ **Disability insurance.** *Members can buy a policy that will pay 70 percent of your average monthly wages up to a $3,000 maximum, tax-free, if you are disabled by accident or illness.*

♪ **Low-cost instrument insurance.** *Members can buy this insurance, which covers not only your instruments but also your computer, recording equipment, PA system … anything you use as a professional musician. Don't think your homeowner's insurance will cover these. Through the union this can cost as little as $75 per year for full replacement value, and covers theft, loss, or damage anytime, anywhere.*

♫ **Union privilege benefits.** *Members have access to low-interest credit cards, discount travel programs, low-cost mortgages, and more.*

♪ **Visa assistance.** *The union can help smooth the way for passage into the United States from Canada by doing the paperwork and filing the application. It takes 120 days to receive a visa.*

♫ **Liability insurance.** *Again, this can be purchased through the union. It protects your business from lawsuits. Some presenters require this and even may ask to be put on as a co-insured. The union recommends a company that tailors liability insurance to AFM members.*

♪ **Other benefits.** *Term life insurance, personal accident insurance, cancer protection plan, and more. The union can help you find the best rates due to collective bargaining.*

♫ **Gigsearch.** *Helps members locate venues in given areas. This is a great tool when building a tour. Members access this service through the Web, where you will need a password that is given by the union.*

♪ **Music Performance Trust Fund.** *This is a granting fund that helps subsidize free musical performances to the public. The fund pays $200 plus 10 percent pension to a solo act or leader, and $100 plus 10 percent pension for each side musician. A co-sponsor must pay at least 60 percent of the budget. Check* **www.mptf.org** *for further information.*

So, call your local chapter or Local 1000, check out their Web sites, get their material, talk to other musicians who are in the union, and think it over. You just might find joining a union to be one of the smartest things you ever did.

Chapter 17
Health

You may be wondering why a chapter on health is included in a book like this. If you are a young musician just starting a career, the excitement and hard work ahead of you consumes all your thinking, and many young people take their health for granted anyway. But I am hoping that you are thinking long-term, of an enduring career in music—unless, of course, you just want to be a "one-hit wonder," a "flash in the pan" who makes the millions, invests wisely, and then gets out! More power to you if you can pull *that* off. But if you want lasting power and the long career, you need to take care of yourself *now*, and every day. No matter what instrument you play, your *main* instrument is your body. Mistreat it, and all those hours, weeks, and years of practicing and hard work will be for nothing.

Diet, Sleep, and Exercise
Starting with the basics: These days, everyone knows how important these three factors are in maintaining health. But how many people actually establish and practice healthy habits, making them part of their lifestyle?

CHOW
If you don't know the effect a poor diet has on your stamina, appearance, and brain, you haven't been paying attention! Although you may need caffeine to get through long nights of performing, too much of it can harm you in both the short and long run. It's basically artificial energy that is addictive, and withdrawal from a serious caffeine habit can cause bad headaches that are much like migraines. A diet of overly fatty or salty foods, too, can affect blood pressure, cholesterol, energy ... a host of vital factors that you need to pay attention to. Karen Sussman, licensed and certified speech pathologist specializing in

voice therapy, says, "Caffeine dehydrates and dries the vocal cords, and also aggravates acid reflux. Too much salt may cause fluid retention and therefore vocal cord swelling ('edema')." It's so easy when on the road to fall prey to fast food, junk food, or not eating at all. You can go on a diet like this for a while, but your concentration and your physical well-being will suffer before too long. Over and over, musicians on the road say it is *crucial* to eat healthfully in order to maintain the grueling pace and keep up their energy and stamina.

Speaking of acid reflux, this can be particularly bothersome to singers. This is where the acid from the stomach comes back up the esophagus, sometimes bathing the vocal cords. Karen asserts that it creates hoarseness, mucous and a feeling of something foreign in the throat, coughing, and throat-clearing, and it is sometimes associated with asthma. A voice therapist or medical doctor can suggest lifestyle changes to combat acid reflux, such as not eating high-acid foods (e.g., tomato sauce and vinegar) or greasy fried foods, avoiding tight clothing around the waist, and losing weight. Furthermore, Karen suggests that one avoid consuming caffeine, alcohol, or tobacco in large doses at all times, as well as eating *anything* for a full two to three hours before lying down. Elevating the head of the bed on six-inch blocks also helps, as does sleeping with your head on a wedge pillow, which can be bought at a medical supply store. Your physician can also prescribe anti-reflux medications if indicated.

When you read the biographies of musicians who have lasted in the business for decades, you will notice that, for the most part, they have discovered that they need to eat sensibly, especially on the road. Many of them are vegetarians, or at least avoid red meat. I know many singers avoid dairy products because of the mucous they produce.

As everyone knows, eating plenty of fresh fruits and vegetables and keeping fats and sugars to a minimum goes a long way towards keeping yourself in top form. We can't afford to be sluggish as a result of being undernourished or overweight. We artists need to think of ourselves as athletes; after all, playing music is, among other things, a very physical job. Also, in some fields of music, appearance is almost as important as musicianship. Pop and rock stars really have to look good and buff—no one thinks someone paunchy is hot! On the other hand, to starve yourself just to fit into someone else's image of "cool" is pretty stupid, too.

CATCHING YOUR Z'S

Sleep is more important than many people realize. And musicians, many who primarily work at night, are notoriously bad about getting adequate amounts.

Not getting enough sleep will affect not only your concentration, but also your appearance and energy. It's well known that sleep deprivation is the cause of many vehicle and work accidents. It's been shown in medical studies that night-shift workers (which many musicians are) suffer from a kind of constant "jet lag," and have higher incidents of a host of problems, from heart attacks to divorce.

The very sickest I have ever been in my life was when I was singing in a club four nights a week until 2:00 A.M., then getting up and working a day job every day, too. After about six weeks of this schedule, I fell ill and was literally unconscious for two days and in bed for several more. Everyone's sleep needs vary, but whatever your optimum amount is, be sure to get it most nights.

Also, pay attention to your own biological rhythms. I am a morning person. When I performed in clubs at night and didn't get home until 3:00 or 4:00 A.M. and slept until maybe noon, even though I was getting the "right" number of hours of sleep, I still felt tired and grumpy all day. Now that I perform in the mornings, getting the same number of hours of sleep feels better when I go to bed early and have to *wake up* at 4:30 A.M. My husband, on the other hand, has always been a night owl, and our early morning performances are hell on him! He can't seem to go to sleep before 11:00 or midnight most nights, even when he has to get up before 5:00 A.M. Again, when you are young, loss of sleep doesn't feel so bad, so it makes you feel more invulnerable to the damage that will inevitably occur over time. So once again, be smart, and think long-term. It's not very attractive to watch a musician who has dark circles and bags under her eyes and looks exhausted!

STAYING FIT

Exercise is the third leg of the pedestal of good health. It's no surprise that Mick Jagger, in his late fifties at this writing, is still prancing around like a young colt—he exercises diligently. As does Madonna. As does anyone who wants to stick around and needs the energy to pull several hours onstage. Non-musicians don't realize how truly physically demanding performing is. Wind musicians and singers know that they have to stay in shape in order for their lungs and muscles to stay in control. Drummers, guitarists, double bass players—we *all* have to stay strong, flexible, and nimble.

I find that stretching just before a performance helps me move better onstage, loosens my muscles, and helps me sing more strongly and with more control. Stretching also helps prevent injuries when lifting equipment or moving around onstage. As a singer, I also always try and do a half-hour of vocal exercises before the gig to warm up my vocal cords. Other singers may do longer warm-ups. Like an athlete, you don't want to start work with cold muscles. Voice teacher Ron Meixsell offers this breathing exercise for singers:

> *Inhaling through your nose, take several short sniffs, then take one deep breath and hold it for as long as you can. Then, blow out through your mouth using short puffs until all the air is gone. Do three to five sets of these. The proper exchange of oxygen in the blood helps calm your nerves and prepares you for performance.*

Some form of aerobics at least three times a week also builds stamina and helps with wind control. For example, the American Heart Association recommends getting a pedometer (they are not expensive, maybe $15–20) and walking at least ten thousand steps a day, about three to four miles. Weight lifting probably feels unnecessary for those who have to schlep their own equipment, but at least some moderate, repetitive weight lifting is excellent for toning and general shaping—not to mention osteoporosis prevention in old age.

Illness

A singer's worst nightmare is laryngitis. I was prone to this for a few years, a time when I seemed relentlessly accident- and sickness-prone. At the lowest point, I was getting sick and losing my voice *every other month*. That wreaked havoc with my performances and my income, since I had to cancel or reschedule many gigs. Since then, I've changed my diet, started exercising as regularly as my schedule allows, and tried to reduce my stress level. My vulnerability to illness decreased dramatically—I haven't had an incapacitating illness for years now.

There are a few easy measures you can take to avoid the common cold and other viruses. First, get a flu shot every year. Before I did this, I fell prey to whatever flu virus was going around and, as a result, lost work. As for colds, you can probably perform with one, but with a fever it just feels miserable. As a matter of course, I take at least 500 mg of Vitamin C every day, along with a multiple vitamin—just in case I don't get to eat adequately at times—and 1000 mg of calcium. (As a small-boned Asian woman, I am particularly susceptible to osteoporosis, and the extra calcium with vitamin D will help me in old age.) I have heard that you can also take the herb echinacea to help build immunity against colds, but I cannot personally vouch for it. When I feel the onset of a cold, I also take extra vitamin C (500 mg at four-hour intervals) and zinc lozenges. I have been told slippery elm is great to suck on for sore throats, but honestly I can't get past the taste. Also, it may seem antisocial and a bit paranoid, but I try not to shake anyone's hand during cold and flu season—after all, that is how viruses get spread, through sneezing, coughing, and contact. Doctors tell us to wash our hands frequently, but if no soap and water are available, you can buy alcohol-based germicidal gel, which is very handy, portable, and non-drying. And, believe it or not, some musicians don't *ever* shake hands with *anyone* because they want to protect their own from over-zealous grips that could ruin their fingers and joints. Remember, like a dancer or actor, your body is part of your livelihood, and if it doesn't work right, you're out of work!

When congested, I use steam, and the easiest method if you don't have a vaporizer is to run really hot water in a sink, put a towel over your head and the sink, and put your face as close to the steam as possible (be careful not to burn yourself). You can also use those facial steamers some people use as beauty aids. Some people advise against using antihistamines, as they not only dry you out but also make you groggy. But *personally* (and I realize this goes against most medical advice), I have found them to be useful for swollen vocal cords due to *illness* (not strain). If I feel swelling, I will take antihistamines at bedtime (because they do make you sleepy) and find they reduce the swelling by daybreak. Karen Sussman adds,

> *A prescription antihistamine such as Allegra (or an over-the-counter one like Claritin) does not cause drowsiness and may be less drying than some other antihistamines. Still, use of oral antihistamines is generally not advisable for singers. Physicians often recommend anti-inflammatory corticosteroid nasal sprays instead.*

These prescription nasal sprays are great because they are often more effective and less expensive than the prescription antihistamines. In any case, with any illness or lingering vocal distress, you should see your doctor for a full evaluation and try not to self-diagnose.

Cold and dryness are a singer's enemies, so be particularly vigilant during the winter months. Inside, try and humidify your house; a simple method for this is putting pans of water or a wet towel over radiators. When outdoors, protect your head and throat with a woolen hat and scarf at all times and try *never* to sing outside in the cold. Inhaling cold air is murder on the vocal cords. My worst case of laryngitis came after agreeing to sing a benefit outdoors in the winter!

If you find you have mucous in your throat, do not "clear" your throat with a guttural sound (the "ahem" sound). This is harsh and bad for the vocal cords. Also, try not to cough it out, as coughing bangs the vocal cords together. Instead, try making a forceful, voiceless "H" sound.

Keeping Your Voice Vocal

Regular visits to the doctor are important to musicians and singers, as they are to everyone. But being self-employed and often uninsured makes it hard to maintain a regular schedule of visits. As soon as I was able, I made sure I had health insurance, not only for those catastrophic injuries or illnesses that can wipe you out financially, but also for the routine checkups (see chapter 18). An ounce of prevention is worth a pound of cure, I say. I just consider it a very basic necessity, like housing and food. I want to know that I am as healthy as I can be, by getting checked as regularly as possible; or, if I'm not healthy, I want to know what's wrong as *early* as possible so that I can do something about it. If you are a woman, you want regular gynecological checkups as well. This is all for peace of mind, if nothing else. You might even be able to find doctors who specialize in treating musicians—maybe they are closet players themselves—who are not only particularly sympathetic but also more knowledgeable about the particular ailments we get because they are interested in our field. Just as there are sports medicine specialists, maybe you can find someone whose expertise is music medicine!

But you may also want other folks on your health team. As was mentioned in chapter 9, singers will definitely want, at least some time during their career if not throughout it, a voice teacher or therapist, or both. It is wise to start with a teacher early in your career so that you don't learn bad habits. A voice therapist, combined with a teacher, will keep your pipes in fine working order for a lifetime.

Another specialist I hope you'll never need is the ear, nose, and throat doctor. But if you are a singer, you just may develop problems, like strained or swollen vocal cords. Sometimes, these problems are less serious and go away through complete vocal rest. (This means no talking or even whispering at all for a few days.) But then there are bad problems like polyps or nodules (also known as "nodes") on your vocal cords. Nodules respond to therapy, but polyps can be resistant to therapy and may require surgery, and that puts you out of business for quite some time.

Again, the best solution is prevention—learning to use the voice properly for voice conservation and for longevity. Voice teacher Ron Meixsell suggests that, for some people, "more damage is done when speaking than when singing. Many people don't realize they are yelling when trying to speak over loud music or other speakers." By the way, yelling and (believe it or not) whispering at *any time* is not a good idea, as both strain the vocal cords. Better to speak softly—not bad advice for anyone!

Occupational Hazards and Work-Related Injuries

Unfortunately, a too-common problem for musicians is hearing loss. This is particularly true for those who play amplified music. I can't tell you how many rock musicians have hearing loss—probably all of them, to some degree or another.

Pete Townshend of The Who, for example, has severe hearing loss now because his group was so loud (they were, in fact, once dubbed "The World's Loudest Rock Band"), and he didn't protect his hearing despite his doctors' warnings about the continuous exposure to those decibels. He also suffered terrifying earaches. Now, he rarely performs live because of the tinnitus (ringing in the ears) that plagues him. For Pete, this only diminishes with rest and a hiatus from loud sounds.[1]

Many young musicians don't think this could happen to them, and if it does, it will be so far down the road that they don't care now. They love their huge stacks of amps, cranked to the max. This is a big mistake. Beethoven notwithstanding, a musician's hearing is one of the most important assets he has. Anyone who has even sat in the audience at a rock concert has experienced the ringing in the ears afterward. This is a sign of hearing damage. Can you imagine the permanent destruction when exposed to this level of sound night after night, right onstage?

Some hearing loss may be inevitable with age, but you sure don't have to help it along. I would urge any musician who plays or is around loud music to wear earplugs consistently. There are various kinds that block out more or less sound. Experiment to find ones that work for you. If you can, make regular appointments with an audiologist to check on any deterioration of your hearing. Something can be done if it's caught early. Karen Sussman offers, "An audiologist can make custom-molded 'musician's earplugs,' which allow music and speech to be heard clearly, while reducing the decibel level."

Ron Meixsell relates this strange story, told in *The Conscious Ear*, a book by Alfred Tomatis. It tells of the great opera star Enrico Caruso, who had an operation that affected his Eustachian tube (a slender tube that connects the middle ear with the pharynx). It actually worked in Caruso's favor, as he was able to hear the higher overtones better, exactly the register where his tenor voice was singing. Conversely, hearing *loss* in any register can affect singing in that register. As Ron says, "The ear is the organ of singing."

For other work-related injuries, musicians may want to have a physical therapist and others handy in their address book. Some health hazards are

[1]Geoffrey Giuliano, *Behind Blue Eyes: The Life of Pete Townshend*, (New York: Dutton, 1996), 27, 159, 297.

carpal tunnel syndrome, tennis elbow, posture-related problems, backaches, and upper-body tension (neck and shoulders). Chiropractors are great for misaligned spines (are you listening, double bass players?). Massage therapists can ease aching muscles and headaches. Many people swear by the Alexander Method, which works on movement and posture. Ron Meixsell finds this method most helpful to both musicians and singers. Some of these occupational hazards can be prevented or cured by therapy, for the aim is to get you back onstage quickly. I have even tried acupuncture in conjunction with massage (successfully, I might add) for particularly stubborn back spasms.

I know most musicians fear arthritis the most, for this crippling disease can put an end to a career. Although there is no known cure at the present, there are remedies that can ease the pain and aid mobility. For instance, at the first signs of pain and stiffness in my hands, upon the advice of a physician I began taking glucosamine and chondroitin sulfate supplements (available without a prescription), which help maintain healthy joints, cartilage, and connective tissue. Some folks take non-steroidals such as ibuprofin or naproxyn for pain, but those with ulcers should take special heed, as these can cause internal bleeding. Seeking a health professional before any of these hazards become totally debilitating should be the goal. There are very few things sadder in this business than a musician's career that is cut short because of negligence, especially if something could have been done if the problem had only been caught in time.

Stress

Stress is a killer for anyone, but it is a demon that especially haunts artists. Being creative and usually sensitive sorts, we may act, react, approach, and feel life somewhat differently than most other folks. We are in a field that is not particularly valued or respected by our society—at least until we reach a certain level in our career, when and if we become "stars." In the beginning of (and sometimes throughout) our careers, we might suffer not only financially, with all the attendant problems that brings, but also from lack of respect, substance abuse, and other problems that come from marching to the beat of a different drummer. Symptoms that may start showing up are insomnia or other sleep disorders, physical pain like headache or muscle aches, and psychological disorders like depression, anger, and compulsions. We become much more vulnerable to illness and injury under stress, as our immune systems become weakened.

With regards to singers, Ron Meixsell observes,

> *Stress shows up in the voice; and when singing, the conflict that arises if you try and hide the effect only exacerbates the stress. The*

muscles in the throat are directly connected to the psyche. They will tighten and the larynx will rise, which will change the tonal quality. This can be alleviated through talking about what causes the stress in the first place, and by vocalizing.

Personally, I know that stress can be greatly debilitating. I almost lost my voice (or at least, could have done some damage) when, during an extremely extended difficult time of my life, I tried to sing with a stress-induced tightened throat. Luckily, I made it through because I was aware of what was going on, tried to reduce what stress I could, concentrated on good technique, and worked diligently with my vocal therapist.

One thing we must do to combat this killer is to recognize it before it becomes too debilitating or damaging. Once you recognize the symptoms and can eliminate medical causes through visits to your physician, you can tackle the problem and act to reduce the stress in your life. Once again, a proper diet, vigorous exercise, and adequate amounts of sleep go a long way in reducing stress.

But more than that, *we have to recognize our place and value in our society.* Artists are just as necessary to a civilized world as doctors and plumbers. We are the architects of emotion and beauty. We take feelings and ideas and sensations and spirit, and manifest them as one of humankind's greatest gifts—music. Don't let anyone tell you that what you are doing is insignificant or frivolous. It demeans our life's work and reduces it to mere entertainment. It is not. Much of the stress musicians feel may come from low self-esteem imposed by the outside world, and the inevitable hardships of the profession. It will be hard, sometimes, to stay the course, what with all the obstacles there are on this path, but if you can just keep this in front of you, your burdens will feel lighter: I believe that what we do is one of the most worthy endeavors that humans are capable of. Remember why you decided to make music in the first place—how much joy and meaning it brings into your own life, not to mention the lives of your audience. Through your talent, you can lift spirits, open minds, and move hearts. Remember to use your music to do that for yourself as well, as it "hath charms to soothe the savage breast." Use your music as your release and a relief.

Substance Abuse Issues

This is a topic that I have extremely strong feelings about. If illness or injury due to negligence makes me sad, substance abuse just makes me mad. This is something that musicians—and others—do to themselves and ostensibly have control over. It may be true that some people are just born with addictive personalities, but I do believe in free will. No one is forced to smoke, drink, or take drugs. With all the experience and knowledge we have these days about the dangers of these substances, and with all the endless stories of musicians dying young or destroying their lives and careers, why people would willingly choose to poison themselves is beyond me. But, I acknowledge that throughout the history of mankind, and probably into eternity, people will do all kinds of stupid and self-destructive things. It is just such a shame that anyone, especially people gifted with talent, should fall into this. But let us assume that this will ever be so. How to deal with this?

CIGARETTES

Smoking tobacco appears to be the "mildest" form of substance abuse. Many artists think smoking is very hip, but, of course, everyone nowadays knows better. Smokers just look clueless, totally unconscious. For singers, smoking can be a career-killer. It can ruin the voice at the least, and possibly give you throat, lung, mouth, or brain cancer at the worst. Joni Mitchell is an example of a beautiful voice altered by tobacco. George Harrison, a lifelong smoker, is another sad example. At age fifty-eight, his life, work, and great talent were cut short because of tobacco-induced cancer. Second-hand smoke is also deadly to nonsmokers. Luckily, now in many parts of the country, smoking is prohibited in restaurants and other places where musicians might work. I now refuse to sing in a room where there is smoking, for my health and for my voice. I won't ride in a car with someone smoking, nor are people allowed to smoke in my house. Years ago, I would have been viewed as a crank (well, years ago I wouldn't have been as aware of the dangers and therefore wouldn't have been so adamant), but these days more and more people are doing the same to protect themselves and their loved ones. There are image issues as well. For instance, nowadays my band and I perform mainly for children and families. My drummer, who is a very considerate heavy smoker, doesn't smoke anywhere around me, in sight of the audience, or even anywhere on the premises of our performances. I, of course, can't control what he does in the privacy of his own space, but as the band leader I can ask that we all watch our public selves, especially since one of our shows is about substance abuse prevention!

DRUGS AND ALCOHOL

Regarding substance abuse, there are separate issues when one is a soloist versus when one is working with a band or as part of a larger group. As a soloist, you would guess that abusing substances would only affect yourself. But that, of course, is not true. The abuser's family, friends, and business associates are also affected. Too many wonderfully talented singers and solo musicians have had their careers and lives cut short by cancer, liver damage, or drug abuse. Had it only affected them, that would be shame enough, but what about people who were depending on them? Because they are more artistically "isolated," soloists especially need to surround themselves with *someone* trusted who will be truthful and protective of them, and they need to heed this person's advice as a "reality check." A soloist does herself no favors if she is insulated by sycophants.

In a group, one person can bring the entire band disaster, either by hurting her own health or by incurring legal problems, thus jeopardizing the future of the band. If one is serious about having a long career in music, the temptations are certainly there and must be dealt with. I would think twice about being in a group with someone who has serious substance abuse issues, no matter how good a friend she may be, or how fantastic a musician. I would hesitate to tie my future with someone so self-destructive. Think of a musical group as all being copilots—would you want your alcoholic or druggy friend to be flying your jet? You could all crash together.

Look, I know that smoking, drinking, and drugs are a large part of the whole music scene and the persona of "musician." In fact, among certain genres (blues, rock and roll, and rap come to mind instantly) it is almost *de rigueur*. Part of the image and legend of many of our musical heroes is built on booze and drugs. But you don't have to buy into that stereotype. So what if "all musicians" use? You don't have to and you won't be ostracized by those who really matter if you don't. After all, don't we all tell our kids to avoid peer pressure when confronted with questionable behavior? The important thing is to be strong and true unto yourself and your art. If you really feel using substances truly enhances your life and art, be sure your use is moderate. You know you have a problem if it begins to negatively affect your work or your personal life.

The music world is rife with stories of drugs and alcohol crashing careers. Be smart—don't be a casualty. You have worked too long and too hard to ruin your career, or that of your associates and friends.

SEEKING HELP

If you or another member of your group has a problem, the kindest thing you could do is try to get help. Addiction is not something that a lot of people can deal with on their own. Of course, there are many organizations, many rehab clinics, many therapists. But the abuser has to *want* to kick. Try and do it not only for yourself but for your loved ones and for your art.

What if someone can't, or doesn't want to, and you all have to live with it? As I mentioned above, there are those who believe that drinking or drugs actually enhance their art and performance, and it's part of the whole musician scene. For example, whether it's true or not, there is a stereotype that many blues musicians and singers are raging alcoholics—perhaps they feel it helps their sound and make their blues more authentic. But if you don't want this as part of *your* career, make it abundantly clear that *their* addictions must not affect your professional life. Whatever they want to do on their own time is their business, but if they appear onstage drunk or high, it becomes everyone's business. As a performing artist, you are very much in public when you work. Again, some circles may consider it "cool" to be looped onstage—in fact, it may be part of their image. But as we all know, time and time again, it proves fatal: to careers, to artists, to families. There are clinics and organizations available that offer support and guidance to those affected by a close family member or friend who is ill from substance abuse; Al Anon is one. Look in your phone directory or go on the Internet to find others in your area.

I can't say it enough: If you are serious about a long career in music, lose the heavy alcohol and drugs. Keith Richards may be one lucky guy (and *he* began to look like death warmed over too early), but not many can escape the ravages these poisons can inflict. The sooner we can kick the idea that these substances are "cool" and worth their price, the better for us all.

Sex

I hesitate to write about this because it is even more personal than the topic above, but it does fall into the health category. I am definitely not a prude, and without getting into moral issues, nowadays casual sex can kill. Musicians seem to attract groupies, so casual sex is really easily available. Especially for touring musicians, life can get lonely and boring, and those backstage cuties are so tempting. I know that committed relationships have sprung from fan-musician liaisons (witness Paul and Linda McCartney), and that's cool. But it's a miracle that someone like Elton John or Mick Jagger, both of whom have admitted to countless sexual partners, hasn't contracted anything worse than the clap. Elton himself says he's amazed he's escaped AIDS, and now works tirelessly as a fund- and consciousness-raiser for that cause.

It's a fact that part of the whole musician/rock star thing is tons of available and willing women and men. Once again, you can choose to be part of that, or not. When temptation rears its pretty head, just remember the whole mortality thing. It's a whole new ballgame out there.

Chapter 18
Insurance

Ugh, another one of those dry topics we artists would rather not think about. But like other topics throughout this book, insurance is something we not only ought to *think* about, but actually *act on*. It's important to be smart and think ahead, anticipating unfortunate or even disastrous occurrences. It's protection for us, our instruments and other possessions, our career, and our loved ones. People doing "straight" work often are protected through their jobs—their employers might pay for some insurance. But we musicians are part of that legion of self-employed folks who, although enjoying a great deal of independence and work satisfaction, also must give *themselves* the benefits that a normal job would automatically bestow.

Now, I know the big issue comes down to, "I would have insurance of all kinds if only I could afford it." Music is a notoriously poor-paying profession until you hit a certain level, and I know many full-time pros who don't even carry any insurance of any kind. This is tempting fate. How does one pay for the "frill" of insurance when many musicians can barely make the rent?

Health Insurance

I consider health insurance to be one of the necessities of life, like food and housing. I don't want to skimp here and do without, because if I am sick or injured, I am out of work, and hey, unlike my brethren at IBM, I don't get sick leave! Not only might I incur medical expenses, but I lose income as well. I want to stay as healthy as possible in order to keep working, or, if I do get sick or injured, I want good healthcare in order to return to work as quickly as possible. Again, I don't want to be bankrupted by either loss of income or sky-high hospitalization and doctor bills. I have heard stories over and over again about famous and not-so-famous musicians who have gotten seriously sick or injured, yet didn't have any insurance. They had to rely on relatives or the kindness of friends who organized benefit concerts for them to pay their bills. This could have been prevented with a little foresight and planning.

One easy way to be covered for health insurance is to be married or otherwise closely related to someone who is already covered by his job. This is the cheapest way to go because you don't have to pay *anything* usually (unless you consider the costs of being married ...); spouses and kids are covered if the policy's a good one. However, if your spouse or parent (if you are a dependent) isn't covered, if his policy doesn't cover you, if you are unmarried, or if you don't have a regular job that covers you, then it's up to you to seek your own policy.

There are organizations you can join (see appendix B) which, for the price of membership, give you the opportunity for low-cost benefits such as health and life insurance, lower travel fares, and so forth. Your local musician's union does the same thing (see chapter 16). Look in your local white pages or on the Internet for the one nearest you. If you own your own business (and self-employed musicians do), you can join the Small Business Service Bureau (SBSB), which has many wonderful benefits for their small membership fee. Investigate which organizations offer what, and then investigate whatever health insurance plans they may offer, if they give a choice. Then go visit facilities, and ask questions about services and fees. If given a choice, you may want a plan that has higher deductibles in exchange for lower premiums. You really want health insurance for the catastrophic events, like serious illness or injury. Most people can handle the smaller expenses.

In New York, my husband and I belong to an HMO, bought through the SBSB. Again, by joining this or a similar organization, you can reap the benefits of a group policy, which is cheaper than getting an individual one on your own. My HMO has the lowest premiums I've found in my area, their facilities are modern and well-equipped, and the service isn't bad. I actually like my doctors for routine checkups or urgent care (there is a small co-pay for each visit). The times I've needed to go to the emergency room at various hospitals around the country, my HMO covered everything completely. This is great for touring musicians. Make sure your plan covers out-of-state emergencies, especially if you tour. I consider the premiums that my husband and I pay to be just part of our overall living expenses. We skimp in other areas, but not on our health. Remember, premiums may be tax deductible; consult your tax advisor.

If you don't want to join an HMO or there isn't one available in your area, you could try a Web site like *www.quotesmith.com*, which searches for the lowest quote on many different things, one of which is independent insurance policies.

If you are truly broke and yet determined to not get a "real job" with its benefits (or are working part-time, which usually doesn't give bennies), investigate low-cost clinics in your area. Most cities and many suburban and rural areas have *some* kind of clinic for lower-income folks, on a pay-as-you-go basis. If you need to see a doctor, either for something routine or for more serious reasons and you don't have insurance, many will either barter, lower their fees somewhat, or allow you to pay over time if you can work out some agreement.

Instrument Insurance

Here is something most of us don't think about until it truly is too late. But how many horror stories have *you* heard about musicians losing their instruments, or instruments getting stolen or destroyed? This can be devastating to an artist, especially those of us who have very good, expensive ones that we are emotionally attached to.

So, what about instrument insurance? A good policy means a damaged instrument will be repaired or replaced at minimal cost to you, and it covers the loss of value of a valuable instrument once repaired. Once again, music-oriented organizations such as the union may offer this. It may come as a shock—it did to me!—but your car insurance won't cover your instrument, even if damaged or stolen from your vehicle. You will find, if you own a home, that your homeowner's policy also will *not* cover instruments if you use them to make a living (or even just perform periodically for money) and take them out of the house. You would need a rider or some such separate coverage, which can be costly. Furthermore, many business insurance policies will not cover professional musicians' instruments, and those that do require a comprehensive list and high premiums. You would have to check with your agent about this (see the section on business liability insurance, below).

All instrument insurance that I've seen requires you to make a comprehensive and detailed list of all items you wish to be covered, down to the year of make, model, value (you may need to pay someone to appraise them), and serial number. It's a good idea to have photos or videos of each one as well, kept in a secure place. If you can, you should try to get insurance to cover the *replacement value* of your instrument. All fine instruments appreciate in value, and you would be very sad if the insurance payment did not afford you the same quality instrument, worth what the lost one was in today's dollars.

Read the whole policy carefully—you want to be able to pick your own repairperson, or, in case of total destruction or loss, your own replacement instrument. Also check the "exclusion of coverage," for events such as theft from a vehicle or damage due to weather, which can void your protection.

Charles Rufino, the violinmaker we met in chapter 4, advises getting devaluation coverage, which provides compensation for permanent loss of value after restoration in the case of severe damage. He advises,

> *Homeowner policies, business policies, and individual music policies generally do not have a devaluation clause, and therefore do not provide such coverage; it has to be added to the policy specifically. Insurance adjusters are not comfortable with the concept of devaluation, so it needs to be clearly spelled out for them in the policy. If your instrument is of moderate value, this coverage may not be necessary for you, but if you have owned a nice instrument for many years, please consider that it may have appreciated considerably in value.*

One company that I know of, Clarion Associates, Inc. (see appendix B) *solely* insures musical instruments. It is a twenty-five-year-old company and very reputable. It has been my experience that using companies like Clarion is the best way to go with regards to cost and comprehensive coverage, over a homeowner's, business, or some other kind of policy. Since they specialize only in musical instruments, they are knowledgeable about all the vagaries of this kind of insurance.

Business Liability Insurance

Why, you might wonder, would a musician need business liability insurance? Because we are living in a litigious society and if someone can sue someone over something, he will. What if you, unintentionally or not, slander someone in an introduction or in song? What if someone accuses you of plagiarism? What if you invite an audience member onstage with you and he falls and breaks a bone? (Good time here to remind you to duct tape down all loose cords onstage, for everyone's safety.) What if there's a brawl in your orchestra and you break someone's jaw and her $100,000 violin? Whatever weird scenario you can think of, someone will sue over a weirder one. Again, you are in public, things happen, and you want to protect your assets and your business from unforeseen misfortune and big disasters. This is especially true if you have a lot to lose, like a house or expensive instruments. Not everything is covered in every instance, so individual policies must be checked for exclusions like personal injury, plagiarism, slander, and so forth.

How much liability should you carry? Well, you need to sit down and figure out how much your personal assets are worth, plus your business assets. If you are not incorporated and someone sues you, he can go after *all* your assets. This is the main reason I incorporated. With a subchapter S corporation, I keep my business entity and assets separate from my personal. I have all incoming checks written to the corporation's name. Likewise, all my promo refers to that name, in addition to my own. If someone were to sue, he would sue my corporation, not me; he could not touch my house.

Again, look, ask, and shop around, especially in trade magazines and organizations, for business insurance with low premiums. Once again, as with health insurance, you might want to opt for high deductibles to get those lower premiums.

Life Insurance

Here is another kind of insurance that you may think is more or less optional. Many people, especially musicians who often don't look into such practical, far-in-the-future matters, think of life insurance as something that only the well-off can afford or even need. But if you have dependants, you probably want to protect them once you are gone. Although I am not an actuary, and as much as I hate to admit it, musicians' mortality rates may be higher than your average professional's, as we tend to be on the road more and take worse care of ourselves for whatever reasons. There's the whole alcohol, suicide, and drugs thing that seems to be endemic to musicians, too. Some insurance companies won't even touch you if you say you are a professional musician. But anyway, if you have a will (and you should if you have dependants and assets you care about, as covered in the Legal Matters chapter) you may also want life insurance … if for no other reason than that it forces you to think about who and what really matters, and how much!

This section is not meant to be a comprehensive treatise on all the different kinds of life insurance—you should have an agent explain the differences between term, whole life, and so on. But it is very reassuring to have *some kind* of life insurance if you have a family that would be financially hurt by your death.

Just briefly and as a point of reference, *term insurance* is the cheapest kind—almost anyone can afford it, especially if you sign up when young and healthy. Your beneficiary doesn't collect unless and until you die, and until then, you "lose" your money. It's like car insurance—you'd rather not use it, thank you very much. It provides protection for a limited period of time, and premiums could rise every year. Or it can be bought, depending on the regulations of the state you live in, for a period ranging anywhere from five to thirty years at a level premium. Either way, it builds no cash value and has no permanent worth.

On the other hand, there is *permanent insurance*, which provides for a tax-deferred build-up of cash values over the life of the contract. It's much pricier than term, but it acts like a forced savings account that you can draw on later in life—you don't need to die to benefit from what you've paid in. Most plans of this sort provide for a payment of a level premium. For those that don't, increases in premiums are usually limited in both amount and duration. *Whole* or *universal life insurance* is a kind of permanent insurance. This kind offers flexible premium payments, an adjustable death benefit, and cash values which include paid interest that is in line with current interest rates. *Variable life insurance* is similar to universal, but the cash values are invested in an equity portfolio, like a mutual fund or bonds. You can usually switch to another portfolio, with some limitations. If you're like me, your eyes are glazing over with incomprehension at this point. But only you, with the advice of your insurance broker, can make the decision about what kind of insurance is ultimately best for you.

During the application process for life insurance, you may be asked to submit to a basic medical exam (blood pressure, blood and urine samples, and the like) and fill out questionnaires. It's important that you are honest about any personal or family history of disease or disability, or drug, tobacco, or alcohol use. Your premiums will be higher if you do have a problematic history, or the company may even deny your application. But better that than to be found fraudulent. That's my opinion based on my "honesty is always the best policy" philosophy.

Disability Insurance

Here, again, is another "optional" kind of insurance, but one that I think *everyone*, especially musicians in particular, should have. This is because it's much more likely, as we age, that we will become disabled before we die. For example, for a male aged forty, long-term disability is *2.9 times more likely than death*.[1] We rely on our bodies and our health in some ways even more than most professionals—after all, a lawyer can still argue a case with a broken hand, and doctors can continue to work with a vocal disability. But short-term or permanent disabilities like these can devastate a musician or singer,

[1] Donald F. Cady, *1999 Field Guide to Estate Planning, Business Planning, and Employee Benefits*, Cincinnati, Ohio: National Underwriter, 1999.

sometimes with dire emotional and financial consequences. Consider this: If you become disabled, your income will fall and your expenses will rise. Disability insurance attempts to make up for some loss of income during the time you are unable to work at your present profession. You might also want to get a waiver of premium rider on your life insurance policy if you have one, which will provide for payment of your premiums after a stated period of disability.

Workman's compensation is a form of disability insurance, except that you must have become disabled *while working*. Unfortunately, disability insurance rarely covers all that you will lose, *plus* all the additional expenses if such an occurrence happens, so it's a good idea to have other plans in mind to tide you over. It really is just a supplement, but as anyone who has barely eked out a living knows, every little bit does help.

So there you have most kinds of insurance that you may need. As I mentioned, some are more crucial than others; the more optional ones can wait until you are making a comfortable living. But other than taxes, I can think of no bigger business expenses that are so necessary. I am constantly amazed at how much of my operating budget goes to all the different kinds of insurance I carry. But it all boils down to this—how much peace of mind do you want, and, in the very worst-case scenario, what will you need to achieve that peace for you and your loved ones?

Chapter 19

Songwriters and Composers

This chapter is specifically aimed towards those who write music. There is big money to be made for the writers of jingles, pop songs, movie scores, and more. In fact, legend has it that Irving Berlin, from the royalties from *one song alone* in his vast catalog, "White Christmas," earned about $50,000 per year! If that's not incentive enough to get on your instrument and pick up a pen, I don't know what is! Plus, there is a certain thrill a composer gets when a piece of hers is aired on the radio or performed live onstage. It's like having children, who will go out into the world and live on after you are gone. There are particular aspects of the music business that these creative people need to know about, including more contracts, rights, and opportunities.

Copyrights

A copyright is a legal recognition of a composer's (or author's or artist's—anyone who creates) ownership of a work and thus gives him legal exclusive right to produce, publish, or sell that work. If you write a song or some other musical piece, you'll want to protect your right to that piece by copyrighting it either formally or informally. Gary Roth, Assistant Vice President of Legal and Business Affairs of BMI, explains,

> *To obtain legal protection, the work must be fixed in a tangible medium of expression, meaning written down or recorded on tape, CD, etc. Although it is not required for protection, you should put a "c" in a circle (©) or the word "copyright," the date of creation (or first publication if published), and your name on any printed or recorded version of the work. Registration of your copyright is a separate matter.*

In order to collect license royalties or sue for infringement, you must register it with the Copyright Office. You can contact them at: U.S. Copyright Office, Library of Congress, 101 Independence Ave. SE, Washington, DC; or call (202) 707–9100. For questions, call (202) 707–5959. You can also go to their Web site (*www.copyright.gov*) and print out the forms—faster than getting them through the mail. To see what these forms look like, refer to the appendix A. For registering songs or other musical compositions, you will need to use form PA. The fee for each submission as of this printing is $30, but check the Web site for more up-to-date information.

You can imagine that if you are a prolific writer, this could add up to quite a hefty sum. I get past this by waiting until December, then copyrighting *all* the songs that I wrote during the year *together* on one form. Under the line "Title of this work," I put something like, "Songs written in 2002"; under "Previous or alternative titles," I put all the titles of the individual songs. If you have many songs that won't fit in the small space, you can use the continuation sheet offered on the Web site. But in this way, I can gang the songs under one title and have to pay only one fee per year. Now, if I ever want to look up or retrieve a song from the office, I will have to know the year I wrote or copyrighted it. No problem—just look at the copyright mark you printed on all versions of the song. Again, this collective registration only indexes your songs by the *collective title*; you would need to complete a form CA and pay another fee if you want to get them indexed individually.

It's been said by those who know, *Never give up your copyrights!* There is a legend about the hit song "Feelings." It seems that the songwriter, some poor, unknown slob who barely had two coins to rub together, sold his song for a mere few hundred dollars. Of course, it went on to be a huge hit and is one of those chestnuts you hear a million times in elevators and dentists' offices, generating untold millions of dollars in royalties. But because the songwriter sold his copyright, *he didn't earn a dime* beyond the initial amount the song sold for. Very sad, but avoidable. It doesn't have to happen to you.

For registering copyrights for recordings, you will need Form SR. You want to register your recordings (cassettes, CDs) for the same reasons that you copyright your music—to give you exclusive rights to the *sound recording*. All this becomes important once you start publishing your work—or distributing it to the public. And it also becomes important once your compositions start earning royalties, or in instances of claims of infringement or plagiarism. Once you've registered the recording, you would put the symbol "P" in a circle (for the sound recording) and "C" in its own circle (for any visuals, like lyrics, artwork, and text on the inserts), the date of publication, and then the copyright holder's name on the recording medium (cassette or CD), as well as on the cover art.

In the United States, the duration of copyright on works created after January 1, 1978, is for the life of the last surviving author plus seventy years. For works created between January 1, 1964, and December 31, 1977, the protection is for twenty-eight years. After that expires, there is an automatic renewal for another sixty-seven years, for a total of ninety-five years. Once the copyright expires, anyone can use the song for free as it goes into the public domain.

Publishing

Publishing simply means that a work is distributed for sale to the public. It can be in a written form such as sheet music, or in recorded form such as on a cassette or CD. Just as you can be your own record company, you can be your own publisher, or you can use an established one. If you opt to self-publish, you'll need to choose a name for your company. If you belong to BMI, ASCAP, or SESAC (see below, under "Performance Royalties"), they will research the name you've chosen to make sure it hasn't already been taken. Or you could hire an attorney to do that for you. That's about all it takes to self-publish. Now, whenever you distribute your work, either through recordings or on the printed page, you will identify the publisher (your company's name) on the work along with your copyright information. This allows people to know that your work is protected and also lets them know whom to contact in case they want to record or otherwise use the work. The advantage to this path is that you get to keep 100 percent of the publishing royalties. The disadvantage to this is, if your song doesn't get out into the world much, 100 percent of nothing is … nothing.

Or, you may choose to find an outside publisher. There are lots of advantages to this. A good publisher will shop your music to other artists who may record it, thus giving you more exposure and royalties than you would otherwise be able to get on your own. The publisher might publish sheet music for you, another source of revenue. And it will do all the administrative work needed if someone else records your music. In exchange for all this, *the publisher* keeps 100 percent of the publishing royalties. If it's a hit song, that share is substantial.

A third option is to share the publishing with an outside house. The advantage of this is that you share in the publishing royalties. In some genres like country and Latin music, not many publishers will consent to this, because if they are doing all the work in trying to get your songs out there, they want to keep 100 percent of the publishing royalties. However, in rock, pop, and R&B music, these split-fee arrangements are quite common. You may be able to work out an administration deal, where the publisher only gets a fee (usually 15 to 20 percent of the publishing) to administer if you have prior releases, but such agreements will generally command little or no up-front advance money. Remember, if you own the writer's copyright, you get 100 percent of *those* royalties.

As in a managerial or recording contract, a clause that you might want to get included in a publishing contract is: If the publisher is not successful in getting your song recorded or otherwise "out there," you get all publishing rights back after a certain length of time—preferably a short one.

Royalties

There are different kinds of royalties that composers need to know about. Royalties are monies that get paid to the writers when their work is sold (as on a CD) or used in some fashion (aired on the radio). But in order to collect these royalties, you need to have some proof or document that you (a) wrote the piece and (b) have allowed its use. We already discussed the copyright, which takes care of point (a); let's take a look at the documents needed for point (b). They are:

MECHANICAL ROYALTIES

When someone else records your music for sale, you are entitled, as the creator of that piece of music, to a share of the proceeds of that sale. Up until the time that *someone* records that piece for the first time (and that someone might be you yourself), another person would have to get your (the copyright holder's) permission to record your work. You may refuse that permission. If you do give your permission, the recording artist would need to get a *mechanical license* (for the first-time use or release of a composition) from you stipulating the terms of the usage, including the royalty rate.

However, once it's been recorded, the song is fair game for anyone else to record, with or without your permission. The recording artists will then need to get from you a *compulsory mechanical license*, which is what it's called after the first recording. Any new recordings of a composition must be faithful to the basic melody and fundamental character of the work; otherwise, if there are any changes, it would be considered a *derivative work* and would require the publisher's approval. A compulsory mechanical license is valid as long as the recording company pays the fees. If it fails to, the license can be revoked.

As of this writing, in the United States the statutory rate is 8 cents per unit sold per song *or* 1.55 cents per minute or fraction of a minute of the playing time of the song, whichever is greater. However, you are free to nego-tiate any rate you can get. Let's say the rate you agree on is 7 cents per piece sold instead. If the other person sells, say, five thousand copies per year, you would get $350 for that year.

The license should also state when or how often the royalties should be paid. The Harry Fox Agency is an arm of the National Music Publishers Association, and as such is the primary organization that specifically licenses, monitors, collects, and disperses these royalties. But if you're at a low level, you can do it yourself for your own work. Mechanical royalties are paid from the record company to the publisher (which might be you), who then in turn pays usually 50 percent to the songwriter. The writer's percentage is spelled out in the agreement he or she signed with the publisher. If the Harry Fox Agency does the administering, the publisher is charged 4.5 percent of the gross mechanical royalties collected.

PERFORMANCE ROYALTIES

If your work gets played over the radio, TV, or Muzak, you are entitled to per-formance royalties. There are still, as of this writing, disputes over the use over the Internet, but to *my* thinking performance royalties should also apply there. In order to get these royalties, you need to join one of the performance rights societies as a writer, and separately as a publisher if you are self-publishing. They are: ASCAP, BMI, and SESAC (see appendix B for contact informa-tion). "BMI will allow you to collect the publisher's share through your writer account without joining separately as a publisher," Gary Roth informs me, wherein you will get "200 percent" of the royalties—i.e., 100 percent of the writer's share of royalties, and 100 percent of the publisher's share. The other two societies may also have a similar deal. Each society has disadvantages and advantages—research each before deciding to sign with any of them.

What they do is monitor the use of their members' songs over the air and in public places such as restaurants. This is done by complicated methods, which, frankly, I have never understood, but it works to a lesser or greater extent. Every time your work, no matter who performs it, is aired, the publisher and the writer get royalties. It's a small amount, but it can add up really fast. Just think of how many times a day you hear a hit song on your favorite radio station. Multiply it by the thousands of stations in the country, then by the world (foreign royalty rates work differently), then by the number of days, weeks, months, or years it continues to get airplay. You can see how writers of hit songs can live extremely comfortably just on royalties alone.

When you or someone else records your music, register *each song* with your society. For instance, BMI will send you work registration forms, which you fill out—one for each song that might get publicly performed. On it, you will put the writer's name as well as the publisher's name. If there is more than one writer, put all the names. The publisher and writer might be the same entity (your company) if you self-publish, or you might have sold the publishing rights. If you've done the latter, you will have to assign the copyrights, but you get a contract for royalties, where you might get a 50/50 split of the publishing. This agreement may be in perpetuity, or you can set a limit on the terms. However, copyright laws as of this writing state that these assignments made since January 1, 1978, will terminate thirty-five years from publication *or* forty years after the execution of the transfer.

Performance royalties will be split 50/50 between the writers and the publishers (or, according to the lingo, 100 percent/100 percent = writer/publisher). Upon copyright, all writers share the writing and publishing rights, in the percentage share that they agree upon. For example, let's say they agree that Writer A gets 30 percent and Writer B gets 70 percent. On the work registration form, you will put the percentage share that each writer and publisher gets. If one writer assigns or transfers his publishing to a publishing company, he will then give up whatever *his* percentage of publishing he has assigned. Using the example above, let's say Writer B splits his publishing 50/50 with XYZ Publishing, but Writer A keeps 100 percent of her publishing. Therefore, Writer A gets 30 percent of the writing royalties and 30 percent of the publishing, and Writer B gets 70 percent of the writing royalties and 35 percent of the publishing (50 percent of his 70 percent), while XYZ Publishing gets a 35 percent publishing royalty.

To complicate matters, if you as a writer collaborate with another writer who is affiliated with a different performing rights society, each writer's publisher must belong to the same society as its writer. In addition, each writer's total writer's share must be the same as the total of his publisher's shares. Therefore, let's take the same example as above, except that Writer A is from ASCAP and Writer B is from BMI. Again, Writer A would earn 30 percent of writer's royalties and 100 percent of publishing, Writer B would earn 70 percent of writing and 35 percent of publishing, and XYZ Publishers (who must be a BMI affiliate) gets 35 percent of publishing. If you *really* want to get crazy, there can be *many* publishers, but each writer can only assign his publishing share *up to the same share of his writing royalties* to his publishers. Each society (BMI, ASCAP, or SESAC) pays its own members.

SYNCHRONIZATION

Gary Roth defines this as "the fee a copyright owner (publisher) is entitled to receive when his or her work is incorporated onto a soundtrack (synchronized with the video)." Almost all movie and TV shows use music. *Someone* had to write it. In addition to whatever fee the composer gets to initially write the music, he or she also gets royalties every time it's aired. Again, this can add up to a huge amount, especially for a hit TV show, which may then go to syndication, or for a movie that goes to video.

OTHER ROYALTIES

Royalties from the sale of sheet music, advertisements, the Internet, CD-ROM, and DVDs go to the publisher, who again in turn pays the writers' share.

Chapter 20
When the Performing Gets Old

Even though the stars in your eyes may have only begun to shine—the gigs are just starting to fill your calendar, and you're just now getting the hang of going on the road for shows in a new town—you may want to give the future some thought *right now*, if you want to continue making some kind of living in music. Someday, the glamour of performing may wear thin, or it's no longer viable. Somehow, I don't see myself jumping around onstage when I am sixty-five. Hey, but who knows—look at Mick Jagger! No signs of slowing down there. And in some fields of music you *can* get away with being an "old codger" performing. In the classical or jazz worlds, not only do you *not* look like an idiot, but you are actually more respected. However, if you are a rock or pop musician, figure on moving on somehow when you get older. There are so many other avenues open, if we only think outside the box. Here are some of my thoughts:

Teach Music
It takes a very special personality to be able to impart knowledge of the art to someone else. Patience is a big plus, as well as a good sense of humor and a generally charismatic way with people. My own dear husband has been teaching guitar for over thirty years in addition to maintaining his full and hectic performance schedule. He loves teaching and excels at it, and his students adore him. Teaching music privately has allowed him to keep his hand in music, stay current with musical trends, and have a stable income. It also allows for a family life, since we don't have to travel constantly. He is very good with all ages, from the very young (he takes pupils as young as six-year-olds) to the not-so-young retirees.

You can have your own private practice and make excellent money, keeping most (after taxes) for yourself because your expenses will be relatively low. You would need a private, quiet space for your studio, which could be in your home.

The downside of private teaching is that you have to do all the administrative duties (scheduling, billing, advertising, and so forth) yourself unless you have help. Plus, it can take years to build up your roster of students to a point where you can live off it full time. An alternative is that you could teach through a music store. If you choose this route, you will have to split your fee with the store, but you will not have the hassle of the administrative stuff and you might be handed a nearly full roster right away. Music conservatories, universities, adult education, and other kinds of educational institutions also offer an outlet to teach. With some of these options, you will probably need a degree of some sort, unless you are Itzhak Perlman.

By the way, if you don't want to teach formally, you can mentor a rising young talent. Newcomers to the business can benefit from your years of experience and sage advice, and in exchange, you'll be enjoying one of the most fulfilling roles one can take, especially later in life.

Represent or Manage Others

You could use all the years of expertise you gained running your own career for the good of other musicians you admire, respect, and support. True, you may not be making music yourself, but you will be helping to put wonderful music that you love out into the world, and that's no small thing. Who else knows better the vagaries and pitfalls of the music business than someone who's been through all the ups and downs herself? I am sure that during your travels you've met extremely talented musicians without representation, who are worthy of a professional career but who can't seem to get there alone. You remember what that's like, right? Approach them with your expertise, offer to work with them for a limited time to see if you can make things click with each other. You might be the next Brian Epstein! Another tactic is to approach an established agency and explain that you have extensive experience in the music industry repping yourself—the agency might be interested in taking you on since you will need very little training.

Join a Group

This could be anything from a theatre or community orchestra to a contra dance band. Change the style that you have been playing, and it opens up a whole world of possibilities, maybe even another career. You may have to start almost from scratch again, but don't discount the value of the reputation you might have built up in your community. You might have to supplement this new livelihood with other kinds of work until (or if) it takes off again. But, in exchange, the pressure on you might be less in a larger or more-established group.

Change Gears

Maybe think about being an arranger, or a musical director for a group or a theatre. If you can write, offer your services as a transcriber (although now, with all sorts of computer programs, most musicians don't even need to know how to write and have no need of a transcriber). Also think of "alternative" audiences—kids, seniors, prisoners—for whom you can develop music programs or concerts, targeting these neglected populations. You don't have to be a rock star performing for screaming teens or twenty-somethings to be fulfilled and appreciated. And you won't need to look forever youthful, either. The opera star Beverly Sills, who can no longer thrill audiences with her gorgeous voice like she used to, went on to serve as general director of the New York City Opera and as chairman of Lincoln Center, guiding them to greater heights with her knowledge of the business and love of the art form.

Own or Manage a Music Store

This is some musicians' dream! And some musicians' nightmare. For those who succeed and love it, they can be surrounded by beautiful instruments all day and, during the slow times, actually get to play them. But be prepared to have to listen to a lot of noise while customers try out various instruments, and have a *very* good head for business. Having good people skills doesn't hurt, either. Think of all the interesting musicians you can meet this way— Paul McCartney needs to buy his basses *somewhere*! You could specialize in your favorite kind of music, too. I know of wonderful stores just for exotic, unusual, and wonderful instruments from around the world. Or, you could just be a dealer in specific instruments such as vintage guitars, acoustic folk instruments, or percussion. But until you become known far and wide, it may be difficult for a specialty store to survive in a small community. Therefore, most community music stores cater to the school band and orchestra crowd, with parents wanting lower-end instruments so their kids can experience music. Depending on where your head is at, this could be a good thing, or not. If you think in too-narrow terms, your business may not survive. So, on the other hand, diversity can be a real plus. Think of all the good your store will bring to your town in terms of helping to put music into the world.

It's not for everyone, however. William "Willie Steel" Casey, a fixture on the Long Island music scene, offers his story. After years of being a professional musician, he decided to open his own music store when his daughter was born. He wanted to be a "stay-at-home dad," but figured if he had a store she could be a "stay-at-the-store" kid. He figured the store would become his main income, and he could still perform his music, earn extra income, and be a dad all at the same time. He did have ten years experience in music retail as well. However, he says, rather than having his performance income supplement the store, it turned out to be *the other way around!* He does admit that his experience is atypical, and says it's probably due to his wanting to play guitar more than run a business. He also doesn't want to deal with computers and the Internet, which he feels have totally changed the climate for brick-and-mortar businesses. But for those businesses that were established and successful before the Internet became so prominent, or who can incorporate it into their traditional methods, running a store can be a fulfilling career in which a musician can flourish. Furthermore, Willie says that having a business legitimizes him with the community much more than when he was "just" a musician. Let's face it, we usually don't have the most sterling image! Owning a business has allowed him to join NAMM (National Association of Musical Merchants), which gives him innumerable perks such as lower airfares, car rentals, and cell phone service, as well as those coveted benefits like health insurance and low interest loans. For those contemplating owning a music store, Willie advises,

> *Don't do it unless you have a lot of money behind you, as you will be competing against those businesses on the Web as well as the big chain stores. Your community needs to support you, too. But the advantages to me are, if I have a gig or need to go to my daughter's teacher conference, I can just close the store. I can do what I want; I am my own boss.*

Own or Manage a Music Venue

You could be that rare club owner who appreciates musicians and treats them with respect and pays well at the same time. This is a wonderful way to promote the kind of music you would like to see live on. It is a very hard business, though, as you can imagine. You may need to acquire the proper permits and licenses for such a venture; scout out a location, preferably in a well-traveled area with plenty of parking or foot traffic; design and build the interior so that it is conducive to the kind of music and crowd you will be getting; purchase or lease furniture and equipment not only for seating and a stage but also for sound and lights, and a bar if necessary. Will you be serving food? That presents a whole other set of challenges. Then you have to book your acts, publicize your events and venue, hire a staff … it's a big, big project, but could be very rewarding. For example, some venues have become famous in their own right, like New York's Bitter End and the Blue Note, or San Francisco's Hungry i. You could be helping to shape musical tastes and promote the kind of sounds you love.

Own or Manage a Record Label or Recording Studio

With digital technology being what it is nowadays, almost anyone can record a CD. There are musicians who have tired of performing and recording themselves, but have all kinds of expertise when it comes to producing. If you are such a person and want to start a studio, chances are you already have some equipment. Your location should be accessible and soundproof. If it's in a residential area, you might want to talk to your neighbors to explain all the strange folks who will be coming and going at all hours of the day and night. Check with your local laws governing the legality of having such a business in your home. Your expenses will be less if it's in your home, but think of the intrusions to your family life.

If you don't yet have equipment, take courses, pick brains, and acquire as much knowledge about a recording studio as you can *before* you invest. Technology changes so much and is so expensive that you don't want to make costly mistakes. Promoting your studio will take time and money too.

If you want to be your own label, it requires registering the name of your label as a business with the proper authorities in your state, finding your artists and recording them, finding (or being) the producers, studio musicians, cover artists, manufacturers, distributors … on and on. There is much more than can be discussed in a book like this, but many artists have traveled this route, and you can, too.

Produce Other Artists or Music Events

Again, using the knowledge you've amassed through your own career, guide others through the mire. Producers work in recording studios, on radio and TV, and in theatres. You could be the next Bill Graham! You should know the music business (and *enjoy* the business end) inside and out. Your musical chops and sensibilities should be impeccable and your reputation respected. If you are producing events, you need to know every aspect of concert production, from the sound and lights to publicity—and by the way, who cleans up? Get known in the music circles in your area, let it be known that you are in the market for artists to produce. Be prepared for many years to go by before you start making money!

Make and Repair Instruments

Looking for that elusive violin with that perfect sound but can't find it anywhere on your budget? Why not try and make one? There are books, courses, and teachers that can be had that could possibly set you on a fascinating career. I know several luthiers (makers of stringed instruments) who are darn good musicians themselves but who have found a lucrative living working with instruments. The same goes for piano tuners and technicians. Hey, if you are a good musician, your hands work well, right? Like any other business, in certain circumstances you may have to obtain a business license and register your business name. But if you want to tune pianos, there may be no need. You could align yourself with a music school or university, or private teachers could recommend you. Network, network, network to find clients. Offer to write for instrument magazines, maybe even donate one of your masterpieces (well, maybe not that deluxe model) to a raffle at a festival or to a famous player, anything to get your name and brand out there. If you had a teacher who guided you in manufacturing and repair, perhaps she could also give you a leg up and put you in contact with the right people to get you started in your own business.

Write about Music

In books, magazines, or newspapers, you could be a reviewer, reporter, or author of books about music technique, business, biographies … your imagination is the limit. Hey, look where my wanderings have led me … here, with you! All you need is a great idea (or several if you want to write a column or for several publications) and good writing skills. Then start compiling your lists of contacts: book publishers (and research which ones accept your kind of book, because otherwise you are wasting your time), trade magazines and papers, general newspapers and magazines. You can go to the bookstore to look up possible niches—find the kinds of books you want to write and jot down those publishers. Or, there are books you can buy, like the *Writer's Guide to Book Editors, Publishers, and Literary Agents* or the *Writers Market* (by the way, there is a similar book called the *Songwriters Market* for you aspiring composers). If you want to write a biography about your favorite musician, if she's still alive, you might try contacting her manager or record company. But

I must warn you, if you don't have a track record in publishing, it's hard to even get your foot in the door. What credentials do you have to offer that artist? It might be easier to start with the trades and/or your local paper. I know not a few musicians who write regular columns for newsletters too. Get a bunch of your writing published *anywhere* and start compiling a résumé. Book publishers want to see a strong outline and at least several chapters of your proposal. It used to be that you could only submit to one publisher at a time, then wait months to hear from them before submitting to another. As you can imagine, this could take years! Nowadays it is acceptable to do multiple submissions. Hey, maybe your best seller will start a bidding war?

I hope I have given you food for thought. Assuming that you continue to love music and are thinking long-term, there is no reason why you cannot use your skills and knowledge until you can no longer. Music is one of those life-long gifts—why not have it bring joy and enrichment throughout your life?

Appendix A
Sample Forms and Contracts

INTAKE/INQUIRY FORM

FEE SCHEDULE

PERFORMANCE CONTRACT

PERFORMANCE FORM

PRODUCT INVENTORY FORM

BOOKKEEPING SPREADSHEETS

CHECKLIST FOR SHOWCASES

COPYRIGHT FORM PA

COPYRIGHT FORM SR

MANAGER'S CONTRACT

INTAKE/INQUIRY FORM

DATE(S) OF CALL(S):

INTAKE/INQUIRY SHEET

NAME OF CONTACT PERSON: PHONE:

ADDRESS TO SEND CONTRACT:

PERFORMANCE ADDRESS: PHONE:

TYPE OF PROGRAM: LENGTH:

DATE: TIME: ARRIVAL TIME:

FEE:

ALTERNATE DATE/SITE:

BACK UP:

AUDIENCE SIZE:

ROOM DESCRIPTION:

stage?

lights?

chairs?

PA SYSTEM:

Electrical outlets?   sell LP?

PLEASE PROVIDE: ☐ *table and volunteers for lp* ☐ *water* ☐ *driving directions*

I SEND: ☐ *bio* ☐ *demo/CD* ☐ *brochure* ☐ *poster* ☐ *video* ☐ *photos* ☐ *promo*
☐ *fee schedule* ☐ *references/quotes* ☐ *contract* ☐ *performance schedule* ☐ *other*

FEE SCHEDULE

The XYZ Band

PO Box 12345, Hometown, N.Y. 67890

(123) 555-3456 phone & fax

email address   www.website.com

2003-2004 FEE SCHEDULE

Block booking fees only apply when sponsors book together

50 MILE RADIUS FROM HOMETOWN, NY	SINGER + 1 ACCOMPANIST	EACH ADDITIONAL ACCOMPANIST
Single concert	$300 + 150	+$150
2 concerts, back to back, same day	$250 + 125/concert	+$125/concert
3-4 concerts, same day (can be different locales)	$200 + 100/concert	+$100/concert

51-100 MILE RADIUS FROM HOMETOWN, NY	SINGER + 1 ACCOMPANIST	EACH ADDITIONAL ACCOMPANIST
Single concert	$400 + 200	+$200
2 concerts, back to back, same day	$350 + 175/concert	+$175/concert
3-4 concerts, same day (can be different locales)	$300 + 150/concert	+$150/concert

ALL OTHER AREAS BEYOND 100 MILES OF HOMETOWN, NY

Please call for prices.

PERFORMANCE CONTRACT

The XYZ Band
PO Box 12345, Hometown, N.Y. 67890
phone & fax: (123) 555-3456
email address@server.net   www.website.com

CONTRACT

NAME OF CONTACT PERSON AND TITLE:

ORGANIZATION/BUSINESS, ADDRESS AND PHONE:

CONTACT ADDRESS & PHONE OF PERFORMANCE PLACE
(IF DIFFERENT FROM ABOVE):

The above organization/business wishes to engage the XYZ Band for the following services:
TYPE OF PROGRAM AND LENGTH:

DATE AND TIME(S):

FEE: *SEPARATE CHECKS, PLEASE SEE COVER LETTER !*
( ) payable on date(s) of concert(s)

ARRIVAL TIME: ALTERNATE SITE OR DATE:

Please have someone available to help unload equipment if necessary

AUDIENCE SIZE (APPROX.):   ROOM SIZE & DESCRIPTION:

SPONSOR WILL PROVIDE: ( ) sound ( ) table for album sales, sales help
( ) electrical outlets ( ) piano ( ) stage/platform ( ) lights ( ) bottles water
( ) driving, parking, unloading directions from Hometown, NY ( ) other

PERFORMER WILL PROVIDE: ( ) sound ( ) other

SOUND REQUIREMENTS:

The organization/business is liable for The XYZ Band's losses due to fire or theft, personal injury or property damage arising in connection with the performance, except to the extent that such claim is occasioned by the negligent acts of the XYZ Band or their employees.

The XYZ Band will not be under liability for act's failure to perform if such failure is caused by physical disability or acts beyond their control, such as weather, strikes, etc.

In case of performance cancellation due to inclement weather or emergencies beyond the organization's control, The XYZ Band will be given at least 24 hours notification. If already en route, organization will reimburse all transportation costs in full. Once the act arrives on the performance premises, they are to be PAID IN FULL, even in the event of last minute cancellations.

THE XYZ BAND BY BOB LEADER, MANAGER   DATE

_____

SIGNATURE VERIFYING CONTRACT   DATE

_____

PERFORMANCE FORM

| DATE | TIME | ARRIVAL TIME |

PRESENTER & LOCATION

| #SETS & LENGTH | | AUDIENCE |

CHECKLIST   SET(S)/SHOW

ACOUSTIC GUITAR

ELEC. GUITAR

BASS GUITAR

OTHERS

GUITAR AMP

BASS AMP

WIRELESSES

MIKE STAND(S)

PA HEAD, SPEAKERS, STANDS

MONITORS, STANDS

GUITAR STAND(S)

MAKEUP

MAILING LIST

PRODUCTS

CASH BOX

BROCHURES

UPCOMING CALENDAR FLIERS

EVALUATION

| ESTIMATED AUDIENCE | WORTHWHILE? |

PRODUCTS SOLD

COMMENTS

PRODUCT INVENTORY FORM

DATE

PERFORMANCE

BROUGHT		REMAIN		SOLD		PRICE		SUBTOTAL
_____ ALBUM #1 TAPES	(-)	_____	(=)	_____	(x)	$15	(=)	_____
_____ ALBUM #1 CDs	(-)	_____	(=)	_____	(x)	$10	(=)	_____
_____ ALBUM #2 TAPES	(-)	_____	(=)	_____	(x)	$15	(=)	_____
_____ ALBUM #2 CDs	(-)	_____	(=)	_____	(x)	$15	(=)	_____
_____ T SHIRTS	(-)	_____	(=)	_____	(x)	$10	(=)	_____
_____ HATS	(-)	_____	(=)	_____	(x)	$10	(=)	_____

GRAND TOTAL _____

BOOKKEEPING SPREADSHEETS

Debit: 2003

DATE	PAYEE	CHK #	AMT.	OFFICE SUPPLIES	POSTAGE	SERVICE	INSURANCE	TAX	CAR/GAS	PHONE	MISC. DESC.	AMT.
Jan. 3	ABC Music	356	50								sheet music	50
	Paper, Etc.	357	22.75	22.75								
5	Post Office	358	37		37							
	Zip Studios	359	300			300					recording time	
9	Phone Co.	360	55							55		
12	Post Office	361	5.55		5.55							
	NYS Tax	362	35					35			sales tax due	
13	Jacks Insurance	363	180				180				business ins.	
14	Joe Smith	364	200			200					brochure design	
16	Texaco	365	20						20		gas	
22	Guitar Magazine	366	20								subscription	20
25	Songwriters Guild	367	25								membership fee	25
	Totals		950.3	22.75	42.55	500	180	35	20	55		95

Credit: 2003

DATE	DESCRIPTION	AMT.	PERFORMANCE	CD#1	CD#2	T-SHIRTS	HATS	SHIPPING	SALES TAX	MISC. DESC.	AMT.
Jan. 4	Rocker Club	500	500								
	sales	150		69.25	69.25				11.5		
7	Big Boys Club	500	500								
	Sales	150		96.95		41.55			11.5		
8	mail order sales	102		41.55		41.55		12	6.9		
9	workshop	300								guitar, ABC University	300
11	Club Zero	1000	1000								
	sales	300		138.5	69.25	69.25			23		
	Totals	3002	2000	346.3	138.5	152.35		12	52.9		300

*Note from author: While they work well for me, these spreadsheets represent my own system of bookkeeping and were not created by a financial professional. Depending on your needs, you may want to consult an accountant for advice about keeping your finances organized.

SHOWCASE PACKING LIST

PROMO PACKETS

_____ BROCHURES

_____ QUOTES

_____ REVIEWS

_____ ARTICLES

_____ FEE SCHEDULES

_____ BUSINESS CARDS

demos: videos, cassettes, CDs to give away
TV, headphones, and laptop
table cloth
backdrop display
mailing list sign up sheet
sample performance schedule
staples, scissors, tape, markers, paper
showcase performance date, time & location sign
any decorations
CD player/tape recorder & headphones
food & drink
duct tape
extension cords
display lighting
giveaways (candy, logos, stickers, etc.)
hand cart
calendar for bookings
cell phone

COPYRIGHT FORM PA

Copyright Office fees are subject to change. For current fees, check the Copyright Office website at *www.copyright.gov*, write the Copyright Office, or call (202) 707-3000.

FORM PA

For a Work of the Performing Arts
UNITED STATES COPYRIGHT OFFICE

REGISTRATION NUMBER

PA   PAU

EFFECTIVE DATE OF REGISTRATION

_____
Month   Day   Year

DO NOT WRITE ABOVE THIS LINE. IF YOU NEED MORE SPACE, USE A SEPARATE CONTINUATION SHEET.

1

TITLE OF THIS WORK ▼

PREVIOUS OR ALTERNATIVE TITLES ▼

NATURE OF THIS WORK ▼ See instructions

2 **a**

NAME OF AUTHOR ▼

DATES OF BIRTH AND DEATH
Year Born ▼   Year Died ▼

Was this contribution to the work a "work made for hire"?
☐ Yes
☐ No

AUTHOR'S NATIONALITY OR DOMICILE
Name of Country
OR { Citizen of _____
     Domiciled in _____

WAS THIS AUTHOR'S CONTRIBUTION TO THE WORK
Anonymous?   ☐ Yes ☐ No
Pseudonymous?   ☐ Yes ☐ No

If the answer to either of these questions is "Yes," see detailed instructions.

NATURE OF AUTHORSHIP Briefly describe nature of material created by this author in which copyright is claimed. ▼

NOTE

Under the law, the "author" of a "work made for hire" is generally the employer, not the employee (see instructions). For any part of this work that was "made for hire" check "Yes" in the space provided, give the employer (or other person for whom the work was prepared) as "Author" of that part, and leave the space for dates of birth and death blank.

b

NAME OF AUTHOR ▼

DATES OF BIRTH AND DEATH
Year Born ▼   Year Died ▼

Was this contribution to the work a "work made for hire"?
☐ Yes
☐ No

AUTHOR'S NATIONALITY OR DOMICILE
Name of Country
OR { Citizen of _____
     Domiciled in _____

WAS THIS AUTHOR'S CONTRIBUTION TO THE WORK
Anonymous?   ☐ Yes ☐ No
Pseudonymous?   ☐ Yes ☐ No

If the answer to either of these questions is "Yes," see detailed instructions.

NATURE OF AUTHORSHIP Briefly describe nature of material created by this author in which copyright is claimed. ▼

c

NAME OF AUTHOR ▼

DATES OF BIRTH AND DEATH
Year Born ▼   Year Died ▼

Was this contribution to the work a "work made for hire"?
☐ Yes
☐ No

AUTHOR'S NATIONALITY OR DOMICILE
Name of Country
OR { Citizen of _____
     Domiciled in _____

WAS THIS AUTHOR'S CONTRIBUTION TO THE WORK
Anonymous?   ☐ Yes ☐ No
Pseudonymous?   ☐ Yes ☐ No

If the answer to either of these questions is "Yes," see detailed instructions.

NATURE OF AUTHORSHIP Briefly describe nature of material created by this author in which copyright is claimed. ▼

3 **a**

YEAR IN WHICH CREATION OF THIS WORK WAS COMPLETED   This information must be given
Year in all cases.

b DATE AND NATION OF FIRST PUBLICATION OF THIS PARTICULAR WORK
Complete this information ONLY if this work has been published.
Month _____ Day _____ Year _____
Nation _____

4

COPYRIGHT CLAIMANT(S) Name and address must be given even if the claimant is the same as the author given in space 2. ▼

See instructions before completing this space.

TRANSFER If the claimant(s) named here in space 4 is (are) different from the author(s) named in space 2, give a brief statement of how the claimant(s) obtained ownership of the copyright. ▼

APPLICATION RECEIVED

ONE DEPOSIT RECEIVED

TWO DEPOSITS RECEIVED

FUNDS RECEIVED

DO NOT WRITE HERE
OFFICE USE ONLY

MORE ON BACK ▶ • Complete all applicable spaces (numbers 5-9) on the reverse side of this page.
• See detailed instructions.   • Sign the form at line 8.

DO NOT WRITE HERE
Page 1 of _____ pages

EXAMINED BY	FORM PA
CHECKED BY	

☐ CORRESPONDENCE	FOR
Yes	COPYRIGHT
	OFFICE
	USE
	ONLY

DO NOT WRITE ABOVE THIS LINE. IF YOU NEED MORE SPACE, USE A SEPARATE CONTINUATION SHEET.

PREVIOUS REGISTRATION Has registration for this work, or for an earlier version of this work, already been made in the Copyright Office?

☐ Yes ☐ No If your answer is "Yes," why is another registration being sought? (Check appropriate box.) ▼ If your answer is No, do **not** check box A, B, or C.

a. ☐ This is the first published edition of a work previously registered in unpublished form.

b. ☐ This is the first application submitted by this author as copyright claimant.

c. ☐ This is a changed version of the work, as shown by space 6 on this application.

If your answer is "Yes," give: **Previous Registration Number ▼**   **Year of Registration ▼**

5

DERIVATIVE WORK OR COMPILATION Complete both space 6a and 6b for a derivative work; complete only 6b for a compilation.

Preexisting Material Identify any preexisting work or works that this work is based on or incorporates. ▼

Material Added to This Work Give a brief, general statement of the material that has been added to this work and in which copyright is claimed. ▼

a

6

See instructions before completing this space.

b

DEPOSIT ACCOUNT If the registration fee is to be charged to a Deposit Account established in the Copyright Office, give name and number of Account.

Name ▼   **Account Number ▼**

a

7

CORRESPONDENCE Give name and address to which correspondence about this application should be sent. Name/Address/Apt/City/State/ZIP ▼

b

Area code and daytime telephone number (   )   Fax number (   )

Email

CERTIFICATION* I, the undersigned, hereby certify that I am the

Check only one ▶

☐ author
☐ other copyright claimant
☐ owner of exclusive right(s)
☐ authorized agent of _____

Name of author or other copyright claimant, or owner of exclusive right(s) ▲

of the work identified in this application and that the statements made by me in this application are correct to the best of my knowledge.

8

Typed or printed name and date ▼ If this application gives a date of publication in space 3, do not sign and submit it before that date.

Date _____

Handwritten signature (X) ▼

☞ x _____

Certificate will be mailed in window envelope to this address:	Name ▼	**YOU MUST:** • Complete all necessary spaces • Sign your application in space 8
	Number/Street/Apt ▼	**SEND ALL 3 ELEMENTS IN THE SAME PACKAGE:** 1. Application form 2. Nonrefundable filing fee in check or money order payable to *Register of Copyrights* 3. Deposit material
	City/State/ZIP ▼	**MAIL TO:** Library of Congress Copyright Office 101 Independence Avenue, S.E. Washington, D.C. 20559-6000

Fees are subject to change. For current fees, check the Copyright Office website at www.copyright.gov, write the Copyright Office, or call (202) 707-3000.

9

*17 U.S.C. § 506(e): Any person who knowingly makes a false representation of a material fact in the application for copyright registration provided for by section 409, or in any written statement filed in connection with the application, shall be fined not more than $2,500.

Rev: June 2002—20,000 Web Rev: June 2002 ♻ Printed on recycled paper   U.S. Government Printing Office: 2000-461-113/20,021

COPYRIGHT FORM SR

Fees are effective through June 30, 2002.
After that date, check the Copyright Office
Website at www.loc.gov/copyright or call
(202) 707-3000 for current fee information.

FORM SR
For a Sound Recording
UNITED STATES COPYRIGHT OFFICE

REGISTRATION NUMBER

SR   SRU

EFFECTIVE DATE OF REGISTRATION

Month   Day   Year

DO NOT WRITE ABOVE THIS LINE. IF YOU NEED MORE SPACE, USE A SEPARATE CONTINUATION SHEET.

1

TITLE OF THIS WORK ▼

PREVIOUS, ALTERNATIVE, OR CONTENTS TITLES (CIRCLE ONE) ▼

2 a

NAME OF AUTHOR ▼

DATES OF BIRTH AND DEATH
Year Born ▼   Year Died ▼

Was this contribution to the work a "work made for hire"?
☐ Yes
☐ No

AUTHOR'S NATIONALITY OR DOMICILE
Name of Country
OR { Citizen of ▶
Domiciled in ▶

WAS THIS AUTHOR'S CONTRIBUTION TO THE WORK
Anonymous?   ☐ Yes   ☐ No
Pseudonymous? ☐ Yes   ☐ No

If the answer to either of these questions is "Yes," see detailed instructions.

NATURE OF AUTHORSHIP   Briefly describe nature of material created by this author in which copyright is claimed. ▼

NOTE

Under the law, the "author" of a "work made for hire" is generally the employer, not the employee (see instructions). For any part of this work that was "made for hire," check "Yes" in the space provided, give the employer (or other person for whom the work was prepared) as "Author" of that part, and leave the space for dates of birth and death blank.

b

NAME OF AUTHOR ▼

DATES OF BIRTH AND DEATH
Year Born ▼   Year Died ▼

Was this contribution to the work a "work made for hire"?
☐ Yes
☐ No

AUTHOR'S NATIONALITY OR DOMICILE
Name of Country
OR { Citizen of ▶
Domiciled in ▶

WAS THIS AUTHOR'S CONTRIBUTION TO THE WORK
Anonymous?   ☐ Yes   ☐ No
Pseudonymous? ☐ Yes   ☐ No

If the answer to either of these questions is "Yes," see detailed instructions.

NATURE OF AUTHORSHIP   Briefly describe nature of material created by this author in which copyright is claimed. ▼

c

NAME OF AUTHOR ▼

DATES OF BIRTH AND DEATH
Year Born ▼   Year Died ▼

Was this contribution to the work a "work made for hire"?
☐ Yes
☐ No

AUTHOR'S NATIONALITY OR DOMICILE
Name of Country
OR { Citizen of ▶
Domiciled in ▶

WAS THIS AUTHOR'S CONTRIBUTION TO THE WORK
Anonymous?   ☐ Yes   ☐ No
Pseudonymous? ☐ Yes   ☐ No

If the answer to either of these questions is "Yes," see detailed instructions.

NATURE OF AUTHORSHIP   Briefly describe nature of material created by this author in which copyright is claimed. ▼

3 a

YEAR IN WHICH CREATION OF THIS WORK WAS COMPLETED

This information must be given
◀ Year in all cases.

DATE AND NATION OF FIRST PUBLICATION OF THIS PARTICULAR WORK

b Complete this information
ONLY if this work
has been published.

Month ▶ _____ Day ▶ _____ Year ▶ _____

◀ Nation

4 a

COPYRIGHT CLAIMANT(S) Name and address must be given even if the claimant is the same as the author given in space 2. ▼

b

TRANSFER If the claimant(s) named here in space 4 is (are) different from the author(s) named in space 2, give a brief statement of how the claimant(s) obtained ownership of the copyright. ▼

APPLICATION RECEIVED

ONE DEPOSIT RECEIVED

TWO DEPOSITS RECEIVED

FUNDS RECEIVED

DO NOT WRITE HERE
OFFICE USE ONLY

See instructions before completing this space.

MORE ON BACK ▶ • Complete all applicable spaces (numbers 5-9) on the reverse side of this page.
• See detailed instructions.   • Sign the form at line 8.

DO NOT WRITE HERE

Page 1 of _____ pages

EXAMINED BY	**FORM SR**
CHECKED BY	
CORRESPONDENCE ❑ Yes	FOR COPYRIGHT OFFICE USE ONLY

DO NOT WRITE ABOVE THIS LINE. IF YOU NEED MORE SPACE, USE A SEPARATE CONTINUATION SHEET.

PREVIOUS REGISTRATION Has registration for this work, or for an earlier version of this work, already been made in the Copyright Office?

❑ Yes ❑ No If your answer is "Yes," why is another registration being sought? (Check appropriate box) ▼

a. ❑ This work was previously registered in unpublished form and now has been published for the first time.

b. ❑ This is the first application submitted by this author as copyright claimant.

c. ❑ This is a changed version of the work, as shown by space 6 on this application.

If your answer is "Yes," give: **Previous Registration Number** ▼   **Year of Registration** ▼

5

DERIVATIVE WORK OR COMPILATION
Preexisting Material Identify any preexisting work or works that this work is based on or incorporates. ▼

a

6

See instructions before completing this space.

Material Added to This Work Give a brief, general statement of the material that has been added to this work and in which copyright is claimed. ▼

b

DEPOSIT ACCOUNT If the registration fee is to be charged to a Deposit Account established in the Copyright Office, give name and number of Account.
Name ▼   **Account Number** ▼

a

7

CORRESPONDENCE Give name and address to which correspondence about this application should be sent.   Name/Address/Apt/City/State/ZIP ▼

b

Area code and daytime telephone number ▶   Fax number ▶
Email ▶

CERTIFICATION* I, the undersigned, hereby certify that I am the

Check only one ▼

❑ author   ❑ owner of exclusive right(s)

❑ other copyright claimant   ❑ authorized agent of _____
                                        Name of author or other copyright claimant, or owner of exclusive right(s) ▲

of the work identified in this application and that the statements made by me in this application are correct to the best of my knowledge.

8

Typed or printed name and date ▼ If this application gives a date of publication in space 3, do not sign and submit it before that date.

_____ Date▶ _____

Handwritten signature (x) ▼
X _

Certificate will be mailed in window envelope to this address	Name ▼	**YOU MUST:** • Complete all necessary spaces • Sign your application in space 8	**9**
	Number/Street/Apt ▼	**SEND ALL 3 ELEMENTS** **IN THE SAME PACKAGE:** 1. Application form 2. Nonrefundable filing fee in check or money order payable to *Register of Copyrights* 3. Deposit material	As of July 1, 1999, the filing fee for Form SR is $30.
	City/State/ZIP ▼	**MAIL TO:** Library of Congress Copyright Office 101 Independence Avenue, S.E. Washington, D.C. 20559-6000	

*17 U.S.C. § 506(e): Any person who knowingly makes a false representation of a material fact in the application for copyright registration provided for by section 409, or in any written statement filed in connection with the application, shall be fined not more than $2,500.

June 1999—50,000   ♻ PRINTED ON RECYCLED PAPER   ☆U.S. GOVERNMENT PRINTING OFFICE: 1999-454-879/48
WEB REV: June 1999

MANAGER'S CONTRACT

Dated:

XYZ Corp.
1234 Management Way
Perfect City, New York

Dear Sirs:
 I have carefully considered the advisability of obtaining your assistance and guidance in the furtherance of my musical, artistic, theatrical and literary career, and have made independent inquiry concerning your ability and reputation. I have determined that your services would be of great value in the furtherance of my career because of your knowledge of and reputation in the entertainment and amusement industries. I have, therefore, determined that I wish you to act as my exclusive personal manager for the term of this agreement, subject to the following provisions and conditions:

1. I hereby engage you as my exclusive personal manager throughout the world for the term of this agreement, and you hereby accept such engagement.

2. You agree to use your best efforts to perform one or more of the following services for me:

    (a) To represent me and act as my advisor in all business negotiations and matters of policy relating to my career; to supervise my engagements and to consult with employers to assure, to the best of your ability, the proper use of my services; to advise and counsel me in the selection of literary, artistic and musical material, in matters relating to publicity, public relations and advertising, in the adoption of the proper format for presentation of my talents and to arrange for interviews or auditions designed to further my career.
    (b) To cooperate with and supervise my relations with any musical, theatrical, literary or other agents employed on my behalf; to advise and counsel me in the selection of third parties to assist, accompany, or improve my artistic presentation; and to make yourself available at reasonable times at your office to confer with me in all matters concerning my career.

3. You are authorized and empowered for me and in my behalf and in your discretion to do the following: approve and permit any and all publicity and advertising; approve and permit the use of my name, photograph, likeness, voice, sound effects, caricatures, literary, artistic and musical materials for purposes of advertising and publicity and in the promotion and advertising of any and all products and services; execute for me in my name and/or in my behalf any and all agreements, documents and contracts for my services, talents and/or artistic, literary and musical materials collect and receive sums as well as endorse my name upon and cash any and all checks payable to me for my services, talents and literary and artistic materials and retain therefrom from all sums owing to you; engage, as well as discharge and/or direct for my, and in my name, theatrical agents, artist's managers, and employment agencies as well as other persons, firms and corporations who may be retained to obtain contracts or engagements of employment for me. You are not required to make any loans or advances to me or for my account, but, in the event you do so, I shall repay them promptly, and I hereby authorize you to deduct the amount of any such loans or advances from my account. The authority herein granted to you coupled with an interest and shall be irrevocable.

4. I agree at all times to devote myself to my career and to do all things necessary and desirable to promote my career and earnings therefrom. I shall at all times engage and utilize proper theatrical agents, employment agencies, or artists' managers to obtain engagements and employment for me, but I shall not engage any theatrical agents, employment agencies, or artists' managers of which you may disapprove. I shall advise you of all offers of employment submitted to me and will refer any inquiries concerning my services to you, in order that you may determine whether the same are compatible with my career. I shall instruct any theatrical agency or artists' manager engaged by me to remit to you all monies that may become due me and may be received by it. (IT IS CLEARLY UNDERSTOOD THAT YOU ARE NOT AN EMPLOYMENT AGENCY OR A THEATRICAL AGENT, THAT YOU HAVE NOT OFFERED OR ATTEMPTED OR PROMISED TO OBTAIN, SEEK OR PROCURE EMPLOYMENT OR ENGAGEMENTS FOR ME, AND THAT YOU ARE NOT OBLIGATED, AUTHORIZED, LICENSED, OR EXPECTED TO DO SO).

5. This agreement shall not be construed to create a partnership between you and me. It is specifically understood that you are acting hereunder as an independent contractor and you may appoint or engage any and all other persons, firms and corporations throughout the world in your discretion to perform any or all of the services which you have agreed to perform hereunder. Your services hereunder are not exclusive and you shall at all times be free to perform the same or similar services for others as well as engage in any and all other business activities. You shall only be required to render reasonable services which are called for by this agreement as and when reasonably requested by me. You shall not be required to travel or to meet with me at any particular place or places except upon my request and then only at your discretion and at my expense.

6. (a) In consideration of your agreement hereto and as compensation for services rendered and to be rendered to me by you hereunder, I agree to pay to you as and when received by me a sum equal to twenty (20%) percent of any and all gross monies or other considerations which I may receive as a result of my activities in and throughout the entertainment, amusement, music, and recording industries, including any and all sums resulting from the use of my musical, artistic, and literary talents and the results and proceeds thereof. Without in any manner limiting the foregoing, the matters upon which your compensation shall be computed shall include any and all of our activities in connection with matters as follows: motion pictures, television, radio, music, literary, theatrical engagements, personal appearances, public appearances in places of amusement and entertainment, records, recordings, music publishing and merchandising (subject to paragraph 6c), publications, and the use of my name or likeness and talents for purposes of advertising and trade. I likewise agree to pay you a similar sum following the expiration of the term hereof upon and with respect to any and all engagements, contracts and agreements entered into or negotiated for during the term hereof relating to any of the foregoing, and upon any and all extensions, renewals and substitutions thereof and upon any resumptions of such engagements, contracts, and agreements which may have been discontinued during the term hereof and resumed within a year thereafter.

(b) The term "gross monies or other considerations" shall include, without limitation, salaries, earnings, fees, royalties, gifts bonuses, shares of profit, shares of stock partnership interests, percentages and the total amount paid for a package television or radio program (live or recorded), motion picture, or other entertainment packages, earned or received directly or indirectly by me or my heirs, executors, administrators or assigns, or by any person, firm, or corporation on my behalf. In the event that I receive, as all or part of my compensation for activities hereunder, stock or the right to buy stock in any corporation or in the event that I become the packager or owner of all or part of an entertainment property, whether as individual proprietor, stock-holder, partner, joint venturer, or otherwise or in the event that I shall cause a corporation to be formed, your percentage shall apply to my said stock, right to buy stock, individual proprietorship, partnership, joint venture or other form of interest, and you shall be entitled to your percentage share thereof. Should I be required to make any payment for such interest, you will pay your percentage share of such payment, unless you decline to accept your percentage share thereof.

(c) Notwithstanding the foregoing provisions of subparagraph 6(a), it is agreed that you shall waive your right to any commission or payment from me pursuant to sub-paragraph 6(a) above, solely with respect to gross monies of other compensation received by me for sales of any record albums, music publishing, or merchandising which are the subject of a production agreement entered into by the parties as of _____ (the "Production Agreement"), but such waiver shall be in effect only for so long as the Production Agreement shall remain in effect. Thereafter, all such gross monies or other compensation shall be subject to this agreement.

7. (a) The term of this agreement shall be for an initial period of one (1) year commencing on the date hereof. You shall have four (4) options to extend the term for an additional consecutive one-year period (each of which, along with the initial period, shall sometimes be referred to as "Contract Periods"), and each such option shall automatically be deemed exercised by you unless you give me written notice to the contrary prior to the end of the then-current Contract Period.

(b) Notwithstanding the foregoing, in the event you have not, within one hundred and eighty (180) days of the date of this Agreement, either secured a Record Distribution Agreement or committed to so-called distribution pursuant to paragraphs 2(a), (b), (c) and (d) of the Production Agreement, I shall have the right to terminate this Agreement on thirty (30) days notice to you provided such option is exercised within thirty (30) days of the end of such on hundred and eighty (180) day period.

8. Upon written notice by either of us to the other, the party to whom such notice is addressed will furnish an accounting to the other party of all transactions between us within thirty (30) days of such request, but not more frequently than once every ninety (90) days.

9. (a) You shall not be required to make any expenditures on my account, but, in the event that you do so, then in addition to the sums required to be paid to you as afore-said, I shall reimburse you for any and all bona fide expenditures incurred by you on my behalf or in connection with my career or in the performance of your services here-under which are substantiated by receipted vouchers or paid bills.

(b) You shall not make any single expenditure on my account of more than One Thousand ($1,000) Dollars without my prior consent.

10. In order to make specific and definite and/or to eliminate, if possible, any controversy which may arise between us hereunder, I agree that if at any time I feel that the terms

of this agreement are not being performed by you as herein provided, I will so advise you in writing by Registered or Certified Mail, Return Receipt Requested, of the specific nature of any claim, non-performance or malperformance and shall allow you a period of thirty (30) days after receipt thereof within which to cure such claimed breach. I agree that no breach of the terms hereof, unless intentionally dishonest, will be construed as incurable. No action may be commenced by me prior to the expiration of the aforesaid thirty (30) day period and no action shall be based upon any complaint except one contained in my aforesaid notice to you.

11. I warrant and represent that I am over twenty one (21) years of age, and that I am experienced and knowledge in the entertainment and amusement industries, and I am free to enter into and perform this agreement and that I have been advised to seek legal counsel to advise me on the benefits and obligations of this agreement.

12. I agree to indemnify and hold you safe and harmless from any and all loss or damage including reasonable attorneys' fees arising out of or in connection with any of the warranties, representations, covenants or agreements made by me herein.

13. You may assign this agreement to an individual who is one of your stockholders, or to a partnership at least one of whose partners is one of your stockholders, or to another corporation. This agreement is personal to me and I may not assign this agreement.

14. This agreement shall be construed in accordance with the laws of the State of New York applicable to contracts made and wholly to be performed therein, and the New York State courts located in New York County or the Federal District Court for the Southern District of New York shall have exclusive jurisdiction of any dispute arising hereunder. In the event that any provision hereof shall, for any reason, be invalid or unenforceable, the same shall not affect the validity or enforceability of the remaining provisions hereof. This agreement is the only agreement between us concerning the subject matter hereof and may not be modified or terminated except by an instrument in writing executed by the parties hereto. A waiver by either of us of a breach of any provision hereof shall not be deemed a waiver of any subsequent breach, whether of a similar or dissimilar nature.

If the foregoing correctly states the terms of our understanding, will you kindly so indicate by signing below at the place indicated.

Very truly yours,

_____

XYZ BAND

ACCEPTED AND AGREED TO:
XYZ MANAGEMENT CORP

BY: _____

Appendix B

Resources and Bibliography

Resources for Managers, Agents, Record Companies, and More

Music Business Registry
Tel: (800) 377–7411
(800) 552–7411 for orders
www.musicregistry.com
ritch@musicregistry.com

Subdirectories where musicians can find valuable resources include *The A & R Registry; The Film and Television Music Guide; Music Publishers Registry*; and *Music Attorney Registry*.

Pollstar Music Industry Contact Directories
Tel: (800) 344–7383
Fax: (559) 271–7979
www.pollstar.com

Agency Rosters, Talent Buyers and Clubs, Concert Venues, Record Companies

Performance Rights Societies

ASCAP
Tel: (800) 95ASCAP
www.ascap.com

One Lincoln Plaza
New York, NY 10023
Tel: (212) 621–6000
Fax: (212) 724–9064

7920 Sunset Boulevard, Suite 300
Los Angeles, CA 90046
Tel: (323) 883–1000
Fax: (323) 883–1049

Two Music Square West
Nashville, TN 37203
Tel: (615) 742–5000
Fax: (615) 742–5020

BMI
www.bmi.com
320 West 57th Street
New York, NY 10019
Tel: (212) 586–2000
Fax: (212) 245–8986

8730 Sunset Boulevard, 3rd floor
West Hollywood, CA 90069
Tel: (310) 659–9109
Fax: (310) 657–6947

10 Music Square East
Nashville, TN 37203
Tel: (615) 401–2000
Fax: (615) 401–2707

SESAC
152 West 57th Street, 57th floor
New York, NY 10019
Tel: (212) 586–3450
Fax: (212) 489–5699
www.sesac.com

55 Music Square East
Nashville, TN 37203
Tel: (615) 320–0055
Fax: (615) 329–9627

Conferences and Showcases

North by Northeast Music Festival and Industry Conference
Toronto, Ontario (Canada)
Tel: (416) 863–6963
Fax: (416) 863–0828
www.nxne.com
inquire@nxne.com

North by North West Music Conference Seattle, WA
Tel: (503) 226–8006
Fax: (503) 226–9613
www.nxnw.com
nxnw@nxnw.com

South by Southwest Music Conference
Austin, TX
Tel: (512) 467–7979
Fax: (512) 451–0754
www.sxsw.com
sxsw@sxsw.com

Emerging Artists and Talent Conference
Las Vegas, NV
Tel: (702) 792–9430
Fax: (702) 792–5748
www.eat-m.com

NEMO Music Conference
Boston, MA
Tel: (781) 306–0441
Fax: (781) 306–0442
www.nemoboston.com
info@nemoboston.com

Performing Arts Exchange Conference
Southern Arts Federation, Atlanta, GA
Tel: (404) 874–7244
Fax: (404) 873–2148
www.southarts.org

Folk Alliance Conference
North American Folk Music and Dance Alliance, Silver Spring, MD
Tel: (301) 588–8185
Fax: (301) 588–8186
www.folk.org
fa@folk.org

North East Regional Folk Alliance Conference
Tel: (215) 546–7766
www.nefolk.org
info@nefolk.org

The Association of Performing Arts Presenters
Washington, DC
Tel: (202) 833–2787
Fax: (202) 833–1543
www.artspresenters.org
artspres@artspresenters.org

Atlantis Music Conference
Atlanta, GA
Tel: (770) 499–8600
Fax: (770) 499–8650

www.atlantismusic.com
atlantis@atlantismusic.com

CMJ Music Marathon Conference
New York, NY
www.cmj.com
showcase@cmj.com
registration@cmj.com

West Coast Songwriter's Association Conference
San Carlos, CA

Tel: (650) 654–3966
Fax: (650) 654–2156
www.ncsasong.org
info@ncsasong.org

Winter Music Conference
Fort Lauderdale, FL
Tel: (954) 563–4444
Fax: (954) 563–1599
www.wintermusicconference.com
info@wintermusicconference.com

Competitions and Contests

There are literally hundreds of contests and competitions for the performance of most instruments (including voice) and in all genres, as well as for songwriting and composition. Some are old and venerable, especially in the classical world; others may just exist for one year. You can check out the Internet for up-to-date information by entering "music competitions" into your search engine. Two sites that I found helpful: www.homoecumenicus.com/music_competitions.htm and www.music.indiana.edu/music_resources/competit.html

Helpful Organizations

US Copyright Office
Library of Congress
101 Independence Ave. SE
Washington, DC 20559–6000
(202) 707–5959 for questions
(202) 707–9100 for forms
www.copyright.gov

Clarion Associates, Inc.
Musical Instrument Insurance
1711 New York Avenue
Huntington Station, NY 11746
(800) VIVALDI or (866) 2-FIDDLE
www.ClarionIns.com

Local 1000
322 West 48th Street
New York, NY 10036
(212) 843–8726
(212) 489–6030 fax
www.local1000.com
office@local1000.com

Harry Fox Agency
711 Third Avenue
New York, NY 10017
(212) 370–5330
(212) 953–2384 fax
www.harryfox.com
clientrelations@harryfox.com

Small Business Service Bureau, Inc.
National Operations Center
PO Box 15014
Worcester, MA 01615–0014
(800) 343–0939
www.sbsb.com

NARAS—National Academy of Recording Arts & Sciences
3402 Pico Boulevard
Santa Monica, CA 90405
(310) 392–3777
(310) 399–3090 fax
www.grammy.com

Universal Product Code (UPC for Bar Codes)

Artists may want to put bar codes on their products for many reasons; two of the most important are that retail stores require them, and Billboard uses them for charting. If you register your products with SoundScan, using the code that is provided by the Uniform Code Council (UCC), then Billboard has access to the sales figures which it uses in determining chart placement. The UCC charges at the time of this writing a minimum of $750 for full membership. This fee is determined by previous sales figures, or, in the case where a company is new, projected sales figures, plus number of items to be sold. Go to their Web site for an application, or you can apply by phone for an extra $25. The UCC will then assign you a unique code for your company and your manufacturer will generate the actual bar code.

Uniform Code Council, Inc.
7887 Washington Village Drive, Suite 300
Dayton, OH 45459
(937) 435–3870
www.uc-council.org

Songwriters Associations

There are many regional songwriters associations, workshops, and other groups throughout North America. To research the ones in your area, type in "[your region] songwriters association" in your search engine. One good Web site is *www.onlinerock.com*.

Trade Publications

It seems that every genre of music and every family of musical instruments has its own set of publications, both on paper and online. There are too many to list here, but you can go to a very useful Web site, *www.music.indiana.edu/music_resources/journals.html*, to find a comprehensive and frequently-updated list with a short description of each and links to their sites. Below are some of the more general interest ones:

AMG: All-Music Guide (in-depth reviews and articles on all genres)
American Songwriter Magazine
ASCAP PlayBack Magazine
Billboard
Music World Magazine from BMI
Contemporary Music Review
Dirty Linen
DownBeat
Entertainment Magazine
Gig Magazine Online
MPA Press (newsletter of the Music Publishers' Association of the US, articles relating to copyright and the current state of music publishing)
MTV Online

Music Connection Magazine
Music Row Magazine (Nashville's music industry publication)
MusiciansNet (online musicians' magazines for most instruments)
Pollstar (the concert hotwire)
Pro-Music-News (news from the music industry and professional recording and PA technology)
Rock & Pop
Rock on the Net
ROCKRGRL Magazine
Rolling Stone
Sing Out! (for folk and acoustic-based, singer-songwriter musicians)
SongLink International Magazine (music industry resource for music publishers, songwriters and composers)
SoundOut (Web magazine of contemporary music)
Static Magazine (for the independent music community)
TalentNews.Com (investigative news site for new talent)
Wall of Sound (reviews, profiles, etc.)

Consultants

Sy Buckner, RFC, CSA
Registered Financial Consultant & Certified Senior Advisor
Buckner Financial Solutions for Retirement & Long Term Care
99 Schoolhouse Lane
Roslyn Heights, NY 11577
Tel: (516) 626–1630
Sy Buckner, CEO of Buckner Financial Solutions, is a member of the Financial Planning Association and President of the Metro New York Society of Mutual Fund Specialists. He is a licensed Life and Health Insurance agent and stock broker, as well as a member of the LIA Health Committee and the Small Business Committee, where he has received several awards.

William T. Casey aka Willie Steel
Huntington Bay Music
288 New York Avenue
Huntington, NY 11743
Tel: (631) 271–8369, (631) 271–8865
www.hbaymusic.com
steeltone@msn.com
Willie Steel has been a professional songwriter and performer on guitar and vocals since 1987. He also owns and manages Huntington Bay Music, a store founded in 1995, and continues to bring his special brand of American music to audiences on Long Island from Montauk to Manhattan.

James Coffey
Blue Vision Music
www.childrensmusicresource.com
www.bluevisionmusic.com
contact@bluevisionmusic.com
James Coffey is an award-winning songwriter, and also runs his own music production company, offering recordings, multimedia, and web design for children's music artists.

Corey Davidson
Davidson Electronics Corporation
1530 Old Country Road
Plainview, NY 11803
Tel: (516) 753–0197
www.davidsonelectronics.com
Corey Davidson is the founder of Davidson Electronics, a full-service pro-audio repair facility specializing in musical instrument, pro audio, reinforcement, and recording equipment repair. Having studied with Joel Chadabe, he carries a B.A. in electronic music and served as a technical assistant to the late composer and "father of tape music" John Cage. Davidson Electronics is a factory-authorized service center for sixty premier manufacturers of professional musical products.

Paul Foley, General Manager
Rounder Records
One Camp Street
Cambridge, MA 02140
Tel: (617) 218–4425
Fax: (617) 876–6133
PaulF@rounder.com
Paul Foley has been the General Manager at Rounder Records since 1998. With more than thirty years of experience in the music business, Paul owned record stores for fifteen years and was Vice President of Sales at Polygram.

Joseph Giardina, Artistic/Education Director
Arts Horizons
One Grand Avenue, Suite 7
Englewood, NJ 07631
Tel: (888) 522–2787
www.artshorizons.org
Arts Horizons is a producing arts-in-education organization and agency, specializing in children and family audiences in the schools of New York and New Jersey. At the time of this writing, it has forty performing groups on its roster.

Paul Kendall
New York
Tel: (631) 243–0814
www.kendalljazz.com
Paul Kendall is a woodwind artist specializing in jazz. He plays soprano, alto, tenor, and baritone sax, flute, piccolo, clarinet, alto and bass clarinet.

Howard Leib, Esq.
271 Madison Ave. Suite 200
New York, NY 10016
Tel: (212) 545–9559
howardleib@aol.com, *www.kidsentertainment.com*
Howard Leib is an attorney specializing in children's and family entertainment. He is the former chair of the New York State Bar Association Committee on Music and Recording Arts, and a contributing editor to Entertainment Law and Finance. Past clients include Whitney Houston, Arista Records, BMG, and Judy Collins.

Scott MacDonald, luthier
S.B. MacDonald Custom Instruments
Huntington, NY 11743
Tel: (631) 421–9056
www.customguitars.com
scott@customguitars.com
Scott MacDonald is a maker of custom fretted instruments, both acoustic and electric. He is also an authorized repairman for the Martin, Gibson, Taylor, Fender, Guild, and Ovation companies.

John McCutcheon
Appalseed Productions
1025 Locust Ave.
Charlottesville, VA 22901
Tel: (434) 977–6321
afm1000@folkmusic.com
www.folkmusic.com
John McCutcheon has been a folksinger since the early 1970s. He is one of that genre's most respected multi-instrumentalists, as well as a world-renowned recording artist and songwriter. John is presently serving as the president of Local 1000, the traveling musicians' chapter of the American Federation of Musicians Union.

George Meier
Huntington Station, NY 11746
Tel: (631) 421–4481
clownhenge@hotmail.com

George Meier is a professional drummer/percussionist and veteran of TV, radio, clubs, and recording studios. He has performed with countless bands, orchestras, poets, and musicians in all styles. His extensive background in theatre and clowning brings a special fun quality to his performances. He also teaches drums and percussion privately.

Ron Meixsell
64 Harrison Drive
East Northport, NY 11731
Tel: (631) 757–1229
Ron Meixsell is a voice teacher who has a Bachelor of Music degree from Susquehanna University, plus graduate credits from Stony Brook University. He has over thirty years of experience in choral conducting and teaching voice, both privately and in public high schools, the Stony Brook Theatre Arts Dept., Upsala College, Dowling College, and Five Towns College. In addition, he maintains a busy performing schedule singing opera, classical, and Broadway music.

John Platt
WFUV, 90.7 FM
Fordham University
Bronx, NY 10458
Tel: (718) 817–4564
Fax: (718) 365–9815
johnplatt@wfuv.org
John Platt is the Development and Marketing Director and host of the "City Folk Sunday Breakfast" at WFUV in New York. His 33 years in radio have included stints as program director of WXRT in Chicago and WRVR in New York. He has produced countless national and local programs (including Pete Fornatale's "Mixed Bag" in New York) and interviewed artists ranging from Randy Newman, Bonnie Raitt, Pete Seeger, and Joan Baez to independent artists.

Lawrence C. Ré, Esq.
Munley, Meade, Nielsen and Ré
Huntington, NY 11743

Gary Roth, Assistant Vice President
Legal and Business Affairs, Performing Rights
BMI
320 West 57th Street
New York, NY 10019
Tel: (212) 586–2000
Fax: (212) 245–8986

Gary Roth joined BMI in 1974 as a staff attorney immediately upon graduation from the College of William and Mary School of Law. Since then he has been Senior Legal Counsel and Senior Attorney in the Legal Department. His duties include supervising the legal matters of the Performing Rights Department in regard to writers and publishers, and counsels on copyright and other legal matters.

Charles Rufino
1841 Broadway, Studio 1118
New York, NY 10023–7603
Tel: (212) 581–6226
www.rufinoviolins.com
Charles Rufino started making violins in 1974, studying instrument-making and restoration in the finest ateliers of Europe and the US. From his studio in New York City, he makes violins, violas, and violoncellos which are regarded by connoisseurs as modern classics. He is a member of the American Federation of Violin and Bow Makers as well as the Entente Internationale des Maitre Luthiers et Archetiers D'Art. For a free copy of Mr. Rufino's brochures, "The Student Guide to Instrument Care" and "The Musician's Guide to Instrument Insurance." You can go to *www. liviolinshop.com* and click on "Advice and Help."

Jeffrey Seader
Santoli and Seader
Certified Public Accountants
400 Townline Road, Suite 150
Hauppauge, NY 11788
Tel: (631) 366–4200
Fax: (631) 366–4267
jfcpa13@aol.com
Jeffrey Seader, CPA, is the managing owner of Santoli and Seader, CPAs (established in 1996) whose areas of expertise include individual and corporate taxation and financial planning for small businesses. Mr. Seader graduated from the State University of New York College at Oswego with a B.S. in accounting.

Karen Sussman, M.A., CCC
Professional Voice Care Center
Hicksville, NY 11801
(516) 433–1822
Karen Sussman is a licensed and certified speech pathologist, specializing in voice therapy. She is the founder and director of the Professional Voice Care Center in Hicksville, N. Y., and is a frequent lecturer at voice and speech seminars. She is also a singer and performer with over 1000 professional performances to her credit.

Fred Wolinsky, Executive Director
Encore Performing Arts, Inc.
Wappinger Falls, NY
Fred Wolinsky is the executive director of Encore Performing Arts, Inc., a New York–based agency that caters to children and family audiences. Presently Encore has twelve performing groups on its roster.

Bibliography

Belleville, Nyree. *Booking, Promoting and Marketing Your Music* (Vallejo, CA: Mix Books, 2000).

Cady, Donald F. *1999 Field Guide to Estate Planning, Business Planning & Employee Benefits* (Cincinnati: The National Underwriter Co., 1999).

Davis, Sarah, and Dave Laing. *The Guerilla Guide to the Music Business* (London and New York: Continuum, 2001).

Galper, Hal. *The Touring Musician* (New York: Billboard Books, 2000).

Giuliano, Geoffrey. *Behind Blue Eyes—the Life of Pete Townshend* (New York: Dutton, 1996).

Miles, Barry. *Paul McCartney—Many Years from Now* (New York: Henry Holt and Company, 1997).

Mitchell, Billy. *The Gigging Musician: How to Get, Play, and Keep the Gig.* (San Francisco: Backbeat Books, 2001).

Naggar, David, Esq. *The Music Business.* (San Francisco: DaJé Publishing, 2000).

Romanowski, Patricia, and Holly George-Warren, eds. *The New Rolling Stone Encyclopedia of Rock & Roll* (New York: Fireside, 1995).

Tomatis, Alfred. *The Conscious Ear* (Barrytown, NY: Station Hill Press Inc., 1991).

Recommended Reading

Koller, Fred. *How to Pitch and Promote Your Songs* (Cincinnati: Writer's Digest Books, 1988).

Rapaport, Diane Sward. *How to Make and Sell Your Own Recording: The Complete Guide to Independent Recording* (Upper Saddle River, NJ: Prentice Hall, 1999).

Rapaport, Diane Sward. *A Music Business Primer* (Upper Saddle River, NJ: Prentice Hall, 2002).

Shemel, Sidney, and M. William Krasilovsky. *This Business of Music: A Practical Guide to the Music Industry for Publishers, Writers, Record Companies, Producers, Artists, Agents* (New York: Billboard Publications, 1985).

The Editors of Songwriter's Market. *The Songwriter's Market Guide to Song and Demo Submission Formats* (Cincinnati: Writer's Digest Books, 1994).

McIan, Peter and Wichman, Larry. *The Musician's Guide to Home Recording* (New York: Amsco Publications, 1994).

About the Author

Patricia Shih wrote her first song at age twelve and hasn't stopped since. At age fifteen she signed a recording and managerial contract with Unicorn Records of Washington, D.C., as part of a folk duo. This marked the start of her professional career. A 45 rpm record was released a year later, and numerous TV, radio, concert, and club performances followed—including an international radio broadcast on the Voice of America and appearances at the legendary Cellar Door, where the duo was runner-up to Emmylou Harris in the competitive *Best of the Hoots*. In 1973, Ms. Shih began her solo career in San Francisco, notably on her own PBS special, *Patty Shih— Music from the Gallery*. Six years later, she returned to the East Coast and settled in Huntington, New York. She began specializing in music for children and families in 1986, while continuing to perform for adult and senior audiences.

To date, Ms. Shih has written over 250 songs, both alone and in collaboration with others, and she continues to tour internationally. She starred for a year on New York Cablevision's *Tell Me A Story* and also wrote and performed the show's theme song. She has appeared in concert with such luminaries as Pete Seeger, Bonnie Raitt, Richie Havens, David Bromberg, Tom Chapin, Livingston Taylor, Odetta, Billy Bragg, Janis Ian, Michelle Shocked, and Peter Yarrow. Her songs are recorded and performed by numerous other artists throughout the world, have been published internationally in magazines such as *Sing Out!* and *Broadside* and the *Rise Up Singing Songbook*, and have won awards and accolades in the American Songwriting Festival, the New York Songwriters Showcase, the Parents' Choice Awards, and the BACCA Songwriting Competition. Articles on Ms. Shih have appeared in the *Oakland Tribune*, *Newsday*, *Acoustic Guitar Magazine*, and the *New York Times*, which has featured her in numerous interviews and spotlights.

Ms. Shih plays six- and twelve-string guitars, piano, Marxophone, Chinese flower drum, and soprano recorder. She has four albums to her credit: two for adults, *Woman with One Closed Eye* (Glass Records) and *Leap of Faith* (Flying Fish Records); and two family/children's albums, *Big Ideas!* and *Making Fun!* on Glass Records. Patricia can be found at her Web address: *www.patriciashih.com*.

Index

Books from Allworth Press

Managing Artists in Pop Music: What Every Artist and Manager Must Know to Succeed
by Mitch Weiss and Perri Gaffney (paperback, 6 × 9, 256 pages, $19.95)

The Quotable Musician: From Bach to Tupac
by Sheila E. Anderson (hardcover, 7 ¹/₂ × 7 ¹/₂, 224 pages, $19.95)

The Art of Writing Love Songs
by Pamela Phillips Oland (paperback, 6 × 9, 240 pages, $19.95)

The Art of Writing Great Lyrics
by Pamela Philips Oland (paperback, 6 × 9, 272 pages, $18.95)

How to Pitch and Promote Your Songs, Third Edition,
by Fred Koller (paperback, 6 × 9, 208 pages, $19.95)

The Songwriter's and Musician's Guide to Nashville, Revised Edition
by Sherry Bond (paperback, 6 × 9, 256 pages, $18.95)

Making and Marketing Music: The Musician's Guide to Financing, Distributing, and Promoting Albums
by Jodi Summers (paperback, 6 × 9, 240 pages, $18.95)

Profiting from Your Music and Sound Project Studio
by Jeffrey P. Fisher (paperback, 6 × 9, 288 pages, $18.95)

Moving Up in the Music Business
by Jodi Summers (paperback, 6 × 9, 224 pages, $18.95)

Career Solutions for Creative People
by Dr. Ronda Ormont (paperback, 320 pages, 6 × 9, $19.95)

Creative Careers in Music
by Josquin des Pres and Mark Landsman (paperback, 6 × 9, 224 pages, $18.95)

Making It in the Music Business: The Business and Legal Guide for Songwriters and Performers, Revised Edition
by Lee Wilson (paperback, 6 × 9, 288 pages, $18.95)

Rock Star 101: A Rock Star's Guide to Survival and Success in the Music Business
by Marc Ferrari (paperback, 5 ¹/₂ × 8 ¹/₂, 176 pages, $14.95)

Booking and Tour Management for the Performing Arts, Revised Edition
by Rena Shagan (paperback, 6 × 9, 288 pages, $19.95)

Please write to request our free catalog. To order by credit card, call 1-800-491-2808 or send a check or money order to Allworth Press, 10 East 23rd Street, Suite 510, New York, NY 10010. Include $5 for shipping and handling for the first book ordered and $1 for each additional book. Ten dollars plus $1 for each additional book if ordering from Canada. New York State residents must add sales tax.

To see our complete catalog on the World Wide Web, or to order online, you can find us at *www.allworth.com.*